Managing Human Forces
in Organizations

Madeline E. Heilman
New York University

and

Harvey A. Hornstein
Teachers College, Columbia University

Managing Human Forces in Organizations

1982

RICHARD D. IRWIN, INC.
Homewood, Illinois 60430

77486

Library of Congress Catalog Card No. 81-85257 (paperbound)
Library of Congress Catalog Card No. 81-71159 (hardbound)

Printed in the United States of America

1 2 3 4 5 6 7 8 9 0 K 9 8 7 6 5 4 3 2

To Our Parents and Mentors

Preface

This book focuses on some of the daily problems confronting men and women who manage people in organizations. In each chapter we explore social and psychological forces which influence both a particular problem and managerial attempts at its solution. Readers are provided with an introduction to relevant social-psychological dynamics, diagnostic frameworks, and, in many instances, action-oriented suggestions. Ideas, not detailed summaries of research, are the basis for organizing chapters. Our paramount concern has been with locating ideas in the behavioral sciences, particularly social and organizational psychology, that are basic, enduring, and germane to managers. These we present to readers in as practical a form as possible. There are hundreds of references in this book, but detailed esoteric refinement of theoretical issues and research findings, requiring elaborate presentations of studies, opposing studies, and synthesizing studies was avoided. We also avoided worrying about whether citations were old and honored or new and faddish. When a useful idea was best represented by a "classic," however old, we discussed and cited the "classic," and when it was best represented by a hot, new item, however au courant, we discussed and cited that item. The age of a reference was less of a concern than our views about its validity and practicality.

Some of our colleagues may be discomfited with our approach. In an effort to speak to managers and future managers, we organized material in terms of managerial problems, not the field of organizational behavior, and we deliberately omitted certain lines of scholarship that are classically included in books like this one. Too often, such issues are interesting to a select few, but without any practical value to the great majority of people who manage and supervise others. In brief, we did not want to write a book structured around material that is only of peripheral interest to most managers, however important it may be to scholars. By and large, before material was included in the book it was tested with members of the book's future audience. We asked them and we asked ourselves, "Can managers use this information to solve problems?" Occasionally, this practical, problem-centered orientation was violated when it became clear that the material concerned issues that are regularly buffeting today's managers, and making the knowledge available softened the blows. The book's last two chapters contain some prime examples of this, but it occurs elsewhere, as well.

Other books are problem centered. Several very good ones contain little informational substance, although they are filled with suggestions that render them useful resources for an experience-based course on organizational behavior. This book could be used in such a course to provide the substance which would otherwise be missing. Some books which are problem centered become chatty and superficial, losing any semblance of scholarly merit. This book does not report any factor analyses, t-tests, or analyses of variance or covariance. Nor are there discussions of multivariate analyses or cross-lag panel correlations. Nonetheless, we have tried to maintain the scholarly standards that we endorse as academics by honestly reporting useful ideas that seem to be continuously confirmed in the behavioral science literature. Finally, a number of books which are problem centered become polemical, eschewing organizational practices which are inconsistent with some sets of values. In the last two decades, these have characteristically been the values of the so-called human relations school. When they are extreme, these polemical pieces neglect the reality of organization life which includes power, politics, competition, self-interest, incompetence, and irrationality. This book does not rejoice in these phenomena, but neither does it neglect them.

Bias undoubtedly crept into our selection. For that we cannot apologize. Authors have a point of view. Such realities cannot be denied, but they can be exposed. When we sensed bias creeping into our efforts, we warned readers and tried hard to share alternative points of view. In the end, we think this book emerged as one that is fair and reasonably wide ranging, even if not a detailed compendium of the whole field. It is a book suitable for use with undergraduates, M.B.A. candidates, students in nonbusiness professional schools, and managers who like to read and profit from so doing.

Writing books can be a chore. The burden was lessened by the coeditors of this series, Larry Cummings and Kirby Warren. They were professional as well as kind. Noel Tichy (University of Michigan) also worked hard to ease our load by reading and commenting on an early draft of the manuscript. Secretarial help from Denise Fennelly, Robin Howe, Regina O'Rourke, and Rita Shiman was an essential and greatly appreciated facilitator of our work. Finally, the whole effort became joyfully pleasant because of our constant companionship and happily successful efforts to manage the human forces in our family organization.

Madeline E. Heilman
Harvey A. Hornstein

Contents

1

Introduction

WHENEVER human beings gather to do a job, there is a danger that the excellence of the whole enterprise will be less than the sum of its individual parts. At one time or another, we have all seen it happen: A committee meets in order to complete some task. As an interested observer, you are impressed by the caliber of committee members. Individually, each person is competent and knowledgeable, a skilled and valued member of the organization. Understandably, you predict success for the group and are simply bewildered as you watch them tumble head over heels into failure.

Despite the wealth of individual talent and the history of individual accomplishment, the group becomes trapped in its own interpersonal mire. The social processes that evolve are all wrong. Human resources are ineffectively used. Communication and problem solving are muddled. Conflict is mismanaged. Leadership functions are left unfulfilled. There is no enthusiastic sense of being part of a team. In the end, individual skills are canceled and the group first flounders, then topples in disaster.[1]

Organizational life is filled with examples like this—where human forces, not technical expertise, affect performance and productivity. Consider the following cases:

1

Organization X develops a new product

For nearly a decade, covering the late 60s and early 70s, one division of a very large multinational firm enjoyed substantial pretax earnings, ranging from $60 million to nearly $100 million. The division was engaged in the manufacture of several products for consumer and industrial markets. Each major product area was headed by a division vice president. During the period discussed, these vice presidents functioned in parallel. That is, management problem solving and planning involved the division president, the relevant vice president, and necessary staff people within a product group, but no one from outside the group. The larger group of vice presidents, collectively called the "executive," met weekly only to ratify decisions which were already made elsewhere. Three events occurred in the mid-70s, however, which rendered this management scheme untenable. First, the profits of the parent company declined substantially, creating major budget problems and placing considerable pressure on the division's cash flow. Second, after many years, a privileged position with respect to raw material prices changed for the worse, adding to the division's financial pressures. Finally, and most important, years of research bore fruit, and a revolutionary new product was developed. The product's potential market was enormous, and it was conceivable that plant, personnel, and materials needs could absorb most of the available cash for several years to come. In addition, the manufacture of this product required as a raw material a second product which this division was selling to industrial customers. Indeed, if sales were as successful as predicted, manufacturing the new product might eventually require this particular material in such amounts that, unless additional manufacturing capacity were developed, the division would lose its position in that market.

The budget questions raised by both the parent company's shrinking profits and the change in raw material prices, combined with those raised by the new product and its potentials all required integrated and coordinated problem solving by the entire executive group. Strategic and operational planning based on answers to these questions would affect each product group. Moreover, each vice president possessed information which should have affected the formulation of any plans. But the group's recent history of working in parallel and the social processes that had evolved left the group ill equipped for the task. Meetings had not been organized to facilitate joint problem solving, and the group itself had not developed its skills as a problem-solving unit. Future success depended on coping with the human forces as well as the technical and business problems that they faced.

Organization Y shifts its marketing approach

A company engaged in the manufacture of hard and soft chemical foams decided to change its marketing strategy from a classical production-oriented one—in which the company produced certain products and the salespeople were expected to sell them—to a more aggressive, customer-oriented approach—in which salespeople were to discover what customer needs existed and then, working with production and R&D people, develop that product more cheaply and quickly than the competitors did. This new strategy created for this company an unprecedented need for cooperation between members of these departments, who in effect now formed a sales team. Of course, it simultaneously created unprecedented opportunities for conflict, which is just what happened. In retrospect, this is not surprising, since, prior to the change, each department was very cohesive (stimulating members' sense of loyalty), and although there had been no overt conflict between departments, each one felt *it* was the company's backbone.

As time passed, the conflict within these sales teams grew. Difficulties and mistakes were always blamed on *them*, the members of the *other* departments. Despite expert skills, work faltered as senior management had to resolve conflicts one by one. Team members remained psychologically tied to their departments and trembled at the thought of being even the least bit disloyal. In this way, they were held captive by human forces which had once worked in favor of organization success. The result nullified individual abilities, and sales teams were unable to collaborate fruitfully to solve organization problems.

Organization Z improves its information system

In the early 1970s, a privately funded social services agency spent considerable time and money to develop a new electronic data-processing system for part of its record-keeping operation. The system, which was developed pretty much without the knowledge or participation of employees, was installed immediately following a bitter labor dispute that involved layoffs of hourly employees. Technically, the system should have saved time and cut costs, but just the opposite occurred. Even after the usual period of time it takes for people to become accustomed to new equipment, difficulties persisted. Errors, turnover, and absenteeism all increased. As so often happens in organizations, a technically excellent solution to an organization problem was failing, not because of its technical adequacy, but because of the human forces which were at play.

Events like these occur in every organization. Tightening budgets, new products, shifts in marketing orientation, and technological innovation are ordinary. On the surface, these all seem only to be commercial, technical, or business problems. But with additional examination it becomes clear that each affects and is affected by the human forces of organization life.

These forces are inevitable intruders into organizations. They cannot be eliminated. Memos, regulations, and proclamations of policy will not rule them out of existence. They do not disappear because tradition, embarrassment, or fear keep them out of management discussions. Like it or not, these forces exist in every human organization, and they can be either a boon or a barrier to managerial success.

Success in management requires an ability to marshal human forces. The effective use of business and technical skills requires an ability to *recognize* and *improve* disruptive organizational conditions of a nontechnical nature. It requires the ability to sharpen and strengthen an organization's capacity to use its human resources.

There is no one right way to accomplish this. No panaceas exist. We are without the 10 or 10,000 commandments which guarantee success in managing human forces. But the behavioral sciences, social and organizational psychology in particular, have produced a wealth of knowledge that is relevant. This book presents that knowledge in order to heighten readers' abilities to both diagnose how human forces affect organizations and to take action that will improve organization performance.

Human forces in organizations

The book's theme is rooted in a systems model of organizations. In its most basic form, this model assumes that all human organizations can be described in terms of three dynamically interrelated events, as shown in Figure 1-1. Organizations receive *inputs* from their surrounding environment; they *transform* some of these in-

Figure 1-1

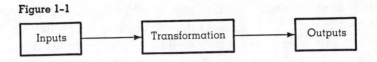

puts as they pass through the organization's internal parts, and produce several *outputs*.[2]

Inputs vary for different organizations, but may include:

The functioning of labor, product, service, and capital markets.

The behavior of key groups such as competitors, suppliers, and customers.

Government regulations and political pressures.

Values, attitudes, beliefs, and customs in the surrounding culture.

The weather (extreme cold, snow, rain, and drought, for example).

Activities and decisions of a larger parent organization.

Resources such as raw material and technology.

The organization's past, its history. (Organizations live and die because of key decisions in the past which place constraints on current functioning.)

Outputs also vary, but may include such things as:

Products and/or services.

Profits.

Market share.

Technological innovation.

Growth of plant and facilities.

Utilization of resources.

Work-related behavior: absenteeism, lateness, turnover, alcoholism, conflict.

Work-related feelings: satisfaction, aspiration, frustration, anger, allegiance.

Capacity to adapt to changing conditions.

Transforming inputs into outputs

Some of these outputs are an explicit part of the organization's *task* or *mission*, which is one of several organizational properties

·that affect *transformation* of inputs into outputs. Every organization and each division, department, section, committee, and task force exists for some purpose. Under ideal circumstances, each directs its activities toward achieving some desired state in the near or distant future. They may want to increase profits or market share. They may seek to service more people, increase plant size, or improve team functioning. Whatever future state they may desire, that state is their task or mission.[3] Smooth organization functioning ordinarily requires that the mission is

Unambiguous in the sense that it is expressed in terms of objective implications and priorities and is not a series of lofty, equally weighted platitudes.

Uniform in the sense that no substantial inconsistency exists between different parts of the mission, e.g., it is often inconsistent to simultaneously attempt to increase profits *and* market share or to service more clients and cut overhead.

Accepted by key members who recognize the mission, its priorities, and the implications of these for their own behavior and performance.

To accomplish its mission, an organization must integrate and coordinate the behavior of individuals and groups. For that reason, some *structure*, a formal organization, is created. Authority and responsibility are explicitly assigned to different jobs, producing a vertical hierarchy as well as lateral relationships. Job descriptions are prepared in an effort to establish some rational and efficient division of labor. Wages and benefits are attached to different jobs. And rules are written to regulate such things as communication, decision making, and problem solving.

This structure, in turn, influences and is influenced by linkages between the tools of the trade, that is, the *technology* that an organization, or any organization subpart, needs to accomplish its task or mission. Hammers, nails, lathes, kilns, computers, filing systems, typewriters, printing presses, and X-ray machines are all tools of some organization's trade. Every organization uses some technology in its attempt to convert inputs into outputs and thereby accomplish its mission. One can therefore characterize the elements of the transformation process discussed thus far as shown in Figure 1-2.

There are at least two schools of thought about how to conclude the building of this model. One suggests that organization per-

Figure 1-2

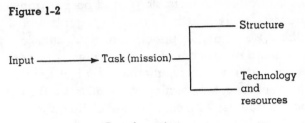

Transformation

formance is the outcome of a completely rational process and possesses nearly algebraic precision. Proponents of this point of view argue: (1) Once the task or mission is fully articulated, it completely determines the technology and resources which must be used and the structure which must be employed; (2) all three—task, technology, and structure—in combination influence the formulation of *objective job demands for individuals and groups;* and (3) these, being prescriptions for work behavior, produce activity which is perfectly consistent with the demands of the task, technology, and structure. This approach is summarized in Figure 1-3. Because everything fits so precisely, outputs are expected to completely satisfy initial task objectives.[4]

But everything does not always fit. Portraying organizational functioning in this manner is naive and idealized. Outputs are not solely determined by such an orderly, static, and mechanical arrangement of events. This model of human organizations neglects what may be the most fundamental component of organization life: people. And this point is emphasized by the second school of thought.

People must formulate, reformulate, and interpret the mission; *people* understand, abide by, and/or change the structure; *people*

Figure 1-3

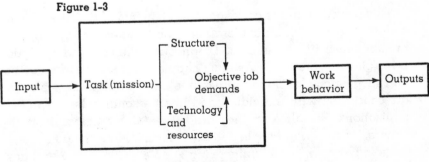

Transformation

use, abuse, and alter the technology; and *people* transform abstract job descriptions into behavior. In organizations, people work together to accomplish the organization's mission. And in working together a filter of human forces is created: a vast organization underworld involving patterns of social process which evolve and affect the interpretation of the mission, the adherence to the structure, the use of technology, and the translation of objective job demands into actual behavior. This more realistic model appears in Figure 1-4.

In the best of times, which is a not-too-frequent occurrence, the social processes that evolve are consistent with organizational needs and support effective functioning. But even this happy arrangement is often lost when change occurs, as it always does, and as it did in the case examples offered earlier in this chapter. Then, the very same social processes which were once beneficial may no longer be so. Instead, they become a hindrance to the achievement of organization success.

All too often, we disregard these facts, acting as if the ideal, naive model were valid. Changes are made in task, technology, and structure neglecting the fit between these elements and the people (human forces) component.[5] Such changes, even when they resolve the original problem, are apt to create new problems because they reflect insensitivity to the social and psychological facts of organization life. When this occurs, if managers aim to remedy problems and to enhance organization performance, then the managers must learn to treat human forces as a tool of work which, like task, structure, and technology, can be examined, altered, and improved.

The human-forces filter

This book's chapters correspond to elements of the filter. Each chapter begins with an exploration of how that component of the human-forces filter operates. Diagnostic schemas and analytic principles are provided. As each chapter proceeds, examples of and suggestions for managerial action are offered. Chapters 2 to 6 are concerned with individual and interpersonal behavior in organizations. Specifically, they are titled, "Communicating With Others," "Perceiving People and Situations," "Motivating People," "Leading People," and "Influencing People." Chapters 7 to 9 are concerned with group and intergroup behavior. They are, "Solving

Figure 1-4

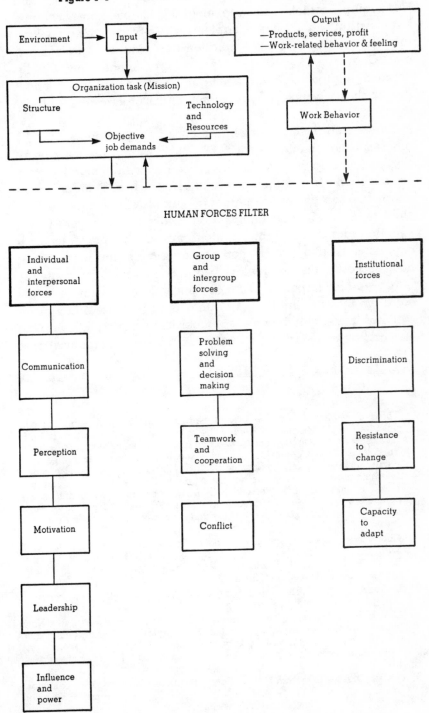

Problems and Making Decisions," "Building Work Teams," and "Managing Conflict." The three remaining chapters are concerned with institutional issues. Chapter 10, "De-Stereotyping," examines the problems of discrimination and bias in organizations, and Chapters 11 and 12, "Managing Change: Individually Oriented Approaches" and "Managing Change: Systems-Oriented Approaches," focus on ways of managing an organization's ability to adapt.

As we said in the preface, this book is organized around the problems that managers face, not the research interests of an academic discipline. Its abiding concern is with human forces in organization life and their power to block or benefit organization progress. These forces are neither immutable nor immovable: they yield to diagnosis and intervention. Books for managers which explain diagnosis and intervention in areas of finance, technology, or marketing, cannot honestly guarantee that readers will have success if they scrupulously study and apply their contents. While we also forbear making any such claim to readers of this book, we freely admit that our aim was to organize and present material in a way that is pleasant, pertinent, and practical to the men and women entrusted with the management of organizations.

Notes

1. These ideas have been expressed by several scholars using different labels to describe the phenomenon. *Assembly effects* is a term used by Collins, B. R., & Guetzkow, H. *A social psychology of group processes for decision making.* New York: John Wiley & Sons, 1964; *imperfect social interaction* is identified as a mediator of performance by Hackman, J. R., & Morris, C. G. Group tasks, group interaction process and group performance effectiveness: A review and proposed integration. In L. Berkowitz (Ed.), *Advances in experimental social psychology* (Vol. 8). New York: Academic Press, 1975; *process losses* is the label applied by Steiner, I. D. *Group process and productivity.* New York: Academic Press, 1972.

2. Churchman, C. W. *The systems approach.* New York: Delta, 1968; Katz, D., & Kahn, R. L. *The social psychology of organizations.* New York: John Wiley & Sons, 1966; Porter, L. W., Lawler, E. E. III, & Hackman, J. R. *Behavior in organizations.* New York: McGraw-Hill, 1975.

3. Beckhard, R., & Harris, R. T. *Organization transitions: Managing complex change.* Reading, Mass.: Addison-Wesley, 1977, pp. 58-68.

4. Gulick, L., & Urwick, L. (Eds.). *Papers on the science of administration.* New York: Institute of Public Administration, 1937; Taylor, F. W. *The principles of scientific management.* New York: Harper & Row, 1911; Weber, M. [*The theory of social and economic organization*] (T. Parsons, trans.) New York: Free Press, 1947.

5. Nadler, D. A., & Tushman, M. L. A diagnostic model for organization behavior. In J. R. Hackman, E. E. Lawler III, & L. W. Porter (Eds.), *Perspectives of behavior in organizations.* New York: McGraw-Hill, 1977.

Communicating with Others

W. L. grumbled as he tried to close his overstuffed attache case. His wife, thinking that he was talking to her, felt annoyed. He was never out of the house on time regardless of how early she awakened him—and she was always up first—or how diligently she tried to organize the morning schedule. Years before, she had reconciled herself to her fate. In a burst of insight, the kind which has personal profundity but no important meaning to anyone else, she told herself, "In the morning, he's a child." Afterward, for a time anyway, the fighting stopped. She told him when it was "time to rise" and "time to shower," or shave, or eat, or dress, and she tolerated his angry accusations as he stumbled about inefficiently collecting this and that in a frantic effort to catch the 8:10 into New York. Her apparent calm collapsed, however, shortly after she returned to work as an insurance salesperson, 11 months ago. Now she, too, had a schedule, and the 8:10 was her target as well as his.

"What?" she shouted, allowing her discontent to show.

"Nothing," he said, closing the case, "I'm ready."

The silence which regularly descended during their 6-minute drive to the station continued all through the 33-minute Amtrack ride into

New York City. Then, as their opposing cheeks nearly touched, hurried kisses were hurled into empty space and on into infinity. Those kisses together with automatically released "good-byes" ended their silence and heralded Mr. and Ms. L's physical separation for the rest of the work day.

Ms. L's office building was only a five-minute walk from the station. The building's express elevators were located directly to the right of the main entrance. Ms. L walked quickly to them and entered one that was waiting, a green light signaling its availability and purpose. The elevator's only occupant saw Ms. L and stepped back as if to make room. Ms. L recognized the woman, a secretary who worked in one of the offices adjacent to her own. A nod in the woman's general direction was quickly truncated when Ms. L's attention was captured by the firm's vice president of finance, who was just entering the elevator. Stepping back, as if to make room for him in the still underpopulated conveyance, Ms. L faced the man, smiled broadly, and said, "Hello. How are you this morning?" He smiled, reported that he was fine, asked about her well-being and, while she was answering, turned to stare up at the number consol which was quickly blinking the floors past which the express elevator was now speeding.

When the doors opened on the 22d floor, Ms. L moved quickly from the elevator saying "Goodbye" to the vice president who nodded without turning his gaze from the consol. Hurrying past the secretary, who had also exited the elevator, Ms. L raced to her office. While unbuttoning her coat with one hand, she lifted a pile of pink message slips from her secretary's desk with the other. Small grunts accompanied her effort to juggle the slips, unbutton her coat, and keep hold of her handbag and briefcase. After a moment, without turning to face her secretary, who stood about 10 feet away preparing the day's first pot of coffee, Ms. L started to question her about selected messages. Not fully understanding the questions, her secretary left the coffee machine, which was now humming and hissing in seeming protest, sped to her desk, and examined the message slips over Ms. L's shoulder, trying hard to recall what the jottings and notations were intended to mean.

Ms. L's day, hardly three hours old, was not an atypical one for her; nor is it likely to be characterized as containing the "extraordinary" by most people. Of course, it was filled with the idiosyncrasies of Ms. L's life. But if we step back from these and examine her day's beginning in more general terms, we see how really typical it is. After waking, Ms. L interacted with her family—her husband, in this case. At work, she communicated with near strangers (the secretary on the elevator and the vice president of finance) and her secretary, with whom she had regular contact. Two of these people were subordinates and one of them was Ms. L's superior. Examine Ms. L's day thus far, and count how many messages she sent and received. In a short space of three hours, without any spectacular events, through word and deed, by gesture, posture, and expression, with acts of commission and omission, Ms. L, as would be the case with any of us, gave and received hundreds, perhaps thousands of messages.

Unfortunately, as most of us know, human communication is dramatically imperfect. The messages which we send and receive are not simply limited to the verbal content of speech. Consider Ms. L's experiences. W.L. grumbled at his attache case and his wife thought that the message was for her. For years, she sent messages to him as if he were a child, and, perhaps as a consequence, he responded like one. "What?" Ms. L shouted in response to her husband's grumble. A simple one-word question? No. Of course not. As so many of us do so much of the time, she "allowed her discontent to show." What of their silence, the hurried kisses, and the goodbyes? What messages did they contain? When Ms. L, the secretary, and the vice president met in the elevator, what messages can you see in their stepping back as if to make room or in the nodding, smiling, gushing hellos, and staring at blinking numbers? And what of the exchange between Ms. L and her secretary? Are yesterday's message slips the only issue, or are other messages also being transmitted by Ms. L as she asks her questions?

Clearly, human communication is a complex event, and we must look past the content of what is being said if we hope to understand what factors are affecting the transmission of messages between people. What is more, it is evident that the sending and receiving of messages between people are different than the sending and receiving of messages which occur when either the sender or the receiver is a machine. The number consol in the elevator blinked information and the coffee machine hissed and hummed in seeming protest. But machines are inanimate. Under ordinary circumstances, we make no inferences or attributions about their feelings, attitudes, values, or beliefs. The number consol may be in error, but it cannot willfully lie, withhold information, or seek domination because we depend on it for information. The coffee pot may sound upset, but it cannot be angry, feign a fit, or plan to "get even."

People are different. We lie, withhold information, and seek domination. We may feel angry, pretend, and plan revenge. With people, the sending and receiving of messages is influenced by our own feelings, attitudes, values, and beliefs as well as by our inferences and attributions about the feelings, attitudes, values, and beliefs of others. These important human capabilities enrich the messages that we send and receive, but they also create the potential for trouble in human communication.

Lewis Carroll recognized the pitfalls of human communication and was teasing us when, in his classic book *Through the Looking Glass*, he had Humpty Dumpty say, "When I use a word, it means just what I intend it to mean, neither more nor less." If Humpty really believed that, then he was indeed doomed to have a great fall, for the process of communication is extremely vulnerable to disturbance. This was neatly illustrated in a 1969 *Harvard Business Review* article titled, "The fateful process of Mr. A. talking to Mr. B."[1]

The article describes a critical event which takes place at an office party. Two men meet. One is an office manager, the other is a truck loader. The following exchange takes place:

Office manager: "You work for United too?"
Truck loader: "Yes, I work in their transport division."

It seems simple doesn't it? A polite, conventional question produced an ordinary, descriptive response. The apparent simplicity is deceptive. Without effort, the article's author destroys it and simultaneously demonstrates the vulnerability of human communication. This brief exchange, and any process of human communication, is conceived of by the author as if it possessed 10 parts. To begin with, the office manager is confronted with:

1. A set of *external stimuli* emanating from the setting which surrounds him, including the stranger to whom he speaks.
2. *Expectations* that he has as a consequence of previous learning, which influence his interpretation of these stimuli and produce. . . .
3. *Inferences* and *attributions* about the stranger, including such things as his status in the company, education, and income.

4. The office manager wants additional information which will either confirm or disconfirm these thoughts and perhaps establish his social standing vis-à-vis the other. But it would be impolite to ask directly, "Are you an office manager like me or only a truck loader?" Hence, he encodes the message in a way that will obtain information without offending.

5. The message that he sends and hears himself send (feedback) is "You work for United too?"

The truck loader's response can be organized into similar components:

6. As a listener, the loader is also presented with an array of external stimuli including the context, the office manager's question, and the total visual picture that the other presents.

7. He, too, has expectations which influence the interpretation of these stimuli producing. . . .

8. Inferences and attributions.

9. More than the words, "You work for United too?" are being responded to by the truck loader. He believes that a game is being played and that the stranger, who he suspects is part of management, wants to establish their relative standing in the company. "He is not simply asking where I work. He is asking if I'm a manager like him." As a receiver of the office manager's question, the truck loader decodes the message, and does so under the influence of current circumstances and personal past experience. Then he must encode a message of his own.

10. The truck loader, understandably reluctant to say "Mind your own business," or "Let's not play these games," or "I just load trucks; you win," finally sends and hears himself send (feedback) the message, "Yes, I work in their transport division." It is a defensive diversion.

The exchange consisted of only two sentences, 12 words. But distortion and inaccuracy are already occurring. The sources of these disturbances are evident and can be identified whenever people attempt to transmit messages to one another. First, human communication, the transmission of messages, involves two or more people, each with his or her own needs, expectations, and intentions.[2] These psychological events affect the perception and interpretation of external stimuli and can produce disturbances in communication.

Second, communication between humans has a history and a future. It is one event in a series. It is a link that is both stimulus and response, cause and effect.[3] Tied, in this way, to a chain of exchanges, any single message can be influenced by more than immediate information needs, and that can produce disturbance in communication.

Third, communication is not limited to verbal messages. At the same time that words are being sent, voice intonations, eye contact, physical distancing, and body posture all send nonverbal messages.[4] In fact, some scholars, after extensive investigation, have offered the following formula to describe the relative contribution of different message sources to one person's perception of another's attitude.[5]

Perceived attitude = .07 (verbal) + .38 (vocal) + .55 (facial)

Forget the specific percentages. They are not critical. What is important is to recognize that words alone do not convey the message in human communication. The multiple sources, their potential for ambiguity and inconsistency, are all possible contributors to disturbance of communication.

Finally, communication is influenced by and influences social relationships. It gives them meaning, and the meaning of messages must be understood in the context of these relationships.[6] This may cause serious distortion in the encoding and decoding of messages and can be a source of disturbance in communication.

Only a fictional character like Humpty Dumpty in an imaginary Alice in Wonderland world would claim, "When I use a word, it means just what I choose it to mean, neither more nor less." That fact presents an enormous problem for managers of organizations. Work requires communication. Job description, goal setting, performance appraisal, problem solving, planning, conflict management, decision making, and almost any other management task that you can think of requires the transmission of messages. Chester Barnard, a great observer of organization life, once wrote, "In an exhaustive theory of organization, communication would occupy a central place, because the structure, extensiveness and scope of organization are almost entirely determined by communication techniques."[7] Less elegantly, but no less profoundly, in their book, *The Social Psychology of Organizations*, Katz and Kahn metaphorically conceived of communication as the "glue" that holds organizations together.[8] Unfortunately, there are ordinary and natural forces in organizations which cause the glue to loosen. Organizational structure, organizational climate, and the individual behavior of organization members are all capable of exploiting the vulnerability of human communication, causing the glue to loosen as disturbances develop.

Organizational structure and communication

Think of an organization with which you are familiar, and imagine that you can map the flow of messages. If this were possible for you to do, then, over time, you would notice patterns emerging. These patterns are called *communication networks*. Three characteristics of these networks affect performance in organizations: (1) whether the communication network is centralized or decentralized; (2) whether one occupies a position at the center of a centralized communication network or at its periphery; and (3) whether the flow of messages is one-way or two-way.

Centralized and decentralized networks

In mapping the flow of messages in an organization, it would soon become evident that, in some instances, messages all flow inward, coming from several positions to one or more central locations. Then they would flow out again, back to the more peripheral positions. The resulting picture might look like one of the following (each of the central positions is identified by a darkened circle):

In other instances, there is no central location. Instead, messages flow freely back and forth between several position. For example:

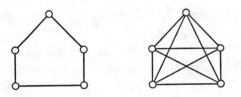

The first group of patterns is called *centralized* communication networks, and the second group, *decentralized* communication networks. In organizations, their formation might be either deliberate and formal or accidental and informal. Influencing their formation are such things as organizationally imposed limits of authority, need and demand for information, access to information, character of tasks, and friendship and status in the organizational hierarchy.

People who occupy central positions in communication networks have an important role to fulfill. It is not unreasonable to claim that group success depends primarily on their performance. Hence, the vulnerability of centralized networks. Incompetence in that position can be disastrous. Even when the person occupying the position is competent, the centralized structure has a built-in fragility. Overload of central positions is increasingly likely to occur as problem complexity mounts.[9]

But, despite these shortcomings, the centralized network is very effective for handling some kinds of tasks. Therefore, it is in a manager's interests to develop skills which will allow him or her to first recognize the contingencies which regulate the effectiveness of centralized and decentralized networks, and then make the required organizational changes, creating a structure which is suitable to the problem at hand.[10] The clearest statement of these contingencies is offered by Marvin E. Shaw. He wrote, "Centralized networks are generally more efficient when the task requires merely the collection of information in one place. Decentralized networks are more efficient when the task requires, in addition to the information collection process, that further operations must be performed on the information before the task can be completed."[11]

How do people feel about these two types of communication arrangements? Here, too, there is consensus among scholars. Regardless of the type of task, decentralized networks are the more satisfying of the two.

Being at the center

Experimental research on the effects of communication networks was originally conducted by Alex Bavelas.[12] The procedure that he used was an artificial, but not an unreasonable simulation of organizational realities. Five people had a problem to solve. They could communicate by writing messages, but experimentally imposed constraints determined to whom they could send these messages. Thus, Professor Bavelas was able to create different communication networks, some that were centralized, with one person "being at the center," and others that were not. The problem people in these two different types of networks had to solve was a simple one. Every person had a card displaying five out of a possible six symbols. One of the symbols was common to all the cards. Each five-person group, working within the confines of its network, had to correctly identify the common symbol.

In organizations, a person's centrality in a communication network may result from physical arrangements, such as the positioning of offices or plant layout. It may be a consequence of having more access to information than anyone else in the network. Or, more familiarly, it may simply reflect one's decision-making authority. For any of these reasons, occupants of central positions in a communication network receive a comparatively greater number of messages than do other members of the network. Consequently, people at the center typically spend their time differently than do those at the periphery. The former compile data, develop solutions, and transmit answers, while those at the periphery spend their time receiving information.[13]

How do people at the center feel about their work? In Professor Bavelas' investigations and in subsequent research these people—who were regularly identified by other network members as the "group leader"—were more satisfied with their work than were people at the network's periphery.[14] Organizationally, this outcome is important because, in time, dissatisfied people may tend to direct their attention from work to nonorganizational concerns.[15]

Bavelas' findings in his artificial simulation clearly capture what others have found in studies of actual organizations. Robert Zajonc and Donald Wolfe, for example, tell us that staff employees with more access to information not only knew more about the firm, they also reported a greater sense of identification with it.[16] A survey of employees at Standard Oil of New Jersey's headquarters produced similar results.[17] These people answered questions designed to assess their satisfaction with material benefits, company reputation, supervisory practices, and job-related opportunities for self-realization. They were also queried about the company's internal policies. Again, satisfaction increased as the degree to which the employees felt that they knew company policies increased.

People at a communication network's center possess information which gives them greater scope in understanding a group's task. Armed with this advantage, they can exert greater autonomy, initiative, and self-control than can the other members of the group. All this contributes to their greater sense of satisfaction.[18]

Recognizing the benefit of information to people at the center of a network helps us to identify actions that managers can take to remedy the disadvantage imposed by communication networks which require some people to occupy peripheral positions. There is evidence that, by increasing information to people who occupy peripheral positions at the outset of a problem-solving effort, managers can heighten these persons' sense of satisfaction with work.[19] As a managerial remedy, this possibility is important. Organizational hierarchies and physical arrangements may lock us into certain networks, but often they do not prevent the distribution of information for selected problems.

One- and two-way channels of communication

Let us return for a moment to the imaginary map that you were creating, the one that charted the flow of messages in some organization with which you are familiar. If arrows were used to illustrate a message's direction, then, between some organization members, you would find arrows pointing in both directions, indicating that the people were behaving alike, both of them sending and receiving messages. Between others, however, most of the arrows would point one way, indicating a disparity in communication with one of the people doing most of the sending and the other doing most of the receiving. The effect would be even more dramatic if the arrows could be distinguished—by color coding for example—so that initiating questions were coded differently from responses, commands from compliance, and criticism from approval. If this could be done, then it would become colorfully clear that some people not only send messages, they also ask questions, issue commands, and offer criticism. Others, in contrast, tend to receive messages, respond to questions, comply with commands, and make approving noises. In short, communication between organization members is not always symmetrical.

The absence of symmetry in message sending has been examined by investigators of organization life. Their conclusions can be succinctly stated; two-way communication is more time consuming than one-way communication,[20] but it is also more accurate and satisfying to the people involved.[21]

Evidence exists to suggest that, when management provides opportunities for two-way communication, the responses from subordinates are favorable.[22] The lesson is not lost on managers and supervisors. It is not uncommon to find them endorsing the need for two-way communication and extolling its benefits. In practice, however, the results do not always conform to the rhetoric. And managers do not always see the gap between what they believe is right and what exists. Indeed, it seems that managers believe that a great deal more two-way communication occurs than do their subordinates. Findings from one study, not at all atypical, illustrate the point: 73 percent of supervisors believed that they received their subordinates' ideas, but only 16 percent of their subordinates concurred. Who is correct is not at issue. The fact that the perceptions are so inconsistent is a problem in and of itself. Unaware that such a problem exists, managers are not likely to take corrective actions.

Misperception by managers is not the only obstacle to two-way communication. Nearly everyone has his/her share of organizational war stories in which some organization members deliberately withheld information which was necessary and useful to other organization members. Almost 30 years ago, an article published in *Personnel Psychology* reported that 68 percent of the executives in one company had information about an organization problem, but only 20 percent shared it, although nothing formal constrained the others from doing so. In a second case, discussed in the same article, 81 percent of the managers in a company knew of a resignation, but only 11 percent told others about it.[23]

Sabotaging two-way communication by withholding information is often a way that managers attempt to maintain control and accumulate power, but the absence of information in organizations has other consequences which those making such Machiavellian moves may not have anticipated.[24] Organizational rumors are frequently stimulated when necessary information is lacking. When communication from management is infrequent, untrustworthy, or lagging in relation to events, rumor finds a fertile breeding ground. The consequences can be very harmful to organizational performance.

In one small, private, metropolitan hospital, moderately sized budget cuts and staff layoffs were deemed a secret by administration, one that had to be kept from the staff lest their morale drop and effi-ciency decrease. The "secret" spread through the hospital like an influenza epidemic. Within days, everyone discussed it all of the time. The secret's content changed with each discussion. Before long, the fact of some budgets cuts and layoffs of recently hired hourly staff was transformed into a major calamity in people's retelling of the secret. People talked about how the hospital was closing or merging, and nearly everyone would be dismissed. People took sick days and vaca-tion days in order to begin job hunting. Union members prepared their case, and community groups were surreptitiously notified of the "se-cret" in its transformed state. Rumor replaced fact, morale dropped, and efficiency decreased.

It is hard to claim that factual information would have pre-vented these costly organizational problems from occurring, but the possibility cannot be dismissed. Rumors and other unofficial, informal exchanges of information can be misleading and inaccu-rate. Sometimes the myth that develops calms people, and some-times it agitates them, but it never allows them to respond effec-tively to the issue at hand. Unfortunately, myth and rumor are commonly identified as the principal sources of organization in-formation.[25] That probably comes as no surprise to anyone who has worked in an organization. Management is often not very eager to direct information downward. And, even when it does, the information's effectiveness is frequently limited because of the failure to create communication systems which contain two-way channels. Consider what we know to be the most familiar forms of communication in organizations: One study showed that 76 per-cent of companies communicate to employees by sending letters, 60 percent use mass meetings, and 72 percent use magazines or newspapers. Other devices commonly used by organizations are bulletin boards, information racks, tours, movies, handbooks, manuals, and reports. None of these effectively permits or encour-ages two-way communication.[26]

Attitude surveys are ordinarily not much better.[27] A classical procedure is for managers (or the consultants that they hire) to ask subordinates questions. Subordinates respond, return the ques-tionnaires, and, from the subordinates' perspective, that is the end of it. They are frequently prevented from having an opportu-nity to discuss the data, its meaning, or appropriate action steps. On occasion, when managers are urged to discuss the data with subordinates, they are typically not given the help or time to make such an effort successful.

Grievance procedures[28] and suggestion systems[29] provide opportunity for employees to initiate communications upward in management, but their availability guarantees neither meaningful participation nor inputs of quality. Making them work takes the energy and commitment of key people. Effort must be put into developing systems that provide for a quick response to grievances or suggestions, which is informative and makes clear the reasons for the company's decision.[30] The importance of having key people committed to such action was illustrated by a survey conducted at Esso Research and Engineering Company. Here, employee participation in a suggestion program closely reflected supervisor support for the program; subordinates were more likely to participate when their supervisors felt positively about the program. In addition, employees themselves were less positive about participation in the program when they felt that making suggestions would bring them into competition with their supervisor, because he or she might interpret their making of a suggestion as a criticism or as an indicator of overambitiousness.[31]

Organizational procedure and management practice do not deserve the total blame for the absence of two-way communication. Ordinary human frailty on the part of subordinates also contributes to the problem. Bad news is withheld from superiors. People act as if they were messengers in ancient Persia who were killed if they returned to the king with bad news. When they have the opportunity, messengers learn quickly. They simply say nothing. This has been called the *MUM* response.[32]

Upward communication of information is especially restricted (1) by people with high need for approval; (2) by those who desire promotion and feel that the information might hurt their chances; and (3) when it may reflect badly on one's self or one's fellows.[33] As the tale of the Persian messenger suggests, we can expect that punitive organizational climates are more likely to exaggerate this MUM response than are nonpunitive ones. That they do that, and more, is a concern of the next section.

Organization climate and communication

Jack R. Gibb's opening sentence in an article titled "Defensive communication" makes a point that should be evident from what we have already said in this chapter.[34] Dr. Gibb says, "One way to understand communication is to view it as a people process rather than as a language process." He is concerned with communication as a people process because he believes that social relationships can cause distortion in both the sending and receiving of messages. Consequently, one remedy for faulty communications is to change people's relationships.

Gibb claims that distortion of communication occurs when people have cause to feel defensive. Such cause exists when the surrounding social context contains a threat to one's well-being. Of course, he is not simply talking about physical threat. Indeed, his principal concern is with social, economic, political, and emotional threats to one's well-being. Under these conditions, people devote energy to defending themselves. They think about how they appear to others and how they may "win, dominate, impress or escape punishment, and/or how (they) may avoid or mitigate a perceived or anticipated attack."[35]

One of the most socially insidious consequences of these thoughts and the behaviors that they create is the defensive response they produce in others, causing relationships to spiral downwards as defensiveness begets defensiveness. Caught in this spiral, people's abilities to communicate effectively are seriously disturbed. Gibb says, "Not only do defensive communicators send off multiple value, motive, and affect cues, but also defensive recipients distort what they receive."[36]

Analyzing tape-recorded discussions of various group discussions, Gibb found evidence that defensive social climates are associated with greater distortion of communication than are supportive social climates. Six categories of behavior are offered by him in order to distinguish defensive and supportive climates:

1. *Evaluative* comments are likely to stimulate defensive climates. *Descriptive* comments, by contrast, are likely to stimulate supportive ones. Gibb's observation is one that is easily recognized in everyday experience. Communication which assesses one's behavior, values, attitudes, or feelings is more likely to provide reason for a defensive reaction than is communication which simply describes events. We can expect this to be especially true when the evaluator has the power to respond punitively to negative assessments.

2. Communication which is aimed at *persuading, influencing,* or *controlling* another tends to generate defensive climates. In contrast, supportive climates occur when speakers maintain a *problem orientation* by communicating a "desire to collaborate in defining a mutual problem and in seeking its solution."

3. Machiavellian moves in which communications are part of a

strategy to manipulate are more conducive to the development of defensive climates than of supportive ones. In these instances, hidden agendas and secret motives guide message sending. Listeners, in turn, quickly realize what is occurring and learn to reinterpret incoming messages. In supportive climates, one feels that the messages being sent are characterized by *spontaneity*.

4. *Neutrality*, which leads listeners to believe that the speaker is detached and uncaring, is a characteristic of defensive climates. In supportive climates, communications are characterized by *empathy* for another's situation.

5. "When a person communicates to another that he feels *superior* [italics added] in position . . . he arouses defensiveness. . . . The person who is perceived as feeling superior communicates that he is not willing to enter into a shared problem-solving relationship, that he probably does not require help, and/or that he will be likely to try to reduce the power, the status, or the worth of the receiver."[37] When a communicator indicates that he and the listener are *equal*, in the sense that they can jointly solve problems, then defensiveness is reduced and a supportive climate can grow.

6. *Dogmatic* communications, stubbornly aimed at winning an argument rather than solving a problem, produce defensive climates. A more *provisional* posture, which communicates that one is prepared to honestly investigate issues in order to solve problems, produces a supportive climate.

Managers undeniably play a central role in determining a work group's climate. During the course of individual and group contacts with subordinates, managers have opportunities to use their own communications as a means of establishing a supportive climate in which the sending and receiving of messages is minimally distorted. In accomplishing this outcome, their ability to remain sensitive to their own behavior and the individual behavior of their subordinates will be crucial. Therefore, let us examine some selected areas of individual behavior that affect communication.

Individual behavior and communication

Words and gestures are symbols. They represent events, ideas, places, and things. Because they are representations, there is room for ambiguity, and the meaning given to words and gestures varies. Individual differences in interpretation is often a consequence of people's social experience. Some of these differences might very well be the cause of faulty communications which observers loosely describe as "people talking past one another." College men and women, for example, have been found to emphasize different things in their descriptions of an identical event. College men were more likely to describe what happened in neutral and objective terms, focusing on the event itself. College women, however, were more likely to describe the style of an event and the feelings it created, focusing on the process rather than the substance of what happened.[38] It seems easy to imagine how this difference might contribute to communication ills both inside and outside of organizations.

Similar problems arise in the nonverbal sphere of communication. Consider gazing into someone's face as a nonverbal behavior, for example. Gazing can be a very useful behavioral adjunct to verbal communication. Researchers have discovered that gazing allows people to (1) regulate the flow of communication by signaling turns; (2) monitor others' responses to messages which are being sent (feedback); (3) express emotions; and (4) communicate the nature of interpersonal relationships.[39] These benefits only arise, however, when gazing, or any nonverbal gesture for that matter, is interpreted similarly by speakers and listeners. That does not always happen. One pair of researchers, for example, found that communication problems between blacks and whites sometimes occurred because of misinterpreted gazing cues. When they are listeners, whites commonly interpreted a pause in speech and a steady gaze from a black speaker as an indication to begin speaking. They did, only to find that the black had also resumed speaking, and now both were speaking at once. When the situation was reversed—the speaker was white and the listener was black—things did not improve. White speakers tried to cue black listeners to speak by gazing at them. But the "cue" was not a cue for the black, and other means for signaling—like a direct question—had to be found.[40]

Just as ethnicity can alter the meaning of a nonverbal behavior like gazing, a person's personality can affect the frequency and motive underlying gazing. The point can be made by first telling you about a personnel specialist for a major utility company. The company calculates its costs for hiring middle-level managers to be in the tens of thousands of dollars. Recruiting, interviewing, testing, and negotiating all require a large outlay of direct and indirect costs. "When several people seem equally qualified and anxious for a position" this personnel specialist was asked, "on what basis do you make the selection?" Without hesitation, he answered, "I pick the person who has looked me straight in the eye. I like someone who looks me straight in the eye." And so do most people. When the gazing does not exceed levels of social appropriateness, people do tend to like others who look them in the eye.[41] Although they may be unaware of the scientific research, this point is not lost on people whose personality incorporates a strong need for approval. They gaze more often than others who do not have this personality characteristic. Unfortunately for those needing approval, people seem to recognize their gazing for what it is. Although they are thought of as warm and friendly, they are also seen as ingratiating.

Status also alters when and how people gaze at another. Remember the story that began this chapter? In it, Ms. L entered an elevator where she met a secretary and a company vice president. She nodded to the secretary and quickly turned to face the vice president. She said hello to him, and he responded while looking at the display consol which registered the passing floors. Exiting the elevator, she bid him farewell, and he nodded silently without diverting his gaze from the consol.

These events, drawn from actual experience, capture a common research finding: low-status people gaze at higher ones more than high-status people gaze at lower ones.[42] When high-status people gaze, it follows a particular pattern called *visual dominance behavior*, which is to say that high-status people gaze more when they are speaking than when they are listening. It is almost as if they were communicating, "When I speak, I'll make sure you listen. When you speak—well, that's not so critical. I can look elsewhere."

From a management perspective, there has been at least one interesting finding about *verbal dominance behavior*; ratings of leadership ability were highest for ROTC officers who showed the strongest patterns of *verbal dominance behavior*. That is, the ratio of gazing when speaking to gazing when listening was very high. Those rated high in leadership ability often did the former, rarely the latter.[43]

There are other nonverbal behaviors which distinguish high- and low-status people. When they are in one another's presence, high-status people tend to assume relaxed postures, low-status people comparatively rigid ones.[44] Think of a corporate executive speaking with a subordinate. Who stretches, leans back, and throws his/her arms wide apart or behind the head? Unless they are deliberately being defiant, it is unlikely that a subordinate would do these things. Touch follows a similar pattern. People who are higher in status do the touching. They have the "power" to initiate. People who are lower in status receive, and are less apt to initiate touching.[45]

None of this should be interpreted as saying that if you are a manager, others will recognize you as a higher-status authority if you slouch, touch, and gaze more when you speak than when you listen. Clearly, other factors enter into the equation. But the results do illustrate how a gesture like gazing can be a powerful influence on people's perceptions of power, status, and ability.

One other nonverbal behavior which communicates a message is the physical distance that is placed between self and others. Two books, *The Silent Language* and *The Hidden Dimension*, both by the noted anthropologist, Edward Hall, describe this phenomenon.[46] We can summarize the ideas by noting that Hall has observed people acting as if four major distance zones exist. On some occasions, by using a given zone, people can influence the course of their relationships.[47] Conversely, the relationships that people have with others whom they encounter can influence the zone which is used.[48] The zones are:

1. *Intimacy zone:* This ranges from zero distance between bodies to about 18 inches. Except when this distance is imposed, as on New York transportation during rush hours, entering this zone with another suggests a special, close relationship.
2. *Personal distance zone:* This ranges from 1½ feet to 4 feet. It is a degree of separation characteristic of relationships between friends and acquaintances.
3. *Social distance zone:* This ranges from 4 feet to 12 feet and is the distance that one can observe in business exchanges and in structured social interactions with strangers, clerks, and salespeople, for example.
4. *Public distance zone:* This ranges from 12 feet to 25 feet. Formal interaction in settings like classrooms and lectures often involves this kind of distance.

These four distance zones exist for all people, although there are cultural differences in how they are utilized. The classic story of the Italian and the Englishman who meet at a party illustrates this point. The Englishman, having a rather conservative interpretation of distance zones, is somewhat appalled when the Italian acquaintance, he met just moments ago, "moves in" too quickly for his tastes. To adjust the distance zone to one of his own liking, the Englishman backs up only to have his Italian friend step toward him once again, abiding by *his* sense of a comfortable distance for conversing. And so it goes. The two, slowly but surely, move across the room in a type of ritual dance, both seeking to maintain the conversational distance they deem appropriate. This vignette, exaggerated as it may be, has a moral worth noting: People differ in nonverbal style. Not only in distancing, but in touching, gesturing, and even eye contact, those from different backgrounds are apt to differ. This is important to remember to avoid misinterpreting another's communicational intent and to avoid having your own misinterpreted.

A final communication

An implicit secondary theme of this chapter is, "organizations benefit from clear communications, therefore, managers are obliged to make communications clearer." Toward that end, we have discussed organizational structure and communication, urging attention to the role of networks, their degree of centralization, and one's position in them. One- and two-way channels of communication were discussed, noting that one-way channels save time, but at the price of accuracy and satisfaction. The effects of defensive and supportive social climates were considered, as was the role of individual differences including sex, ethnicity, personality, status, and cultural background. Even physical distance was examined as a factor which can support or confuse communication from message sources. All of these issues were mentioned in the hope of increasing your awareness of human forces which distort the sending and receiving of messages in organizations.

But the elimination of distortion in communication is not always a goal that managers seek. Some believe that unclear communication has its uses and can even yield benefits for themselves and their organization.[49] By withholding information, increasing ambiguity, and selectively distorting interpretation, for example, members of organizations avoid mentioning what is dangerous and unacceptable. In so doing, they hope to avert unpleasant and potentially destructive confrontation.

Another example of faulty communication's benefit can be

drawn from the familiar saying, "Knowledge is power." Without commenting on the ethics, it is clear that by limiting the distribution of information, individuals and groups can maintain control of an organization's goals and operations.[50] For these people, clearer, more comprehensive communication could be a cost. Information can also be withheld by low-power groups. Misleading emphasis, half-truth, and confusing detail are often used by low-power groups to escape punishment, maintain autonomy, and keep annoying managers off their backs. In these instances, information control acts as a power equalizer.

A final example of faulty communication's possible benefits occurs during organization conflict. It has been observed that vague, ambiguous statements defining mutual interests and aims often allow parties in conflict to avoid destructive exchanges and continue negotiating.[51]

It would be wrong to conclude that distortion and deception in communication are desirable additions to organizational life. That is not so. But these last few observations make it clear that organization members sometimes face realities which cause them to take refuge in faulty communication. Whether that outcome is a consequence of an already malignant communication process or an unavoidable necessity of organization life we will leave as a question for readers to consider.

Notes

1. Johnson, W. The fateful process of Mr. A talking to Mr. B. *Havard Business Review*, 1969, *31*, 49–56.
2. Scott, R. L. Communication as an intentional, social system. *Human Communication Research*, 1977, *3*, 258–267.
3. Fisher, B. A. *Perspectives on human communication*. New York: Macmillan, 1978.
4. Miller, J. G. The current status of theory and research in interpersonal communication. *Human Communication Research*, 1978, *4*, 164–178.
5. DePaulo, B. M., Rosenthal, R., Eisenstat, R. A., Rogers, P. L., & Finkelstein, S. Decoding discrepant nonverbal cues. *Journal of Personality and Social Psychology*, 1978, *36*, 313–323; Merhabian, A., & Weiner, M. Decoding of inconsistent communications. *Journal of Personality and Social Psychology*, 1967, *6*, 109–114; Merhabian, A., & Ferris, S. R. Inference of attitudes from nonverbal communication in two channels. *Journal of Consulting Psychology*, 1967, *31*, 248–252.
6. Miller, F. E., & Rogers, L. E. A relational approach to interpersonal communication. In G. R. Miller (Ed.), *Explorations in interpersonal communication*. Beverly Hills, Calif.: Sage Publications, 1976; Parks, M. R. Relational communication: Theory and research. *Human Communication Research*, 1977, *3*, 372–381; Rogers, L. E., & Ferace, R. V. Analysis of relational communication in

dyads: New measurement procedures. *Human Communication Research,* 1975, *1,* 222-239.

7. Barnard, C. R. *The functions of the executive.* Cambridge, Mass.: Harvard University Press, 1938.

8. Katz, D., & Kahn, R. *The social psychology of organizations.* New York: John Wiley & Sons, 1966, 1970.

9. Shaw, M. E. Communication network. In L. Berkowitz (Ed.), *Advances in experimental social psychology* (Vol. 1). New York: Academic Press, 1964.

10. Glanzer, M., & Glaser, R. Techniques for the study of group structure and behavior. II: Empirical studies of the effects of structure in small groups. *Psychological Bulletin,* 1961, *58,* 1-27; Guetzkow, H. Communications. In J. March (Ed.), *Handbook of organizations.* Chicago: Rand McNally, 1965, pp. 525-573; Heise, G. A., & Miller, G. A. Problem solving by small groups using various communication nets. *Journal of Abnormal and Social Psychology,* 1951, *46,* 327-335.

11. Shaw, Communication network, p. 144.

12. Bavelas, A. Communication problems in task-oriented groups. In D. Cartwright & A. Zander (Eds.), *Group dynamics: Research and theory.* New York: Harper & Row, 1968.

13. Guetzkow, H., & Simon, H. A. The impact of certain communication nets upon organization and performance in task-oriented groups. *Management Science,* 1955, *1,* 233-250.

14. Bavelas, Communication Problems; Shaw, Communication Network, p. 144.

15. Kelley, H. H. Communication in experimentally created hierarchies. *Human Relations,* 1951, *4,* 34-56.

16. Zajonc, R. B., & Wolfe, D. M. Cognitive consequences of a person's position in a formal organization. *Human Relations,* 1966, *19,* 139-150.

17. Stuhr, A. W. Some outcomes of the New York employee survey. *Social Science Research Reports. IV: Surveys and inventories.* Standard Oil of New Jersey, 1962.

18. Leavitt, H. J. Some effects of certain communication patterns on group performance. *Journal of Abnormal and Social Psychology,* 1957, *46,* 38-50; Mulder, M. Power and satisfaction in task-oriented groups. *Acta Psychologica,* 1959, *16,* 178-225; Trow, D. B. Autonomy and job satisfaction in task-oriented groups. *Journal of Abnormal and Social Psychology,* 1957, *54,* 204-210.

19. Gilchrist, J. C., Shaw, M. E., & Walker, L. C. Some effects of unequal distribution of information in a wheel group structure. *Journal of Abnormal and Social Psychology,* 1954, *49,* 554-556.

20. Barrett, G. V., & Franke, R. H. Communication preference and performance: A cross-cultural comparison. Technical Report No. 29. Pittsburgh: Management Research Center, University of Pittsburgh, 1969.

21. Tesch, F. E., Lansky, L. M., & Lundgreen, D. C. The one-way/two-way communication exercise: Some ghosts laid to rest. *Journal of Applied Behavioral Science,* 1972, *8,* 664-673.

22. Habbe, S. Does communication make a difference? *Management Record,* 1952, *14,* 442-444.

23. Davis, K. A method of studying communication patterns in organizations. *Personnel Psychology,* 1953, *6,* 301-312.

24. Martin, N. H., & Sims, J. H. Thinking ahead: Power tactics. *Harvard Business Review,* 1956, *34,* 25.

25. Householder, F. J. A railroad checks on its communications. *Personnel,* 1954, *32,* 413-415.

26. Opinion Research Corporation. *Public opinion index for industry.* October 1953.

27. Sirota, D. Why managers don't use attitude survey results. *Personnel,* January/February 1970.

28. Sayles, L. R. *Behavior of industrial work groups: Predictions and control.* New York: John Wiley & Sons, 1958.

29. Alger, L. J. *Suggestion statistics.* Production series 165. New York: American Management Association, 1946; Bellows, R. M. *Psychology of personnel in business and industry.* Englewood Cliffs, N.J.: Prentice-Hall, 1954; Scott, W. D., & Clothier, R. C. *Personnel management* (3rd ed.). New York: McGraw-Hill, 1941.

30. Bellows, *Psychology of personnel in business and industry.*

31. Johnson, R. E. Results of the 1958 C.Y.I. opinion survey. *Social Science Research Reports IV: Survey and Inventories.* Standard Oil of New Jersey, 1962.

32. Rosen, S., & Tesser, A. On reluctance to communicate undesirable information: The MUM effect. *Sociometry,* 1970, *33,* 253–263; Tesser, A., Rosen, S., & Conlee, M.C. News valance and available recipient as determinants of news transmission. *Sociometry,* 1972, *35,* 619–628.

33. Johnson, R. E., Conlee, M. C., & Tesser, A. Effects of similarity of fate on bad news transmission: A re-examination. *Journal of Personality and Social Psychology,* 1974, *29,* 644–648; Read, W. H. Upward communication in industrial hierarchies. *Human Relations,* 1962, *15,* 3–15.

34. Gibb, J. R. Defensive communication. *Journal of Communication,* 1961, *11,* 3, 141–148.

35. Gibb, Defensive communication, p. 141.

36. Ibid., p. 141.

37. Ibid., p. 146.

38. Baron, R. A. Reducing the influence of an aggressive model: The restraining effects of discrepant modeling cues. *Journal of Personality and Social Psychology,* 1971, *20,* 240–245; Cashell, D. J. *Sex differences in linguistic style.* Unpublished doctoral dissertation, Purdue University, 1978.

39. Argyle, M., Fugheur, R., Alkema, F., & McCallin, M. The different functions of gaze. *Semiotica,* 1973, *7,* 19–32; Knapp, M. L. *Nonverbal communication in human interaction* (2nd ed.). New York: Holt, Rinehart & Winston, 1978.

40. La France, M., & Mayo, C. *Moving bodies: Nonverbal communication in social relationships.* Monterey, Calif.: Brooks/Cole, 1978.

41. Kleinke, C. L., Bustos, A. A., Meeker, F. B., & Staneski, R. A. Effects of self-attributed and other-attributed gaze on interpersonal evaluations between males and females. *Journal of Experimental Social Psychology,* 1973, *9,* 154–163; Kleinke, C. L., Staneski, R. A., & Weaver, P. Evaluation of a person who uses another's name in ingratiating and non-ingratiating structures. *Journal of Experimental Social Psychology,* 1972, *8,* 457–466.

42. Exline, R. V. Visual interaction: The glances of power and preference. In J. K. Cole (Ed.), *Nebraska Symposium on Motivation* (Vol. 19). Lincoln, Neb.: University of Nebraska Press, 1971, pp. 163–206; Exline, R. V., Ellyson, S. L., & Long, B. Visual behavior as an aspect of power role relationships. In P. Pliner, L. Krames, & T. Allowey (Eds.), *Nonverbal communication of aggression* (Vol. 2). New York: Plenum Press, 1975.

43. Exline et al., Visual behavior.

44. Merhabian, A. Significance of posture and position in the communication of attitude and status relationships. *Psychological Bulletin,* 1969, *71,* 359–372; Merhabian, A. *Nonverbal communication.* Chicago: Aldine-Atherton, 1972; Scheflen, A. *Body language and the social order.* Englewood Cliffs, N.J.: Prentice-Hall, 1972.

45. Henley, N. M. *Body politics: Power, sex, and nonverbal communication.* Englewood Cliffs, N.J.: Prentice-Hall, 1977.

46. Hall, E. T. *The silent language.* New York: Doubleday, 1959; Hall, E. T. *The hidden dimension.* Garden City, N.Y.: Doubleday, 1966.

47. Merhabian, Significance of posture and position. Rosenfeld, H. M. Affects of approval-seeking induction on interpersonal proximity. *Psychological Reports*, 1965, *17*, 120-122.

48. Sundstrom, E., & Altman, I. Personal space and interpersonal relationships: Research review and theoretical model. *Human Ecology*, 1976, *4*, 47-67.

49. Keisler, S. *Interpersonal processes in groups and organizations*. Arlington Heights, Ill.: AHM Publishing, 1978.

50. Crozier, M. *The bureaucratic phenomenon*. Chicago: University of Chicago Press, 1964; Thompson, J. D. *Organizations in action*. New York: McGraw-Hill, 1967.

51. Kursh, C. O. The benefits of poor communication. *Psychoanalytic Review*, 1971, *58*, 189-208; Okon, M. A., & DiVesta, F. J. Cooperation and competition in coacting groups. *Journal of Personality and Social Psychology*, 1975, *31*, 615-620.

3

Perceiving People
and Situations

LOOK at the drawings in Figure 3-1. Can you answer the questions accompanying them? Most people think they can, and do, and in so doing dramatize a basic psychological principle: perceptions often are erroneous. If, in any of the three examples, you identified a longer line, then you made a mistake. In fact, the focal pair of lines in each of the drawings is exactly equal in length.

In viewing people and situations, there also is a tendency to assume that what we experience is "the truth." If we experience

Figure 3-1

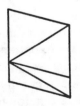

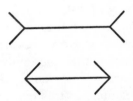

Which line is longer?   Which diagonal is   Which line is longer?
                             longer?

Source: Kimble, G. A., & Garmezy, N. *Principles of general psychology.* New York: Ronald Press, 1963, p. 324.

an individual as loud, uncouth, and stupid, we assume that he or she *is* loud, uncouth, and stupid. Similarly, if we experience a situation as exciting, potentially rewarding, and providing an opportunity for creativity, we assume that this experience is a direct result of the situation—we do not stop to realize that our minds intervene in the stimulus-experience chain, often resulting in a somewhat less than accurate view of the world.

Examples of errors in perception are common enough. Nearly everyone has had the experience of dialing a phone number, hearing a voice, and proceeding to talk only to find, after an embarrassing lack of response, that you have dialed a wrong number and the voice that you thought you heard was not the one that you actually heard. One account executive told how, on one occasion, she met her superior as they were both leaving the office. The superior, an unusually formal person, seemed particularly elated and the new, young, aspiring employee interpreted this behavior as an indication of the superior's satisfaction with her rather than as a reaction to other events. The misperception encouraged a friendly, informal response which resulted in months of effort aimed at repairing the relationship. A similarly embarrassing and costly episode occurred when the manager of a branch bank wrongly assumed that a colleague agreed with his political views because the two of them "thought alike" about company issues. Each of these examples highlights the personal contribution we make to perception, and the potential distortions it can produce.

But what we *perceive*, not what *is*, is all we have to go on. We consider it to be truth. And it is this perception of reality, not reality itself, which forms the basis of our actions. Failure to recognize this can have devastating consequences in organizational life.

Differences in perception

Because there is not necessarily a one-to-one relationship between what we see and how we experience it, people often hold different perceptions of the same event. Sometimes these perceptions are not only different, but actually contradictory. A good example of this can be found in a study conducted in 1954 documenting student reactions to a particularly brutal Dartmouth-Princeton football game.

A few minutes after the opening kickoff, it became apparent that the game was going to be a rough one. The referees were kept busy blowing their whistles and penalizing both sides. In the second quarter, Princeton's star left the game with a broken nose. In the third quarter, a Dartmouth player was taken off the field with a broken leg. Tempers flared both during and after the game. The official statistics of the game, which Princeton won, showed that Dartmouth was penalized 70 yards, Princeton 25, not counting more than a few plays in which both sides were penalized.[1]

Asked after the game who had started the rough play, only 36 percent of the Dartmouth students but as many as 86 percent of the Princeton students indicated that Dartmouth was at fault. Furthermore, after viewing a film of the game, Princeton students reported seeing twice as many infractions by Dartmouth players as did Dartmouth students.

This study makes evident that different people viewing the identical physical event often arrive at totally different conclusions. Other examples of this phenomenon abound. It is well known, for instance, that the favorite food of an individual from one culture may absolutely disgust a person from another culture. Similarly, the same weather may be comfortable for someone from Florida but unbearably hot for someone from Maine. Who the viewer is, his/her history, and current circumstances all influence perception.

Thus, what is self-evident to a manager may not be so to a subordinate, superior, or someone in a different function. Their view of the facts are biased much as the manager's is. Assuming otherwise is a common and often deadly mistake. For all of these reasons, it is impossible to influence behavior or respond adequately to it without some understanding of the other's experience of the world. It also is crucial to recognize and come to grips with one's own blinders, which are apt to distort perception.

Perception-biasing factors

Needs

In 1947, a study was done in which children from an upper-class Boston school and children from a settlement house in one of Boston's slums were asked to estimate the size of a penny, a nickel, a dime, a quarter, and a half dollar.[2] The children from poor homes estimated each of the coins to be far bigger than did the others. A common interpretation of these findings is that needs were guiding the perception of money and, for the needy children tested, the coins loomed "larger than life." Some years later, researchers showed that people who were thirsty judged slides with pictures of thirst-quenching drinks to be brighter than equally vivid slides not displaying such pictures.[3] Here, too, the need of the individual was found to interfere with his/her perception. Things of value, it seems, are accentuated.

Similar findings have been discovered in organizational research. It is interesting to note, for instance, that when asked to describe the people they work with, employees talk more about their bosses than about anyone else, despite the fact that they may interact with others as often or even more often than they do with bosses.[4] But bosses, of course, are the people most important to satisfying a worker's needs and, like a 25-cent piece in the minds of small, poor children, they too sometimes "loom larger than life."

The tendency to accentuate need-satisfying aspects of situations can create problems on the job. Consider the following event:

Ms. H has just begun work after completing her M.B.A. She has been at company X for three months and, after overcoming her initial anxiety, seems to be doing quite well. But she is a perfectionist; she is not entirely satisfied with her output and believes that she should be getting more work out of her subordinates. She also is convinced that they do not like her very much, and she resolves to sit down with each of them individually to go over their projects. In this way, she hopes to build relationships with them and, in the process, eliminate the awkwardness she now senses whenever they talk.

When leaving work one evening, she bumps into one of her subordinates, Mr. B. As they ride down in the elevator together, he comments on her "superb performance" and tells her that since she has arrived things have been more effectively managed than ever before. He also mentions how different she is from her predecessor.

As Ms. H hails a taxicab to take her home, she mulls over Mr. B's words. "Wow," she says to herself, "was I reading that situation wrong! They love me." As the taxi pulls up, she decides to postpone her tête-à-têtes with each of her subordinates. "We all have to set priorities," she notes, "and this issue evidentally is not one which heads the list."

Ms. H has chosen to focus upon and magnify the favorable comments that Mr. B made. Without knowing whether his views are shared or even whether he really believes what he is saying (after all, there are several motives that may be driving him other than veracity), she accepts what she wants to hear as truth. Her desire to hear good things about herself may, in this case, backfire. Her original feelings about the state of her working relationships may be on target, and doing something about them might, in fact, be of very top priority if she is to be successful in her job.

Thus, needs make valued aspects of individuals or situations salient. We tend to see what we wish is so. But how about what we wish is not so?

Sometimes we have our ears and eyes particularly attuned to hear and see negative information. This occurs particularly when we sense danger afoot. The juices get going and we become vigilant, ready to recognize the faintest suggestion of threat to ourselves and our well-being. This sense of being on guard does not prevail at all times, however, and more often there is a tendency to overlook what is undesirable.

Surely everyone has had the experience of forgetting an appointment with someone he/she really does not want to see. Remembering seems to be selective. And so is perception. People tend to ignore the unpleasant in life or to avoid it for as long as they can. It even has been demonstrated that, when flashed on a screen for only a few seconds, words that are unpleasant are recognized less readily than words that are pleasant.[5] It thus would seem that, just as we avoid *doing* things that are unpleasant, we avoid *seeing* things that are unpleasant to us. This is known as *perceptual defense.*

Perceptual defense can promote effective work behavior. It allows us to screen ourselves from events and people who might potentially distract or hinder us from accomplishing our goals. However, perceptual defense can also render us psychologically deaf and blind to events and/or people to whom we should be attending. Not hearing the warning in the words of a superior, for instance, may have very serious consequences for career advancement—it is hard to heed a warning that is not heard. Similarly, not noticing a memo regarding a telephone call from an important client who happens to "bug" you can severely harm your work effectiveness. Therefore, just as it is important to carefully examine one's perceptions of positive events for possible exaggerations, it is important to remain alert in the hope of making oneself aware of whom and what we choose to ignore.

In summary, it appears that needs bias perception in several ways. They accentuate what we desire to see and hear and tend to screen us from what we do not desire to see and hear, except when we are alert to potential danger. Need-based errors in perception are, therefore, systematically directed at producing a positive state of mind, even if it is at the cost of accuracy.

Category schemes

When we first meet another person, we are likely to categorize him/her on certain dimensions. Questions are asked: Is he/she attractive? Intelligent? Interesting? Situations also are classified into categories, e.g., complicated, threatening, pleasant, etc. Such categorization helps make the word more manageable—it gives us a quick way of sizing things up and enables speedy response.

But the categories that are important to one perceiver do not regularly coincide with those that are important for another.[6] For some people, good-bad is a critical category in perceiving people, for others, intelligent-stupid may be more important. Research in person perception shows that categories do, in fact, derive from the perceiver, not from the person being perceived.[7] The preference for some categories over others reflects the implicit theories we have about people and situations.

There are consequences of this selective use of categories in perception. For example, those of us for whom sociability is a critical dynamic will be prone to see the world in terms of acceptance and rejection. These sociability-oriented people are predisposed to attend more to whether another is friendly than whether he/she is effective or high-powered. No doubt, they will find only certain individuals attractive, and when, for instance, hiring decisions are made, they may be insensitive to aspects of a candidate's makeup that are far more critical to successful performance. Similarly, managers who focus on efficiency may be insensitive to interpersonal aspects of individuals that also are important in determining work effectiveness.

It would thus seem that the type of categories a manager brings to bear are important determinants of what he/she sees. It also seems likely that the greater the number of categories that a manager uses in processing what he/she sees, the better off he/she will be. In fact, there are research findings which suggest that the degree of differentiation in the perception of others is related to managerial effectiveness.[8]

Not only are the type and the number of category dimensions used of importance, but the weighting attached to each also is critical. Even when people use the same categories for perceptual organization, they sometimes give radically different weights to the dimensions they use in common. This can result in very different overall evaluations. For example:

Mr. J has been involved in training in a multinational chemical company for some time. He has just completed a workshop for a major affiliate of the company, and, in reviewing the evaluations done by participants, his superior comes across a very curious fact. Of the 20 overall ratings (given in response to the question, "Generally, how effective was Mr. J?)" 8 were extremely high (6 or 7 on a seven-point scale) and 9 were extremely low (1 or 2 on a seven-point scale). Mr. J's supervisor was puzzled. All the workshop participants had experienced the same Mr. J. How could their reactions differ so?

At the next conference Mr. J conducted, a more detailed rating form was administered. In addition to asking for a general rating of each of the workshop leaders, it requested some specific descriptive material. Then the reason for the split vote became clear. Mr. J, it seemed, was superb at one-to-one counseling with the participants and was seen as warm, sympathetic, and humane. But, at the same time, Mr. J was seen as a poor lecturer and deadly boring in front of a group. Everyone agreed on his strengths and weaknesses.

Evidently, when Mr. J was given his overall rating, different weight was attached to his characteristics by different people. Those to whom the counseling skills were of great importance gave him a high effectiveness rating; those to whom the teaching skills were of importance gave him a low rating. And, in some sense, both points of view were correct.

Given the impact of categorization processes on how we perceive the world, it seems essential for every manager to become aware of (1) the number of categories he or she uses in sizing up a person or a situation; (2) what these categories are; and (3) the importance attached to each of these categories in forming perceptions.

One way to uncover these issues is to examine a list of bipolar adjective dimensions such as that in Table 3-1 and rank them according to their importance to you in judging others in work settings. The best way to go about this is to consider what you would want to know if you had only one question to ask about someone you did not know, then two, then three, and so on, and rank the corresponding dimension accordingly. Afterward, you might decide at what rank you feel the added information you get from asking a question about the next dimension is not particularly useful; that is, the point at which you already have formed a fairly firm impression with the information you have.

This exercise helps you become aware of your perceptual schema. It provides you with an opportunity to assess whether you are attending only to a narrow band of attributes, whether your preferred dimensions are appropriate to the situations in which you employ them, and whether some of the dimensions at the bottom of your rank order should, in fact, be given more weight. A similar procedure can be used to identify your schema for perceiving situations rather than people, although a different list of adjective dimensions would then be needed.

In summary, perception can be biased by the category dimensions that we use to size up people and situations. The type, number, and importance we attach to such dimensions all influence what we see. Furthermore, these dimensions tend to be connected to a whole constellation of others. For example, those who

Table 3-1
Example of some adjective dimensions

gutsy-timid	loyal-fickle
energetic-lethargic	ambitious-unambitious
passive-assertive	sophisticated-provincial
attractive-unattractive	stimulating-boring
strong-weak	effective-ineffective
cold-warm	prompt-tardy
intelligent-stupid	decisive-indecisive
knowledgable-ignorant	hardworking-lazy
loud-quiet	happy-depressed
hard-soft	nervous-calm
fast-slow	outgoing-introverted
simple-complex	competitive-cooperative
friendly-unfriendly	dependent-independent
erratic-dependable	kind-nasty
	aggreable-disagreeable

saw Mr. J primarily as a poor lecturer might also assume that he is unsure of himself and introverted. And those who saw Mr. J primarily as a fine counselor might assume he also is mature and sensible in his approach to life. Thus, any bit of data about a person or event has implications for a whole host of attributes. Stereotypes, which will be discussed in detail in Chapter 10 of this book, are the outcome of just such a process.

Perspective

Remember the story of the blind men and the elephant? Each one of them, standing in his unique position vis-à-vis the elephant, reached out and touched a different part of the enormous animal. Consequently, each had a different impression of what an elephant is like.

And so it is with those of us who are not blind. Our unique perspective highlights some aspects of what we see and obscures others. Thus, our perceptions are flawed by our vantage point for observation. Organizational affiliation, position, and professional orientation each contribute to the bias of perspective.

Organizational affiliation. Consider the situation of Mr. B, the production supervisor, and Mr. T, the maintenance supervisor in one division of a large assembly plant:

They were called to a joint meeting by their superior, Mr. K, who was himself recently called into his immediate supervisor's office. Productivity in the division had been down for nearly two weeks. The drop was now starting to be felt by other groups in the plant. Mr. B's and Mr. T's superior was an easy-going fellow. No recriminations or explanations were encouraged. After a discussion of the issues, Mr. K said that they were "to go all out in keeping equipment operating. It was essential to push production levels beyond normal quotas."

Mr. B, the production supervisor, heard the message clearly, especially the last part. It meant that maintenance schedules and shutdowns could be reduced so that equipment could remain in operation for longer periods. Mr. T also heard the message clearly, especially the first part. As he left the meeting, he wondered how he would juggle his crews in order to handle the increased number of maintenance checks and shutdowns that would now be required.

Thus, as with the blind men and the elephant, the very same message had different contours for Mr. B and Mr. T. This state of affairs is not uncommon. Because individuals belong to different units of an organization, they view the same event from different vantage points and that leads to selective perception—focusing on different aspects of the same event. The aspect most salient is, of course, the one that touches the individual most closely.

Position. Much as different organizational affiliations can result in differential perception of the same event, a manager's position in the organization's hierarchy can influence how or what he/she "sees." What is self-evident to him or her may not be so to a subordinate or superior.

If one were to ask both a manager and his/her subordinates about his/her supervisory style, for instance, it is highly likely that there would be disagreement. By and large, supervisors tend to see their supervisory style as looser and more democratic than do their subordinates.[9] Interestingly, if you were then to question the same managers about *their* superiors, you would be likely to find the same pattern; they would see their superiors as less democratic than their superiors see themselves.

And supervisory style is not the only thing supervisors and subordinates see differently. Supervisors tend to believe that their subordinates have more of a role in decision making than their subordinates feel they have.[10] Supervisors also tend to see themselves as using primarily rewards and other positive incentives to motivate subordinates, while subordinates are more likely to see coercion and threat as the keystone of their supervisor's influence strategy.

All of these examples make clear that the role one occupies in a hierarchy exerts a powerful influence on perception. Evidently, subordinates have some uniform perceptions no matter how high or low they are on the organizational hierarchy in an absolute sense. Similarly, supervisors seem to have a consistent pattern of perception regardless of the organizational level at which they are functioning. This, of course, means that the same individual, who is both a supervisor to someone and a subordinate to someone else, will probably view events differently as a function of the particular hierarchical role he/she is occupying at the time.

Professional orientation. People with different professional orientations are likely to have different styles of operating; their training and education often emphasize different approaches to problems. Thus, what may appear to be a perfectly reasonable course of action to one individual may appear to be foolish and wasteful to another. Consider the following situation:

There has been a outburst during a meeting of the long-range planning group in a publishing company. The group is very varied in composition—it consists of individuals from the legal, accounting, sales, production, and personnel departments. Meetings, which have been occuring monthly for five months, have been tense. This is not a group of people who are used to working with one another.

The outburst, which was not entirely unexpected, involved the sales and production people. The relationship between these two departments had been deteriorating in recent months, with each one accusing the other of being responsible for its problems. Sparked by a financial report detailing the past quarter's earnings, the representatives of each of these departments went after each other. In front of the total group, insults were hurled and caustic accusations launched.

The group was immobilized. Finally, after an embarrassed silence, the individual from accounting suggested that the group move on to the "real" business of the day. But the individual from personnel, trained in psychology, insisted that the issue between the sales and production departments be aired and perhaps resolved. He claimed that no constructive work could be done by the planning group until the problem between these two members was explored. The accountant became increasingly irritable. The meeting ended with everyone feeling frustrated.

The reactions of the accountant and the psychologist reflect their different perceptions of what has happened. The accountant sees the episode between the sales and production people as irrelevant to the task at hand; the psychologist sees it as directly related to the work of the group. The backgrounds and training of each almost guarantees that they will view the world differently.

Thus, organizational affiliation, hierarchical role, and professional orientation are some of the factors that can affect one's perspective in perceiving people and situations. Each of these put a particular slant on what one looks at and how it is interpreted. As such, they bias perception in quite systematic and predictable ways.

Values

We all make assumptions about what makes people tick. As managers, these assumptions are likely not only to guide our behavior (see Chapter 4 on motivating others), but also to bias our perceptions. It is common to make the assumption, for instance, that all subordinates want to be promoted. The symbolic value of promotion as a reward is considered to be universal. However, many managers are currently discovering that promotion, in and of itself, is not always well received. This is especially so when relocating is required:

Bill Jones has a sick feeling in the pit of his stomach as he pulls into the driveway of his house in a suburb of New York City. He has just been told that he has been promoted. That's the good news. The bad news is that he will have to move to a small town in Arizona where a new plant is being built. He dreads telling his wife Marcy about it. She is in the third year of doctoral study at a New York university and is determined to complete her dissertation within the next two years. Kathy, his daughter, is also going to be upset. She has been taking dancing lessons at a first-rate ballet school and has her heart set on trying out for the Christmas performances of the *Nutcracker Suite* next fall. Even. his son Jeffrey is apt to be upset. He was just chosen to be a starting forward on his high school's basketball team, an honor for which he has worked long and hard. Bill knows that Mr. X, his boss, had every intention of doing him a favor by recommending him for this promotion but, as he approaches his front door, he wishes that there were some way to turn it down without ruining forever his chances to move up in the company.

The situation of Bill Jones is becoming increasingly common.[11] With two-career families on the rise and more attention to the needs of the family as a whole, the needs of others can overshadow one's own desire for advancement. In such situations, the gift of a promotion may turn into the burden of a major family problem.

There also are instances in which promotion is a bane rather than a boon. An example is when the more prestigious job is one which holds less challenge or is removed from the type of work one really likes to do. Here, one is reminded of a well-known television news anchor in a large eastern city who, after several years at the pinnacle of his success—his own news show—gave it all up to return to pounding the pavement, being just a reporter because, he claimed, that is what television journalism is all about. In another case, an acquaintance, who was the CEO of one operating unit of a large multinational corporation, complained to this book's authors in disgruntled, depressed tones about his promotion to vice president. It was a promotion that brought him out of the field, back to New York headquarters, for "paper pushing and politics."

Thus, a manager's perception of an event, here a promotion, may not be shared by his subordinates. And the consequences of this may be exactly the opposite of what the manager had intended. The manager's attempt to reward his/her subordinate may, rather than make the subordinate happy, create problems and distress.

The promotion issue is an example of how, in today's world, there is a shifting pattern of commitment to investment in one's career. More and more, young people starting out in the job market are seeing work as merely one aspect of their lives, not the only one. Nonwork has taken on a new importance, and in doing so, may create a value disparity. Refusing to work overtime, for instance, may be perceived as perfectly reasonable to those who place their families above their work, but may be perceived as irresponsible to those who do not. Taking sick days when one is ill rather than braving it out and coming in to work is another example. It may seem the only sensible course of action to those who put themselves and their physical well-being above work, but greedy and exploitative to those who do not. In each case, the value orientation of a manager leads to one perception rather than the other. And the consequences of the two perceptions are apt to be quite different.

Expectations

Have you ever heard the story about the man who gets a flat tire at 2 A.M. on a deserted road, only to find that his spare has been stolen? The man (let's call him Mr. Smith), being a sensible fellow, starts to walk in the direction of the nearest town, all the while looking for a telephone so he can call for assistance. After walking for about half an hour, he sees a house several hundred yards in front of him. The house is completely dark, although obviously inhabited—there is smoke puffing from the chimney. Mr. Smith, who by now is cold and tired, is elated at the sight of the house. That is, at first he is. But as he gets closer and closer to it, he begins to play out an imagined scenario; he gets to the door, rings the bell, and, after some time, the head of the household, a man clad in a robe and looking very sleepy, comes to the door. Mr.

Smith asks to use the phone. The man whose house it is, after uttering some furious words, slams the door in his face.

This scenario plays itself over and over again in Mr. Smith's head. As he trudges up to the door of the house and rings the bell, he feels the anger welling up in him—anger that is a reaction to his imagined scenario. The door finally opens, and before the surprised resident can inquire as to his needs, Mr. Smith gruffly yells, "You can take your lousy phone and go to Hell!" And with that, he turns on his heel and stalks off into the night, leaving the man in the doorway openmouthed and baffled.

This story captures a truism; our expectations often influence what we perceive. Sometimes our expectations, or *perceptual set*, cause us to view the world selectively and see only the parts of events or people that we anticipate. At other times, such as in the example with Mr. Smith, our expectations cause us to actually distort what we see so it fits our preconceptions.

The role of expectations on the perception of people has been well documented. In a very influential study conducted by Harold Kelley in 1950, a class of students enrolled in a psychology course at M.I.T. were told that the regular instructor was out of town and a new instructor would be replacing him for the day.[12] The guest instructor then led the class in a discussion, immediately after which the students were asked to describe their impressions of him on a brief questionnaire. Before meeting the guest instructor, however, a one-paragraph biographical description of him was handed out so the class could get "some idea of what he's like." Two descriptions, differing only in a single detail, were distributed. One set of descriptions read:

> Mr. _____ is a graduate student in the Department of Economics and Social Sciences here at M.I.T. He has had three semesters of teaching experience in psychology at another college. This is his first semester teaching Ec. 70. He is 26 years old, a veteran, and married. People who know him consider him to be a rather cold person, industrious, critical, practical, and determined.[13]

The second set of descriptions was identical except for the last sentence. It read:

> People who know him consider him to be a very warm person, industrious, critical, practical, and determined.[13]

Thus, only the phrases "rather cold" and "very warm" distinguished the two descriptions.

Offhand, one would think that such a minor difference in descriptions would have very little consequence. But this is not what Kelley found. Students who were told that the instructor would be "rather cold," consistently rated him less favorably than did those who were told that he would be "very warm". The former group saw him as less considerate of others, less informal, less sociable, less popular, less good-natured, less humorous, and less humane. Additionally, the students who were led to expect a cold person were less active in the class discussion than those who were led to believe that he would be warm. It is remarkable that one simple difference in a description could cause such massive differences in impressions of the very same man, in the very same classroom, running the same discussion. It is even more remarkable that not only were impressions affected, but behavior as well.

The importance of this research is great. It demonstrates the tremendous influence of previous information on our perceptions. The relevance of the findings to organizational life is extensive. Consider, for example, the following instances: a newcomer to an organization asks a co-worker for information about the boss; or an employer contacts a prospective employee's character reference and requests an evaluation prior to interviewing him/her. In both of these cases (and many, many more), Kelley's findings would suggest that the previous information given will shape how one individual perceives the other and the nature of future interaction with him/her.

Kelley's research also demonstrates that expectations can cause different individuals to perceive the same event in different ways. If ambiguous, a person or situation will be perceived in accordance with preconceptions.[14] Thus, if one person expects a situation to be pleasant and another expects it to be unpleasant, it is likely that the two will experience the same situation quite differently. This, too, has important implications for organizational life. If one college recruiter, for instance, believes that graduates of the Wharton School are well trained and another believes they are poorly trained, their subjective reactions to a job candidate with a Wharton degree are apt to differ considerably.

Expectations originate from many different sources. Some arise from previous information; thus, where you are, what you are doing, and who you have contact with can all create expectations. Others arise from individual histories, background characteristics, and personality dispositions (e.g., optimists and pessimists). And still others arise from societal stereotypes. The latter source of expectations is potentially profound as well as pernicious, and its organizational consequences will be discussed in more detail in Chapter 10, "De-stereotyping."

Tendency toward constancy

Often when a person is perceived to have one favorable quality, he/she is assumed to have a whole host of other favorable qualities, as well. This is known as a *halo effect*. Sometimes this also is known as the "teacher's pet" phenomenon: if Sally is a fine student regarding conduct in the classroom, the teacher may assume she also is a fine student in reading and math, is considerate of others, is respectful of her elders, and is incapable of being responsible for the most recent school theft.[15]

And so it is with the perception of people in organizations. A favorable impression of one characteristic of a subordinate can spread to all other characteristics. Often, this is an error of reasoning—people are rarely indiscriminately "good" on all dimensions. Being intelligent, for example, does not necessarily indicate a tendency toward honesty and/or patience. Yet, in an effort to impose some stability on the world we encounter, these errors abound.

Halo effects are not limited to favorable characteristics. Negative halo effects also occur. Thus, a superior who is known to be very hard driving and to put a great deal of pressure on subordinates to produce, may wrongfully be identified as insensitive to their problems, stingy with bonuses, and selfish about giving credit and praise. Here, too, a total picture is drawn on the basis of one bit of information, a picture which, in this case, is consistent in its unfavorableness.

The halo effect is one type of *logical* error that is often made in perceiving others. A logical error is the tendency to see a group of traits as "belonging together" when, in fact, they logically do not.[16] Halo effects are logical errors with regard to evaluation, i.e., favorableness or unfavorableness. But, as we discussed in an earlier section, other traits also are thought to "go together," and information about one leads to assumptions about others. Thus, shy people are often assumed to be polite and unambitious, and glamorous-looking people are often assumed to be shallow and not hard working.

The operation of the halo effect and other logical errors of perception can lead to errors of judgment. In selecting a person to do an important task, or to represent one's department on a task force, a wrong choice may be made. Halo effects can result in an overblown assessment of an individual's skills. Similarly, negative halo effects can result in the failure to capitalize on a subordinate's talents and capabilities. Rather than giving him or her opportunities, we "write off" the individual on the basis of one negative trait.

Yet another type of perceptual bias that is prompted by the tendency toward constancy is that of perceiving the behavior of others as consistent across situations. Thus, it is assumed, for instance, that a co-worker who is outspoken and confident in her dealings with her peers will be similarly outspoken and confident in her dealings with her superiors. Although it seems only reasonable to assume that this individual's behavior in one situation should be indicative of how she will act in another, this assumption often is incorrect.[17]

One reason for this error is the general proclivity to see others' behavior as prompted by personality traits rather than by the particular circumstance in which they find themselves.[18] Thus, to continue with our example, we see the co-worker as an outspoken and confident *person*, not as outspoken and confident when she is comfortable and in a nonthreatening situation. We do not realize that, when tense and nervous, this same co-worker is quite shy and diffident. And, because we are likely to see her in only a limited set of situations (e.g., with her peers), our theory about what she is like is repeatedly supported; the behavior we see does not span all the variability in her behavior that truly exists.

As with the other excesses of the tendency toward constancy in perception, the assumption of cross-situational consistency in behavior also can lead to errors of judgment in organizational life. In this case, too, inappropriate personnel decisions can be made because of the failure to recognize that individuals are not the same with all people under all conditions. Indiscriminate assumptions of effectiveness or of ineptitude are almost certain to result in a less than optimal use of human resources.

Attributional processes

For three years, Carol Granger was a relatively inconspicuous young woman at company M. She worked in the customer-relations department and recently had become engaged to an attorney. Then came the confrontation. She accused her boss of sex discrimination. She claimed he had promoted men whose work was of lesser quality than her own, who handled fewer accounts than she, and whose attendance records were far more spotty than hers. Soon after, she began legal proceedings against company M.

Why did Ms. Granger wait so long to complain? Why did she not use grievance procedures within company M set up expressly for this purpose? Did her imminent marriage to an attorney have anything to do with her legal action? These questions, and the many others this real-life example prompts, demonstrate that we rarely are content to passively note an episode. Rather, we tend to make inferences about why it has occurred. This tendency to ask "why" reflects our belief that events are *caused*, they do not simply happen. The process by which we answer this question has come to be known as the *attribution process*.

There are several attributional errors and biases that have repeatedly been discovered in research. The most pervasive attributional error is that which we have briefly mentioned in the last section—the error of underestimating the situational causes of another's behavior and overestimating the role played by personality characteristics. There is a tendency to perceive people as the cause of events, unless evidence to the contrary is overwhelming. Thus, if an employee, Mr. Jones, talks on the phone most of the day, regularly comes in late, and already has used up his sick days for the year although it is the beginning of March, we generally will assume that his behavior is caused by his laziness, irresponsibility, and lack of commitment to his job. We do not immediately assume that Mr. Jones has an ailing wife or some other personal problem unless we have known him awhile, and his present behavior is a departure from what we know him to be like. But, in many cases, behavior *is* caused by the situation—by forces external to the individual.

Interestingly, almost the opposite distortion in attributional processes occurs when we seek to explain our own behavior.[19] Here, situational forces, not our own personalities, are emphasized. Thus, the Mr. Jones in our example will most likely see his own behavior as a result of the tremendous stress he is under, not as reflecting an enduring characteristic of himself.

Harold Kelley has identified another source of attributional error in the judgment of causation.[20] The *illusion of external constraint* is the illusion whereby an individual does not recognize his/her own part in prompting the behavior of others. As with the driver who continually sees accidents in his rearview mirror and constantly complains about "bad drivers," never guessing that his own driving is causing others to career into one another, many of us are blind to the effects we are having on others. In organizational life it is quite usual, for instance, for a person to discount the fact that his/her own aggressiveness has sparked the aggressive behavior of others. Rather, he/she is under the illusion that the others' personalities or the situation in which they all find themselves is the reason for the aggression. His/her own role in the process is disregarded. Such illusions predominate, particularly when the events being explained are undesirable and thus one's role in sparking them is unpleasant to admit, even to oneself.

In their classic work, "From acts to dispositions," Edward Jones and Keith Davis discuss two additional sources of distortion in attributional processes.[21] Both influence the formation of inferences about others. The first, *hedonic relevance*, regards the importance of another's behavior to oneself. If, for instance, you are greatly committed to the idea that those in business should be attentive to environmental issues, someone whose behavior is unmindful of the environment is hedonically relevant to you. Consequently, you will be more likely to infer personality characteristics of that individual (such as selfishness or short-sightedness) than would someone for whom such behavior is not hedonically relevant. The second influence on the formation of inferences about others, *personalism*, concerns the effects of the observed individual's behavior on the perceiver. You would feel more strongly that a person is rude if he/she snubbed you than you would if you saw him/her snub someone else.

Each of the attributional biases identified here operates when we seek to explain why a given event has occurred. Since engaging in the process of attributing causes for events is virtually automatic and essentially unconscious, such biases are very insidious. Only by forcing ourselves to make conscious the way in which we explain events can these errors be identified and corrected.

Conclusion

Perceptual biases abound. They come in many shapes and forms. But does perception actually influence behavior? In Kelley's research, classroom participation was found to be affected by the perception of the instructor. In a more recent research effort, reward allocation was found to be affected by the type of attributions made about a worker.[22] It seems that how one views another or a situation is very influential in determining how that individual behaves.

This raises the possibility of a vicious circle operating between perceptions and behavior. Theodore Newcomb, in discussing this idea in 1947, termed one aspect of this vicious circle *autistic hostility*.[23] In other words, unfavorable impressions of someone result in a restriction of interaction and contact with that person, which, in turn, makes it extremely unlikely that the initially unfavorable impression will ever be disconfirmed. If, for example, a co-worker ignores a greeting because he/she is preoccupied, you may assume he/she is unfriendly and a snob. Consequently, you avoid him/her in the future, and when, on rare occasions, he/she has an opportunity to be friendly, you discount the behavior, being suspicious about his/her interest. Thus, there is little opportunity for you to discover that your initial impression has been in error.

The same type of vicious circle can occur with regard to perception of situations. If, for instance, your first presentation to the top management group is a disaster, with a great deal of anger and hostility directed toward you, you may assume that all such meetings are dangerous and threatening. Consequently, you walk on eggshells when making subsequent presentations, saying no more than is necessary and taking no risks. If the group encourages you to freely discuss your ideas, you are suspicious and do not comply. You, therefore, never have the opportunity to disconfirm your original impression of these meetings, even if the particular day you first made a presentation was anomalous and not at all representative of the typical meeting.

This chapter has discussed the many ways in which perception is vulnerable to distortion. The fact that such distortion can potentially result in mistakes in judgment and action suggests that being sensitive to one's own selectivity and biases in perception is essential if management skills are to be optimized. It also suggests that being cognizant of the unique personal, organizational, and situational pressures that affect how others in the work setting perceive the world is critical to good management. For, the more accurate his/her perception of people and events, the more effective a manager is apt to be in directing, influencing, and bringing about change in the work environment.

Notes

1. Hastorf, A. H., & Cantril, H. They saw a game: A case study. *Journal of Abnormal and Social Psychology*, 1954, *49*, 129-134.

2. Bruner, J. S., & Goodman, C. C. Value and need as organizing factors in perception. *Journal of Abnormal and Social Psychology*, 1947, *42*, 33-44.

3. Gilchrist, J. C., & Nesberg, L. S. Need and perceptual change in need-related objects. *Journal of Experimental Psychology*, 1952, *44*, 369-376.

4. Leavitt, H. S. *Managerial psychology*. Chicago: University of Chicago Press, 1978, p. 27.

5. McGinnies, R. Emotionality and perceptual defense. *Psychological Review*, 1949, *56*, 244-251.

6. Kelley, G. A. *Psychology of personal constructs*. New York: Horton, 1955.

7. Dombusch, S., Hastorf, A., Richardson, S., Muzzy, R., & Vreeland, R. The perceiver and the perceived: Their relative influence on categories of interpersonal perception. *Journal of Personality and Social Psychology*, 1965, *1*, 434-440.

8. Fiedler, F. E. *Leader attitudes and group effectiveness*. Urbana, Ill.: University of Illinois Press, 1958.

9. Evidence for this comes from the authors' experiences in working with individuals in a wide range of roles in a wide range of companies.

10. Toffler, B. L. Occupational role development: The changing determinants for the individual. *Administrative Science Quarterly*, 1981, *26*, 396-418.

11. Rapoport, R., & Rapoport, R. Dual-career families re-examined (Rev. ed.). New York: Harper & Row, 1977.

12. Kelley, H. H. The warm-cold variable in first impressions of persons. *Journal of Personality*, 1950, *18*, 431-439.

13. Ibid., p. 433.

14. Rosenthal, R. *Experimenter effects in behavioral research*. New York: Appleton-Century-Crofts, 1966.

15. Leeper, R. A. A study of the neglected portion of the field of learning: The development of sensory organization. *Journal of Genetic Psychology*, 1935, *46*, 41-75.

16. Amabile, T., & Hastorf, A. H. Person perception. In B. Seidenberg & A. Snadowsky (Eds.), *Social psychology*. New York: Free Press, 1976.

17. Bruner, J. S., Shapiro, D., & Taguiri, R. The meaning of traits in isolation and combination. In R. Taguiri & L. Petrullo (Eds.), *Person perception and interpersonal behavior*. Stanford, Calif.: Stanford University Press, 1958.

18. Bem, D. J., & Allen, A. On predicting some of the people some of the time: The search for cross-situational consistencies in behavior. *Psychological Review*, 1974, *81*, 506-520.

19. Jones, E. E., & Nisbett, R. E. The actor and the observer: Divergent perceptions of the causes of behavior. In E. Jones, D. Kanouse, H. Kelley, R. Nisbett, S. Valins, & B. Weiner (Eds.), *Attribution: Perceiving the causes of behavior*. Morristown, N.J.: General Learning Press, 1972; Heider, F. *The psychology of interpersonal relations*. New York: John Wiley & Sons, 1958.

20. Kelley, H. H. The processes of causal attribution. *American Psychologist*, 1973, *28*, 107-128.

21. Jones, E. E., & Davis, K. E. From acts to dispositions: The attribution process in person perception. In L. Berkowitz (Ed.), *Advances in experimental social psychology* (Vol. 2). New York: Academic Press, 1965.

22. Heilman, M. E., & Guzzo, R. A. The perceived cause of work success as a mediator of sex discrimination in organizations. *Organizational Behavior and Human Performance*, 1978, *21*, 346-357.

23. Newcomb, T. M. Autistic hostility and social reality. *Human Relations*, 1947, *1*, 69-86.

4

Motivating People

JAMES THOMPSON, a remarkably talented computer programmer, has recently been making serious errors in his work. He also has slowed down considerably, and his desk is piled high with work that shows little sign of being completed in the near future. A rush job has just been delivered to him, and his boss has called him into her office to inform him of its importance and its urgency. James looks deenergized, his walk is slow and plodding, and his usually alert demeanor is not at all evident. "I just am not motivated to get anything done," he says, "I don't even feel like coming to work in the morning."

What does James mean? How can such an able employee fail to work effectively? What can be done about it? This chapter addresses these questions.

What is motivation?

Motivation is the individual's *desire* to work. It must be distinguished from *ability*. For, while being able to perform a job effectively is a necessary ingredient of work performance, an individual has to want to perform accurately and sufficiently if a good job is to be done.

There are several blocks to developing an easy understanding of work motivation. For one, there is no single reason why people work. Studs Terkel, in his book, *Working*, makes this point with great clarity.[1] Over a period of seven years, he interviewed hundreds of workers about their jobs, and a quick glimpse at their responses displays great diversity in their reasons for working. For some, money is key, but others work because they enjoy what they do, and still others work because of the status it affords them. To further complicate matters, people's reasons for working are different at different times; thus, when first hired, a person may work hard to impress his/her supervisors, but after a while may do so because the job is satisfying. Or, when young, an individual may work hard because a job is challenging, but, with the passing of years, the primary reason for work may shift to, for instance, the satisfaction that arises from working with others whom one likes. Thus, understanding what motivates people to work is a far more complex question than it might at first appear.

Theories of work motivation abound. In a chapter reviewing articles on behavior in organizations, written in 1979, nearly one fourth of those cited were concerned with motivation—and for good reason.[2] Motivation is one of the most fundamental of all issues in organizational psychology. While not all of the theories and research efforts are of use to managers, it is important to understand some of the many different ways in which researchers and scholars have formulated their ideas. For they form the bases of organizational programs and managerial strategies designed to motivate others.

Steers and Porter, in their book, *Motivation and Work Behavior* identified three components of motivation: (1) an energizing component, (2) a channeling component, and (3) a maintenance component.[3] A motivated person is, therefore, someone who is activated to engage in work behavior, who has a goal toward which he or she is heading, and who has the inclination to sustain the behavior over a period of time. We will use these three components of motivation to organize the brief presentations of the major theoretical points of view which follow.

Motivational theories

Energizing people

If managers are to motivate people, they need to understand what makes people active and ready to engage in work behavior. Several theories provide suggestions.

Need theory. Motivational theories which focus on needs assume that there is some internal state which provokes the individual to act. Abraham Maslow is the best-known theorist of this school.[4] Using informal observation and clinical experiences, Maslow drew up a list of five needs that individuals strive for during their lives. He also ranked these needs; that is, he put them in the order of their urgency to an individual. The result is a need hierarchy. The basic principle of the theory is that needs lower in the hierarchy are more powerful than those higher up. And an individual does not become concerned with any need until the one preceeding it is satisfied. The hierarchy of needs begins with physiological needs and peaks with self-actualization needs:

Self-actualization needs

↑

Ego needs

↑

Social needs

↑

Safety needs

↑

Physiological needs

Physiological needs, which are taken as the starting point, include the basic needs of food, water, shelter, and the like. Safety needs are concerned with protection against danger, threat, and deprivation, and are commonly considered to include the need to be safe from injury, whether physical or psychological. These two needs are defensive. In other words, they are directed at protecting the individual from damage.

Once the physiological and safety needs are fulfilled, social needs come to the fore. Rather than focusing only on self, individuals focus on contact with others. This includes the need for belonging, for association, for acceptance, for friendship, and for love. The need entails not only the receiving but also the giving of affection and companionship.

At the fourth level of the need hierarchy are the ego needs. These are generally classified into two subsets: the needs that relate to one's reputation—such as needs for status, recognition, appreciation, and respect—and the needs that relate to one's self-esteem—such as needs for self-confidence, achievement, and competence.[5] Thus, esteem needs encompass both the need for the respect and esteem of others and the need for personal worth.

One behavior is apt to meet both of these needs simultaneously, such as doing a difficult job effectively, but some behaviors serve only to meet one or the other of these ego needs.

Highest on the need hierarchy is self-actualization. If the first four needs are satisfied, then, according to Maslow, the individual will need to realize his or her potential. This is the need to discover exactly who one is and work toward the expression of this identity. That is, when our physical needs and our needs for love and respect and esteem have been met, what remains is the need to become all one is capable of becoming.

Although Maslow did not develop his theory specifically for work motivation, its implications for work situations were quickly recognized. The theory has received wide acceptance because of its intuitive appeal, but empirical support for it is disappointing. Because Maslow posits that, as lower-order needs become satisfied, people go on to the next need in the hierarchy, to adequately test the theory individuals must be tracked over time. Two studies in which changes over time were examined did not provide support for the theory. Hall and Nougaim, who hypothesized that, as a need became satisfied, its importance would decrease, followed 49 AT&T executives over several years.[6] The predictions were not only disconfirmed, but just the opposite was found to occur; the more satisfied people were with a particular need, the more important it was seen to be. In another study, the satisfaction of a lower-level need was found not to be related to the increased importance of the next need on the hierarchy, as Maslow's theory would suggest.[7] Thus, there is little evidence that anything like a need hierarchy exists. Finally, research using factor analysis, a statistical tool for identifying groupings of correlated items, has failed to reproduce a set of five needs that match Maslow's list, leading many to conclude that there is nothing inherently sacred about Maslow's typology.

Alderfer has proposed an alternative to Maslow's need theory.[8] He calls his Existence, Relatedness, Growth (ERG) theory. Rather than five levels of needs, this theory argues for three, each corresponding to a name in the theory's title. Existence needs, lowest on the hierarchy, are concerned with physical needs; relatedness needs are concerned with social needs; and growth needs, highest on the hierarchy, are needs for personal development and improvement. Unlike Maslow's, ERG theory does not adhere to a rigid progression through the hierarchy. That is, more than one need can be active at a time, and the satisfaction of a need does not necessarily lead to a concentration on the next need on the ladder. In fact, some needs may increase in strength when they are satisfied, for example, a challenging job increasing rather than decreasing growth needs. But this is not the major innovation of ERG theory. It is the notion that the lack of satisfaction of higher-order needs can lead to regression, with an increase in concern for needs lower on the hierarchy. The regression effect has interesting implications for behavior at work. It suggests that, if relatedness and/or growth needs are not being met at work, rather than persevering in attempting to meet these needs, people may show an increased concern about salary, working conditions, vacations, and other existence needs. Thus, the apparent concern is not necessarily indicative of the real concern.

Building upon the work of the need theorists, and his own research, Hall has put need theory in a different framework. He suggests that it is not a hierarchical progression that is key in determining people's needs, but their career stage. According to Hall, people's needs change as they advance in their careers.[9] Early on, a person has a need for identity formation and essentially is involved in *exploration*. The next stage, the *establishment* stage, is the time that people become concerned with intimacy and forming attachments. A third stage, known as the *maintenance* stage, focuses the individual on generativity—the desire to produce something meaningful to be passed on to the next generation. The last stage, termed the *decline* stage, is characterized by a need for integrity in the form of satisfaction with life. Thus, Hall believes that the needs which energize people shift during the course of a person's work life.

How can these need theories be useful to managers? Whichever theory one uses, it is suggestive of ways of categorizing individuals, and in so doing helps the manager in directing his or her motivational effort. If, for instance, a manager knows a subordinate is striving for acceptance, then the possibility of recognition and attention on the part of the organization may facilitate the work performance of this person far more than will, let us say, an additional week's salary. Thus, the point to be learned is that an individual's needs can be assessed at any point in his/her career, and by being sensitive to these needs, motivation for increased productivity can be sparked.

Need for achievement. Focusing on one particular motivational need, McClelland formulated the concept of the need to achieve (n-Ach).[10] The theory of need achievement is concerned with predicting the behavior of those individuals who either have a high or low need to achieve. To determine who is high or low n-Ach, McClelland had managers tell stories about ambiguous pictures and then picked out the relevant themes in the stories they related. A typical picture might depict an architect seated at a desk which contains blueprints, drafting materials, and a photograph of his family. The respondent is asked to make up a story about what led up to the scene, what the architect is thinking, and what is likely to happen later. The assumption underlying the use of this technique is that, given an ambiguous stimulus, people will *project* into it their own needs, desires, and goals. A strong need for achievement is evidenced by themes in the related story which indicate striving for excellence in task accomplishment. In the example given, for instance, the high n-Ach respondent would talk about the work the architect is doing and its challenges and problems.

It has been posited that those who have high n-Ach are attracted by tasks for which there is a reasonable probability of success and avoid those tasks which seem too easy—because they are not challenging—or too difficult—because of the fear of failure. They also prefer tasks for which outcomes depend on their own individual efforts. Last, they have a need for feedback on how well they are doing, and the more concrete it is, the more it is appreciated.

McClelland and Winter have found that effective entrepreneurs and managers are very likely to have high n-Ach.[11] This is so regardless of whether the country the subject is in is socialist or capitalist and whether his or her organization is publicly or privately owned. The authors also claim that n-Ach can be raised by training and experience. This, of course, raises a very critical question: Do organizations succeed because the people staffing them are high in need achievement, or do successful organizations create achievement-oriented people? This question remains unanswered.

Unlike the hierarchical needs discussed before, the need for achievement is a chronic need, one which is not readily satisfied. It is persistent and stable over time, preoccupying an individual with achievement goals and predisposing him or her to react in a particular way to certain work situations. In a sense, then, need for achievement is a personality characteristic rather than a need in the more usual sense. Managers would do well to capitalize on this need in their subordinates, structuring tasks so that concrete standards by which employees can measure their own performance are available and providing specific quantitative feedback about subordinates' accomplishments. Again, being aware of the need category can be a useful device in enhancing motivation.

Activation theory. It is not only the internal need state of a person that can be energizing. The variety and complexity of the work setting can also determine how much energy an individual directs at his/her work. In this vein, a number of researchers have proposed that a person's *degree of activation* is a determinant of his/her performance.[12] The term *activation* refers to the degree of excitation of the brain. Noise, bright colors, and variety all are examples of things that tend to heighten the activation level, whereas muted tones, dull colors, and routinized activity tend to reduce it.

The relationship between activation level and performance is thought to be U-shaped. At low activation levels, performance is negatively affected because of boredom, a decrease in sensory stimulation, and a lack of muscular coordination. High activation levels also are a detriment to effective performance, here, because of stress, loss of muscular control, and disorganization. Intermediate activation levels are, however, thought to be optimal—providing enough energy for the individual to act alertly and vigorously, but not so much as to be immobilizing (see Figure 4-1).

While managers cannot control the internal needs of their subordinates, they can often affect the context in which work is occurring. In doing so, it is useful to keep in mind the relationship

Figure 4-1
The consequences of level of arousal on performance

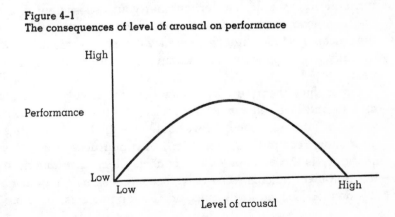

depicted in Figure 4-1. Arousal, it seems, is a spur to performance when it occurs in moderate doses. Thus, challenge, activity, and variety are apt to facilitate motivation. But, when the work setting becomes so arousing that it is frantic, or when it is dull enough to be boring, optimal performance is not apt to result.

Channeling the energy

Once a person is energized to act, he or she has many choices about what to do with that energy. There are a number of theoretical formulations that attempt to explain why a person chooses to engage in one activity rather than another.

Expectancy theory.   The assumption underlying expectancy theory is that people operate on a cost-gain principle, acting to maximize their gains and minimize their losses. Although the roots of this assumption go far back in history, Victor Vroom first applied it to work motivation in his influential book, *Work and Motivation*, written in 1964.[13] Since that time, many have expanded upon expectancy theory and modified it, but, today, it still remains a very important theory of motivation in work settings.

According to expectancy theory, the effort an individual exerts to do a particular task (force) is a multiplicative function of the *expectancy* that effort will lead to outcomes and the *valence* (perceived positivity or negativity) of the outcomes:

$$\text{Force} = \text{Expectancy} \times \text{Valence}$$

In short, expectancy theory predicts that you will work harder (1) the more you believe that effort will result in a desired outcome, and (2) the more desirable you think you will find the outcome. It incidentally does not matter whether your assessment of either the likelihood of the outcome or the anticipated attractiveness of the outcome is inaccurate; expectancy theory is based not on what actually will happen but on what an individual believes will happen.

Expectancy theory distinguishes between first-level outcomes and second-level outcomes. Typically, the first-level outcome is work performance. Second-level outcomes include rewards such as money, recognition, promotion, or group acceptance. *Instrumentality* is the concept which connects them. Instrumentality is the first-level outcome's perceived usefulness in bringing about the desired second-level outcome. Performance is therefore in-

strumental if increases in it are believed to lead to attractive rewards. It is not instrumental if performance is believed to be unrelated to such rewards (e.g., in an organization with a fixed salary
schedule based only on seniority, increased performance will not
be expected to better one's pay), or negatively related to such
rewards (e.g., in a cohesive group with norms against productivity, increased performance will be expected to result in social
ostracism and negative feelings). As is obvious from these examples, performance can lead not only to positive outcomes, but also
to neutral or negative ones. Therefore, the valence of performance
is a function of the desirability of these second-level outcomes and
the extent to which they are believed to be associated with performance. If an individual perceives a high degree of association
between performance and desired rewards, the valence of performance itself is high. If, however, nothing much of value is associated with performance, its valence will be neutral. And last, if
increases in performance are believed to result in undesirable
conditions, the valence of performance will be low.

To illustrate how the expectancy formulation works, let us return to the problem of James Thompson presented at the beginning of this chapter. Thompson knows from past experience that
his effort to get his work done will indeed result in heightened
work accomplishment. However, this greater productivity is perceived to be negatively related to the outcomes he desires. The
more he accomplishes, for instance, the more work he feels that he
is assigned. Furthermore, he has in the past been asked to forego
his three-week vacation "for the good of the company" because he
is so indispensable and been asked to take it in three, one-week
parcels instead. And even worse, the other computer program-
mers seem to avoid James when he is working at peak efficiency—once he even caught them whispering about his
"apple-polishing." Since he has let things go a bit, he feels he has
been included more readily in lunches, midmorning chats, and
even outside social activities. Clearly, for him, increased performance is not positively valenced, and although he knows he
can produce more, he is unmotivated to do so.

To continue with our illustration, Thompson's plight can be contrasted with that of one of his colleagues, Lou Royce. Lou sees
increased performance as the gateway to advancement. He believes that, if his output were increased dramatically, he would be
promoted, given a raise, treated with more respect, etc. But Lou's
expectancy is low. That is, he is certain that, regardless of how

much energy he puts into his work, his performance will not be appreciably bettered because of the ineptness of his current assistant which thwarts him at every turn. Thus, despite the high valence of performance, his low expectancy that effort will, in fact, result in a performance increase stops him from trying.

These two examples make clear that motivation can be deterred by either (1) the nonpositive valence of high performance; or (2) the low expectancy that working hard will lead to heightened performance.

Support for the expectancy model of motivation is mixed, although in total it tends to be positive.[14] There is evidence, for instance, that the greater the importance (valence) attributed to pay, the greater the work effort expended, that low-expectancy individuals perform at a lower level than high-expectancy individuals, and that high reward instrumentalities for performance are related to higher production.[15]

Expectancy theory has been very controversial. There are two principal criticisms. First, the assumption that human beings engage in such a complex cognitive process to arrive at decisions about how to behave has been assailed. Second, there are those who fault the theory because of the assumption that people base their behavior only on cost-gain considerations.[16] These criticisms aside, however, the ideas introduced by the theory have been found to be extremely useful in understanding motivation and in thinking about work behavior more generally.

The principles of expectancy theory suggest a number of prescriptions for managers:

1. *Rewards for performance must be desired by the employee (positively valent) if effort is to be exerted.* Remember, there are no absolutes here. You must keep in mind that what you consider a desirable reward may not at all coincide with how the employee sees things.
2. *Variations in performance must be seen as producing variations in the amount of reward obtained.* That is, heightened performance must be seen as instrumental. This means that the manager must be able to control the magnitude of at least some important rewards enough to produce a linkage between performance and reward.
3. *Employees must believe that effort will affect performance.* Just tempting employees with a very attractive reward will be of no service in enhancing motivation if the employees do not believe that there are actions they can take to achieve it.

4. *If either expectancy or reward valence is low, effort expenditure will be minimal.* Both attractive outcomes and the belief that effort will lead to them are necessary in order to motivate employees. If either one is absent, the motivational force is nil. If one component is very high and the other very low, e.g., a large bonus is offered (high valence) for an impossible task (low expectancy), or a minor benefit (low valence) is offered for a very manageable task (high expectancy), motivation also will be low.

5. *Specific actions into which employees can put their effort should be made as clear as possible.* Simply creating the conditions to motivate people does not inform them about what behaviors in particular are valued. Performance can be increased in a variety of ways, all of which may not be equally acceptable to you, e.g., increasing quality versus increasing quantity of work.

Reinforcement theory. Reinforcement theory also is based on the idea that people perform in ways which are most rewarding to them. But, unlike expectancy theory, the focus is wholly on the environment; there is little concern with the internal workings of the individual.

The basic proposition of reinforcement theory is a simple one—that behavior is controlled by its consequences. The consequences are called *reinforcers*. A reinforcer is anything which follows after a behavior and influences the likelihood that that same behavior will be repeated again. Reinforcers come in many forms. They can be positive or they can be negative. Positive reinforcers enhance the likelihood and negative reinforcers decrease the likelihood that a behavior will recur. For example, an employee whose boss says, "good work" after he/she has taken the initiative to follow up a lead is reinforced for the behavior and is likely to take such initiative again in the future. The reinforcer is the praise given him/her by the boss. Similarly, an employee who is reprimanded for being late may then make a special effort to be on time. Here, the reinforcer is the criticism, and the employee changes his/her behavior to avoid such negative reinforcement in the future.

By and large, those who apply reinforcement theory to motivating people at work have focused on positive reinforcement, or reward. Assuming that the behavior a manager wants is, in fact, evidenced by an employee, it is predicted that rewarding the individual for the behavior will cause him/her to repeat that behavior.

There are a number of rules that one can identify in the use of reinforcement theory which can serve as guidelines to managers:

1. *Make distinctions in how employees are rewarded.* People should be rewarded in accordance with their performance. Treating everyone in the same way, while ostensibly an equitable policy, really insures that everyone performs at only an average level. Those who are high performers feel they are unacknowledged and will not continue to perform so effectively; those who are poor performers are rewarded for their minimal success, thereby encouraging their unwanted behavior to continue.

2. *Inaction has consequences.* The failure to respond to heightened performance and the efforts to achieve it can have deleterious consequences. It also can modify behavior. Many managers find it difficult to praise employees. Others find it difficult to tell an employee about what he/she is doing wrong. Not doing these things, however, reduces a manager's effectiveness.

3. *Make clear which behavior is being reinforced.* Simply telling someone that he/she is doing well is not as effective in terms of reinforcement theory as is telling him/her what exactly is being referred to. If this is not clear, the reinforcement may be attached to the wrong behavior, with the result that the latter behavior, not the one of interest, will be increased.

4. *Use multiple reinforcers.* Fortunately, managers have many different types of reinforcers at their disposal. Different people may find different consequences rewarding, and thus, there should be flexibility in reinforcer administration. Also, any one reinforcer may lose its value if it is used repeatedly. Thus, managers must be sensitive to what is a reinforcer for whom if they are to effectively use reinforcement as a motivational strategy.[17]

The effectiveness of reinforcement is additionally thought to be influenced by the schedule of its administration. There are many different schedules of reinforcement that a manager can use to reward his/her workers. Schedules can be *continuous* or *partial*. If, every time an employee demonstrates a desired behavior, he/she is rewarded, this is a continuous schedule of reinforcement. With a continuous schedule, the desired behavior is very quickly established—in other words, the message that that behavior is viewed positively is loud and clear. But, when and if the reinforcement is not administered, the behavior quickly disappears. Because it is impossible (and inconvenient) to reward a desired behavior continuously, the continuous schedule of reinforcement is unwieldy to implement.

Partial reinforcement, in contrast, is a schedule by which reinforcement is administered only intermittently. It works far more slowly in establishing behavior, but, once the behavior is in place, it is more permanent. Partial reinforcement can be based on the time that has elapsed since a previous reinforcer was administered, or it can be based on the number of desired responses that occur. Moreover, the schedule can be fixed (the same time interval or the same number of desired behavior passes before the next reinforcement), or can be variable (the administration of the reward fluctuates around some average).

While managers clearly cannot control the schedule of all reinforcement administered, it is suggested that they give some thought to this problem. Moreover, it is likely that different schedules will be used for different types of reinforcers because of feasibility, convenience, and organizational constraint.

Reinforcement theory as a motivational device was given a lot of credibility by the well-publicized behavior modification program at Emery Air Freight. (This will be discussed in Chapter 11.) Research conducted in more controlled settings also attests to the theory's efficacy. Reinforcement has been shown to increase behavior more than does no reinforcement, and schedules of reinforcement have been found to have different effects.[18] It is clear that reinforcers influence behavior.

According to reinforcement theory, all behavior can be determined by the environment. Aspects of the individual such as needs, motives, values, and beliefs are considered unnecessary and in some sense irrelevant to influencing behavior. For some, this denial of the internal aspects of human beings is irksome and nonsensical. Other theories stress rewards without excluding these internal states as factors in motivation, and Locke, for one, has questioned whether reinforcement theory has therefore actually added anything new to our understanding of work behavior.[19] Nonetheless, if only because it makes such an exaggerated argument, reinforcement theory is useful because it forces us to look at the work environment itself as a source of motivation for workers.

Goal-setting theory.   In contrast to the assumptions of both expectancy and reinforcement theories that people act to maximize gain and minimize loss, some have argued that the basis of work motivation is the striving to attain goals. A work goal is what the employee intends to accomplish by some specified time in the future. Thus, the goal of a sales manager may be to establish a certain number of new accounts, to begin a new product campaign, and to sell a specific number of products, all in six months time. The major figure in goal-setting theory is Edwin A. Locke, whose impressive theorizing and research have encouraged many other investigators to work in this area.[20]

Goals affect performance in two ways. First, they provide information about how much effort must be expended. Feedback about how much one is accomplishing allows the individual to modulate his/her behavior by slowing down, speeding up, or continuing to work at just about the same pace and intensity. Secondly, goals direct behavior. They are informative about the behavior that an individual must engage in if the goal is to be met. If, for instance, your goal is to write a series of reports over the next few weeks, the goal would direct you to make few appointments, have large chunks of writing time, and cut down on other behaviors which, although relevant to your job, are inappropriate to your goal.

Goals can be set by an individual or handed down to him/her by a superior. If it is not self-set, the individual must be made aware of the goal the other has for him/her and exactly what is supposed to be accomplished if the goal is to be adopted. In fact, the more specific the goal, the more informative it is. And, of course, the goal must not only be understood, but accepted. For unless it is accepted and therefore incorporated into one's intentions, the goal does not seem to direct work behavior.

A considerable amount of research verifies the link between goal setting and performance.[21] Generally, the higher the goal set, the more effective is performance. Even those individuals with goals so high that they are virtually unattainable have been shown to perform better than those who set easy goals. But caution must be exercised. When goals are known to be impossible to reach, performance tends to plummet.[22]

Maintaining behavior

Once energy has been created and channeled to produce behaviors that facilitate effective work performance, the question of how to sustain these behaviors arises. For, in work settings, employees are expected to maintain high performance as long as they have their jobs. One theory we have already discussed, reinforcement theory, is useful in explaining not only how motivational energy is directed but also how it is maintained; the schedules of reinforcement are of particular relevance to the issue of maintenance. There are, however, several other theories which address the question of maintenance, each to be discussed below.

Two-factor theory. Frederick Herzberg asked 200 engineers and accountants in the Pittsburgh area to answer two simple questions.[23] He asked them to tell him about a time when they had felt exceptionally good about their jobs and to tell him about a time they had felt exceptionally bad about their jobs. When the data were analyzed, it was found that feeling good about the job was related to the content of the job. Feeling bad about the job, however, was related not to the job itself but to the job environment. Accordingly, Herzberg called the job-content factors, satisfiers, and the job-environment factors, dissatisfiers. A list of these factors follows:

Satisfiers	Dissatisfiers
Interesting and important work	Poor interpersonal relations with supervisor, peers, or subordinates
Opportunity for achievement	
Recognition for achievement	Supervision that is incompetent
Possibility of advancement	Company policies that are wasteful
Responsibility for important tasks	Lack of job security
	Bad working conditions
	Insufficient salary

Herzberg found that the same types of factors tended to be associated only with good or bad experiences, not with both. Thus, job security was rarely mentioned as a contributor to a good experience but was often cited as a contributor to bad experiences, whereas the opportunity for responsibility was rarely mentioned as a contributor to a bad experience but was often cited as a contributor to good experiences. This finding is very important. It suggests that satisfaction and dissatisfaction are not opposites. Because something does not cause satisfaction, it does not automatically cause dissatisfaction or vice versa.

Based on these findings, Herzberg called the dissatisfiers *hygiene factors*, because they merely prevent dissatisfaction, and the satisfiers *motivators*, because they motivate the employee to be more productive. Herzberg saw these two factors as independent of one another. According to the theory, the presence of hygiene factors results solely in the absence of dissatisfaction, not in satisfaction. Only motivators can produce satisfaction.

The implications of the theory are clear enough. If you provide employees with good working conditions, pleasant interpersonal relationships, high salaries, or job security, it will *not* motivate them. It simply will keep them from being dissatisfied. Although not being dissatisfied is a condition for performing optimally, it alone cannot create an incentive for excellence on the job. Only the presence of factors such as opportunities for achievement, recognition, responsibility, and so on (the motivators), will create this incentive. Thus, two-factor theory argues for the necessity of designing work so as to increase the motivators in work settings.

But how much support has two-factor theory received? Although there has been a vast amount of research on the subject, the results are far from uniform. Evidence refuting the theory is as extensive as evidence supporting it. Herzberg, himself, has supported his theoretical predictions.[24] But, when they tested the theory by methods other than the job story-telling one, other researchers have been unable to duplicate the results. Despite this very serious problem, however, two-factor theory has had a major impact on management thinking and practice.

Theory X and Theory Y.   Although it is not really a theory of motivation but rather a philosophy of management, it is important to know about Douglas McGregor's Theory X and Theory Y.[25] McGregor distinguished between two entirely different and contradictory sets of motivational assumptions that can be held by managers. The theory a manager holds is said to then affect his strategies for motivating employees. So, in contrast to all of the theories we have thus far reviewed, Theory X-Y focuses on the one trying to induce motivation, not on the individual who is being motivated.

Theory X, a traditional management conception of how to motivate others, makes the assumptions that people dislike work, that they avoid responsibility whenever possible, that they have little ambition, and that they seek safety and security above all else. Because of these assumptions, Theory X dictates that the prodding, coercing, or manipulating of subordinates is necessary if they are to perform adequately. For, if left to their own devices, employees would not accomplish anything at all.

Theory Y is a set of assumptions about individuals that differs sharply from those of Theory X. According to Theory Y, people do not dislike or avoid work, they can and do learn to accept and even seek out responsibility, they are creative and capable problem solvers, and they are not motivated by security alone, but in fact strive for self-esteem and self-actualization through work if such opportunities exist. Theory Y, then, has a much more positive view of human nature than does Theory X. It therefore dictates that the role of management is to provide an open and flexible work environment in which individuals' potential can be realized, and to encourage participation whenever possible so employees can play an active role in determining their own fates. In this way, employees will motivate themselves rather than be motivated by external sources, with the result being greater work productivity and effectiveness.

Theory X and Theory Y have not really been tested. Nor is it easy to do so. Nonetheless, McGregor's formulation has been popularized and is a common way of describing people and organizations. Moreover, the ethic underlying McGregor's ideas, that people can motivate themselves if the organizational conditions are facilitative of this process, has been one contributor to the notion of participative decision making (PDM), which will be discussed later in this chapter.

Equity theory.   So far in this chapter, we have treated motivation as if it is a private affair based only on the interaction between the manager and his subordinates. But this is not so. People constantly compare and contrast themselves with others in the work setting, and the outcomes of these comparisons can affect the degree of motivation to maintain a given behavior.

Equity theory, which is attributed to J. Stacy Adams, concerns the inputs and outcomes people feel they put in and get out of their jobs.[26] Inputs include all of the factors that people feel they have "invested" in their jobs, including effort, education, ability, and so forth. Outcomes of the job include pay, fringe benefits, status, recognition, or any other valued outcome. The relationship of our perceived outcomes to our perceived input can be formulated into an *equity ratio:*

$$\text{Equity ratio} = \frac{\text{Outcomes}}{\text{Inputs}}$$

Equity ratios allow people to determine how much they are getting out of the job as compared to how much they put in.

But, according to equity theory, people are not content to merely calculate their own outcome/input ratios. Whether consciously or unconsciously, they compare themselves to others in the work setting. If we perceive the equity ratios of others to be equal to our own, then we feel as if we have been treated equitably by those in authority. If, however, we perceive the equity ratios of others to be different from our own, a condition of inequity is experienced.

An example is useful here. Assume, for a moment, that Susan J and Michael B both work in the same department doing the same tasks at X company. Both Susan's and Michael's inputs into their jobs are sizable; they both come into the office early every day, they both take on a good deal of responsibility, they both take work home, and they both complete all assignments with care and speed. However, Susan and Michael are not paid the same salary—Michael is earning $2,000 more per annum. Thus, although the inputs are identical for Susan and Michael, their outcomes clearly are not. Consequently, Susan is likely to experience inequity.

Inequity has motivating properties. To continue with our example, Susan has several options:

1. She may work on changing Michael's equity ratio. She might, for instance, try to get him to increase his inputs even beyond what they are currently.
2. Susan may distort her perception of either her own or Michael's inputs or outcomes. She may, for instance, decide that Michael really is working much harder than she is. Or she may decide that despite appearances, she really has not been giving so much of herself to her work.
3. She may change her own inputs or outcomes. She may decide to slacken her efforts a bit because little is affected by working as hard as she is. Or she may try to convince her superior of her greater deservedness of reward.
4. Susan may stop using Michael as a comparison. She may pick someone else, and thereby create a new equity formulation.
5. Susan may opt for leaving the situation entirely if all of the other coping strategies fail to reduce the inequity she is experiencing.

Of course, not all of these modes of inequity reduction are always feasible. It is unlikely, for instance, that Susan will be able to distort her perceptions of her inputs—she is too much in touch with them. And, of course, not all of these modes of inequity reduction are equally desirable.

Most of the work testing equity theory has been concerned with pay. There are two types of inequity regarding pay. *Underpayment* is the situation when an individual believes he or she is not receiving sufficient pay for the input he/she has invested in the job. This can be because others who seem to be putting in less are receiving the same (or even more) pay. *Overpayment* is the situation in which an individual believes he/she is receiving more pay than his/her inputs warrant. This can be because those who seem to be putting in more are getting paid the same (or even less), or because those whose inputs seem equivalent are receiving less pay.

Equity theory elicited a good deal of interest.[27] It has consistently been found that underpaid workers tend to lessen their effort to reduce the inequity they experience. However, it is the inequity due to overpayment that sparked the most interest. For the notion that people can be dissatisfied because they are receiving too much money is counterintuitive and not consistent with a conception of human beings seeking to maximize their gains. Equity theory, in contrast to, for instance, expectancy theory or reinforcement theory, would predict that overpaying people relative to others would increase their input and thus reduce the inequity between inputs and outcomes. For the most part, the data collected reflect this counterintuitive result, and therefore provide strong support for the theory.[28]

There are a number of problems which limit the use of equity theory in management practice. They are in the form of unanswered questions which have not really been addressed by the theory or the research. One is the question of when people will, in fact, adjust their input (in the form of effort) to right a perceived inequity. Distorting what we see to undo an inequity may be easier than working harder (if overpaid) or may be less risky than working less (if underpaid). When people choose which route to inequity reduction is not clear. A second unanswered question which limits the practicality of equity theory is that concerning the others who are used for comparisons—who are they? Without knowing the likely referent of a social comparison, it is difficult to utilize inequities in the service of inducing motivation. Lastly, it is not clear how the sum total of inputs and outcomes is calculated. While most of the research has focused on pay, it is conceivable that there are other beneficial outcomes that can counteract or enhance the effects of pay on performance.

Nonetheless, there are some practical recommendations which derive from equity theory. The most important is that managers must not ignore the social elements of motivation. People do not work in a vacuum, and their assessment of their situations and their resulting performance are greatly affected by others around them. Also, the equity formulation suggests that organizational outcomes be tied closely to individual inputs to reduce incorrectly arrived at inequity calculations. Finally, managers should be aware that different types of employees probably select different others for comparison. There is some evidence, for instance, that professionals compare their inputs and outcomes to those of other professionals.[29] In this case, the individual may be being rewarded equitably by the standards of his or her organization but be underpaid by the standards of the profession as a whole; for that individual, an inequity exists. Sensitivity to this and other choices of comparison others can help a manager to recognize when an employee experiences inequity and can help a manager to alleviate the detrimental effect of such "hidden" inequities on performance.

Motivational programs

The theories we have reviewed attempt to explain what motivates employees and how motivation operates in work settings. Several of the theories have become the basis of organizational programs and practices directed at motivating employees. It is important for managers to know something about these programs, their benefits and limitations, if such programs are adopted. In this way, managers can become informed consumers of whatever menu of choices their organization provides. However, because most managers have very little control over the decisions to institute these programs and sadly small influence in shaping how they are implemented on an organizationwide basis, the knowledge of the specifics of any of these programs is probably less useful than is an understanding of the ideas that gave rise to them. A brief review of some of the most popular work-motivation programs follows. Several others are discussed elsewhere in the book.

Participation in decision making (PDM)

PDM has its theoretical roots in the humanistic theories of Maslow and McGregor. But support for it comes from other quarters, as well. Politically, many see it as a vehicle for avoiding the nefarious effects of unbridled management. Pragmatically, many believe that if people participate in making decisions, they will be more committed to these decisions and will work harder to implement them. There is, in fact, support from social psychology theory and research in this regard.[30] Consequently, the reasons for using PDM as a motivational program are diverse and so are the many forms that PDM can actually take.

In essence, PDM is the process by which employees participate in decisions about the work they are doing. But participation can vary in a number of ways.[31] First is *degree*. That is, there can be no participation, partial participation in the form of consultation or nonbinding advisement, or full participation in which the employee actually is involved in considering and arriving at the final decision. Second, participation can vary in *content*. That is, the decisions in which employees participate may be limited to routine ones, may or may not involve the issues concerning the work itself or work conditions, and may even encompass company policy. Finally, participation can vary in *scope*. PDM is great in scope if employees at all levels of the organization participate in all management decisions; PDM is small in scope if limited to the particular issues faced by the individuals making the decision.

At its extreme, PDM is exemplified by the workers' councils in Yugoslavia where employees even at the lowest levels of a company have representatives on a council which makes all major policy decisions. Japanese quality circles also utilize PDM principles, although in a very different way. (More about this is contained in Chapter 12, which focuses on managing change.) Taking other shapes and forms, there are innumerable examples of PDM programs being used in American industry. The success of all these programs is dependent on the types of individuals involved and how they function as a decision-making group, the nature and content of the decisions being made, and the way in which PDM fits into the larger organizational context.[32]

Behavior modification

The principles of reinforcement theory have been applied to organizational settings in the form of behavior modification programs. Perhaps the best-known example of such a program is the one reported by E. J. Feeney, formerly a vice president at Emery Air Freight.[33] Although more about this and other behavior modification programs is presented in Chapter 11, which is devoted to individually oriented strategies for managing organizational change, it is important to state here that, with an emphasis on programmed learning procedures, frequent feedback, and positive reinforcement, annual company sales increased from 11 percent to 27.8 percent. This dramatic increase stimulated a good deal of interest in behavior modification in industry throughout the 1970s.

Management by objectives (MBO)

The research and theory concerning goal setting have given rise to management by objectives programs. These programs ideally involve supervisors and subordinates in at least two formal meetings. First, they work together, set specific performance goals, and agree on how to measure whether the goals have been achieved. Then, at the end of an established time interval, a second meeting is held in which performance is measured against the goals which were set. In the MBO process, this latter step is crucial. For goal setting, in and of itself, is not sufficient to motivate continued achievement. Evaluation of subordinates' performance in light of the goals and giving feedback about performance are essential to developing the desirable motivation.

MBO has gained popularity not only as a motivation tool but also as a method for performance evaluation. Its appeal is its concreteness. Specific behavioral objectives are set and the evaluation of whether they have been met is quite straightforward. Problems arise, however, when objective measures of performance are not possible or do not adequately reflect what is most crucial about a work product. Furthermore, because implementing an MBO program effectively requires a good deal of skill on the part of both the supervisor and the subordinate, training often is required. Nonetheless, the MBO approach has been widely used in American industry in recent years, often with very favorable results.

Job enrichment

Herzberg's two-factor theory suggested that rather than simplify jobs, we should increase their scope and complexity if we are to motivate employees. In this way, organizations would emphasize and develop job characteristics that are the "motivators,"

namely, recognition, achievement, responsibility, and the satisfaction intrinsic in the work itself. Consequently, programs designed to increase one or more of these job characteristics were
set up, and, in the mid-1960s, many successful job redesign efforts
in major companies (e.g., American Telephone & Telegraph, and
Texas Instruments) were widely publicized.[34]

Improving on the controversial two-factor theory, the work of
Hackman and Oldham resulted in a model identifying particular
job dimensions which can, in fact, "enrich" a job.[35] The model
posits three psychological states that are key if a person is to be
motivated (and satisfied with a job). First is *experienced meaningfulness* or, more simply, the extent to which one's work is seen as
important and valuable. Second is the *experienced responsibility*
an individual feels for his/her work outcomes. Third is *knowledge
of results* of performance. The more these three states are experienced by a worker, the more motivated he or she is predicted to
be. The variety of skills a job requires, the degree to which a
whole unit of work is completed, and the perceived significance of
the work all contribute to the meaningfulness that one experiences. Autonomy affects experienced responsibility; the more control individuals have over how they work, the more responsible
they feel for the outcomes. And knowledge of results is dependent
on receiving timely, credible feedback. This model, known as the
Job Characteristics Model, has been extremely useful in providing
a framework for job-design efforts—it indicates what, specifically, should be done if the scope of a job is to be broadened.

Reviews of research on job-enrichment programs have demonstrated their utility in creating job satisfaction, although performance increments are not always an accompaniment.[36] But they
also make clear that job enrichment works best for particular
types of people. Individuals who have high needs for growth,
creativity, and challenge are, for instance, more likely to respond
favorably to job-enrichment efforts than those who are not. This
latter group is apt to view such efforts as a tricky means of getting
more work out of employees. Job enrichment also seems to work
best in particular types of job situations. There is some indication,
for instance, that it is only when issues of pay, security, and social
relationships are adequately cared for that employees will become concerned about the nature of their jobs.[37] There also is the
potential danger that enriching one person's job can diminish the
job of his or her superior, causing enormous on-the-job problems,
and ultimately a failure of the job-enrichment effort. Thus, while

job-enrichment programs can indeed have a positive effect on motivation, when used indiscriminately—without attending to the individuals involved, the types of jobs they have, and the work system as a whole—such programs are unlikely to be effective.

Motivation in perspective

Even this brief review of the major theories of work motivation and the programs they spawned makes it evident that the concept of work motivation is a complex one. It also is evident that no one theory, by itself, can adequately describe the phenomenon in its entirety. Nor can any one theory prescribe with precision what a manager should do to motivate employees. Each theory is useful in its own way—pinpointing critical factors managers should be aware of in embarking on their efforts to motivate subordinates. No doubt, as a reader, you will find that the theories we presented do not have equal appeal. This is possibly because your own native assumptions about why people work may coincide more with some of the ideas presented than with others. And this is fine. One need not accept the assumptions of all motivational theories to be an effective motivator. But, at the same time, there are likely to be dangers if the repertoire of assumptions one accepts is too limited, dangerously constraining managerial options.

The motivational programs we have reviewed are quite diverse, haboring very different assumptions about human beings. Some, such as job enrichment or PDM are based on humanistic views of people, views which depict individuals as desirous of growth, challenge, and responsibility. Behavior modification and like-minded incentive programs, in contrast, are based on the notion that people seek to maximize their gains and minimize their losses in work situations. Finally, MBO is based on a view of people as achievement oriented, as challenged by and working toward goals. Just as all of the motivational theories are not similarly attractive to all individuals, all of the motivational programs are not similarly attractive to all organizations. And, for the most part, managers have no control over the selection of a program. Organizational decisions, made at points remote from most managers, cause their organization to embark on one rather than another of these programs.

Perhaps, for managers, the greatest usefulness of the motivational theories and the programs they have generated is the checklist of causal factors they suggest. The checklist can help the manager locate the source of the motivational problem and then act on it. An example of a checklist one might extract from the theories and programs presented here follows:

What are the employees' needs and desires? Perhaps sitting down and talking with him/her would clarify this. Knowing what he/she wants may help you, as a manager, to provide it.

Is the work environment properly activating? That is, are people sufficiently aroused to work, but not so aroused that they are immobilized? If not, can one act on the environment to modulate the degree of arousal experienced?

Is it clear to the employee that working hard will lead to more effective performance? Is it clear that such effective performance will lead to desirable outcomes? If the answer to either of these questions is "No," then alterations in the objective situation or in the employee's inaccurate perception of it should be attempted.

Are reinforcers provided for effective work? Managers have dozens of possible rewards at their disposal, many of which they overlook. Is it clear what they are rewarding? Such clarity, which is easy enough to establish, is essential.

Does the employee have distinct, realizable goals? If not, why not give him/her some? If yes, are you sure they have truly been accepted by the employee as his/her own goals? Perhaps a joint goal-setting discussion would be useful periodically.

Is there a way an employee can assess how he or she is doing? Are there concrete standards for evaluating performance? If not, is feedback given on a regular basis? Providing such information, even if it only is in the form of subjective impressions, can be very effective as a motivational device.

What is the actual content of the employee's job? Are there opportunities for challenge, responsibility, and pride in the work? If not, are there things that are under your control that can enhance these?

Does the employee ever participate in decision making? If not, it is because you really believe he/she would not have the organization's interests at heart? You might want to examine some of your assumptions about what makes your employees "tick"—they influence much that you do.

Are there disparities in the treatment of employees who are co-workers? Are the disparities based on their work performance? If not, and you have no control over the way pay is determined, you can try to supplement unjustifiably low salaries with other benefits and privileges which are under your control.

If James Thompson, the computer programmer described at the beginning of this chapter, were to walk into your office in his ennervated state, using such a motivational checklist would be extremely helpful. Although you might not be able to instantly motivate him, you would have some excellent clues about where to look for causes of his motivational problem and some avenues for working on it. Remember, to effectively motivate others, you must look carefully not only at the individual and his/her needs, goals, and desires, but also at the job situation—the nature of the tasks required, the reward system, the social context in which work takes place, and the job setting itself. And, finally, managers must look critically at themselves to determine how they are contributing to motivational problems. For they, too, are part of the work environment. And built-in biases about how others approach their work and/or a limited view of the motivational process can inhibit managers from utilizing all the motivational strategies that are, in fact, accessible to them.

Notes

1. Terkel, S. *Working: People talk about what they do all day and how they feel about what they do.* New York: Pantheon, 1972.

2. Mitchell, T. R. Organizational behavior. *Annual Review of Psychology.* Palo Alto, Calif.: *Annual Reviews,* 1979, *30,* 243–282.

3. Steers, R. M., & Porter, L. W. (Eds.). *Motivation and work behavior.* New York: McGraw-Hill, 1975.

4. Maslow, A. H. *Motivation and personality.* New York: Harper & Row, 1954; Maslow, A. H. *Motivation and personality* (2nd ed.). New York: Harper & Row, 1970.

5. McGregor, D. *The human side of enterprise.* New York: McGraw-Hill, 1960.

6. Hall. D. T., & Nougaim, K. E. An examination of Maslow's need hierarchy in an organizational setting. *Organizational Behavior and Human Performance,* 1968, *3,* 12–35.

7. Alderfer, C. P. Effects of task factors on job attitudes and job behaviors. II: Job enlargement and other organizational context. *Personnel Psychology,* 1969, *22,* 418–426.

8. Alderfer, C. P. *Existence, relatedness, and growth: Human needs in organizational settings.* New York: Free Press, 1972.

9. Hall, D. T. *Careers in organizations.* Pacific Palisades, Calif.: Goodyear Publishing, 1976.

10. McClelland, D. C. *The achieving society.* Princeton, N.J.: Van Nostrand, 1961.

11. McClelland, D. C., & Winter, D. C. *Motivating economic achievement.* New York: Free Press, 1969.

12. Scott, W. E., Jr. Activation theory and task design. *Organizational Behavior and Human Performance,* 1966, *1,* 3–30.

13. Vroom, V. H. *Work and motivation.* New York: John Wiley & Sons, 1964.

14. Pritchard, R. D., & Sanders, M. S. The influence of valence, instrumentality and expectancy on effort and performance. *Journal of Applied Psychology,* 1973, *57,* 55–60.

15. Arvey, R. D. Task performance as a function of perceived effort-performance and performance-reward contingencies. *Organizational Behavior and Human Performance,* 1972, *8,* 423–433; Georgopoulos, B. S., Mahoney, G. M., & Jones, N. W. A path-goal approach to productivity. *Journal of Applied Psychology,* 1957, *41,* 345–353; Jorgenson, D. O., Dunnette, M. D., & Pritchard, R. D. Effects of the manipulation of a performance-reward contingency on behavior in a simulated work setting. *Journal of Applied Psychology,* 1973, *57,* 271–280.

16. Locke, E. A. The nature and causes of job satisfaction. In M. D. Dunnette (Ed.), *Handbook of industrial and organizational psychology.* Chicago: Rand McNally, 1976.

17. Several of the suggestions listed were adapted from Hamner, W. C., & Organ, D. W. *Organizational behavior: An applied psychological approach.* Plano, Tex.: Business Publications, 1978, pp. 49–50.

18. Komaki, J., Waddell, W. M., & Pearce, M. G. The applied behavior analysis approach and individual employees: Improving performance in two small businesses. *Organizational Behavior and Human Performance,* 1977, *19,* 337–352; Pritchard, R. D., Leonard, D. W., Von Bergen, C. W., Jr., & Kirk, R. J. The effects of varying schedules of reinforcement on human task performance. *Organizational Behavior and Human Performance,* 1976, *16,* 205–230.

19. Locke, E. A. The myths of behavior needs in organizations. *Academy of Management Review,* 1977, *2,* 543–553.

20. Locke, E. A. Toward a theory of task motivation and incentives. *Organizational Behavior and Human Performance,* 1968, *3,* 157–189.

21. Ibid., Latham, G. P., and Yukl, G. A. A review of research on the application of goal setting in organizations. *Academy of Management Journal,* 1975, *18,* 824–845.

22. Stedry, A. C., & Kay, E. The effect of goal difficulty on performance. *Behavioral Science,* 1966, *11,* 459–470.

23. Herzberg, F., Masner, B., & Snyderman, B. B. *The motivation to work.* New York: John Wiley & Sons, 1959.

24. Herzberg, F. *Work and the nature of man.* Chicago: World Publishing, 1966.

25. McGregor, *Human side of enterprise.*

26. Adams, J. S. Inequality in social exchange. In L. Berkowitz (Ed.), *Advances in experimental social psychology* (Vol. 2.). New York: Academic Press, 1965.

27. Campbell, J. P., & Pritchard, R. D. Motivation theory in individual and organizational psychology. In M. D. Dunnette (Ed.), *Handbook of industrial and organizational psychology.* Chicago: Rand McNally, 1976.

28. Adams, J. S., & Rosenbaum, W. B. The relationship of worker productivity to cognitive dissonance about wage inequities. *Journal of Applied Psychology,* 1962, *46,* 161–164.

29. Goodman, P. S. Social comparison processes in organizations. In B. M. Staw & J. R. Salancik (Eds.), *New directions in organizational behavior.* Chicago: St. Clair Press, 1976.

30. Coch, L., & French, J. R. P. Overcoming resistance to change. *Human Relations*, 1948, *2*, 512–532; Lewin, K. Frontiers in group dynamics. *Human Relations*, 1947, *1*, 5–41.

31. Locke, E. A., & Schweiger, D. M. Participation in decision making: One more look. In B. M. Staw (Ed.), *Research in organizational behavior* (vol 1). Greenwich, Conn.: JAI Press, 1979.

32. Vroom, V. H., & Yetton, P. W. *Leadership and decision-making*. Pittsburgh: University of Pittsburgh Press, 1973.

33. New tool: Reinforcement for good work. *Business Week*, 18 December 1971, p. 76.

34. Lord, R. N. *Motivation through the work itself*. New York: American Management Association, 1969; Weed, E. D. Job enrichment "cleans up" at Texas Instruments. In J. R. Maher (Ed.), *New perspectives in job enrichment*. New York: Van Nostrand Reinhold, 1971.

35. Hackman, J. R., & Oldham, G. R. Motivation through the design of work: Test of a theory. *Organizational Behavior and Human Performance*, 1976, *16*, 250–279.

36. Katzell, R. A., & Yankelovich, D., with M. Feen, O. A. Ornati, & A. Nash, assisted by J. A. Berman, R. A. Deliberto, I. J. Morrow, & H. M. Weiss. *Work, productivity and job satisfaction: An evaluation of policy-related research*. New York: Psychological Corporation, 1975.

37. Oldham, G. R., Hackman, J. R., & Pearce, J. L. Conditions under which employees respond positively to enriched work. *Journal of Applied Psychology*, 1976, *61*, 395–403.

5

Leading People

ON one occasion, when a prominent "football school's" team had an unusually poor season, the school's students as well as its faculty and board joined a chorus of editorials from the college and local newspapers in an attack on the team's coach. "Drop Smith," they shouted. "Out with Smith." "Smith leads team to disaster." Leaders often inherit the blame or the bounty that is a consequence of their team's performance.

Sports is not the only setting in which this occurs. To an audience of observers, generals win or lose battles, police commissioners suppress crime or allow it to escalate, mayors are the cause of a city's deterioration or its growth, and a company's managers are identified as the principal reason for their organization's poor or profitable performance. Whether leaders are always as directly responsible for group, organizational, and institutional performance as this response suggests can be questioned. It is possible to argue, for example, that the response may simply reflect people's preference for understanding complex events by praising or blaming the activity of one person.[1] Even if this is true, however, and the response is a wrongful exaggeration, it must not distract us from recognizing the concern that most cultures have with leadership. With almost axiomatic rigor, it is commonly assumed that being an effective leader is perhaps the most critical aspect of a manager's job. Leaders, it is assumed, create the context in which groups work; they influence the climate and ambience of relationships among group members and the way in which tasks get done. Leadership is, therefore, key to productivity and worker satisfaction.

Not surprisingly, then, the role of leader has been extensively examined, thought about, and discussed. In fact, it is certainly one aspect of managerial activity that has not been subject to the frequent ebbs and flows of fad and fashion in this area of study. In every decade since the turn of the century, leadership has been a major preoccupation of behavioral scientists.

Despite the attention leadership has received, however, there still is little consensus about who good leaders are or what it is that they do. In an attempt to pin down this phenomenon, theorists have approached the issue of leadership from a number of different perspectives These approaches, although different from one another, are individually informative, each emphasizing and capturing a different part of the whole. A review of each of the major approaches follows, and some attention is paid to their implication for managerial functioning. Rules of thumb, which can serve as practical guides to action, can be gleaned from various approaches to leadership, and one such group of rules is shared at the chapter's end.

The trait approach

On request, most of us can paint a picture of our image of an effective leader—someone who, more than most, epitomizes what leaders are like. This person, who may be a composite of several people, is easily distinguished from a group that we call "followers." Indeed, it is easy to observe that people regularly speak as if most of humankind could be divided into two groups—leaders and followers—each distinctly different from one another. We hear people talk about so-and-so being a "born" leader or a "natural" leader, and we soon learn to accept the fact that there is a definable cluster of traits associated with leadership.

This way of thinking about leadership results in very powerful assumptions which have far-reaching organizational consequences. If, in fact, we could identify those traits that are essential to effective leadership and measure them reliably, then we could devise a simple test for preselecting leaders. The test could be used to make hiring decisions, identify those with management potential, and provide a basis for promotion and upward movement in companies. It could even be used by institutions of higher learning to ferret out those applicants who truly are likely to have an impact on their environments. With such a refined measurement tool available, the "risk" would be taken out of selection decisions and, accordingly, the world would be a better place.

But what are a leader's attributes? For obvious reasons, one early group that addressed this question sought to answer it by analyzing the traits possessed by great men in our history. (The sexual bias in the selection of their sample is evident and will receive no additional mention.) They were notably unsuccessful in identifying any reliably consistent set of traits possessed by these heroes. Others, guided by similar assumptions, examined differences between nonleaders and those in positions of leadership. Scores of studies were conducted. They compared bishops and clergy, insurance executives and policy holders, and military officers and recent recruits. These studies involved old people and young ones, and they were conducted in settings as unlike one another as college campuses and prisons.[2]

Again, no consistent findings emerged. In fact, both careful and casual examinations of this literature quickly lead to the disappointing discovery that no feature differentiating leaders from nonleaders has emerged with strong, unequivocal support. Although extroversion, dominance, interpersonal sensitivity, adjustment, and ambition have each distinguished leaders from nonleaders on some occasions, there are other instances in which these very attributes are, in fact, more characteristic of followers than of leaders.[3] There is some recent evidence that managerial effectiveness is more evident among those who possess greater self-assurance, intelligence, initiative, and need for self-actualization and power over others, and less need for financial reward or job security.[4] But the association between these traits and effectiveness is not strong, and it is not possible to unhesitatingly deny the possibility that these individual characteristics are the result, not the cause, of being an effective manager. How can this be? Why hasn't a common set of leadership traits emerged with concreteness and clarity? Certainly this situation does not accurately reflect our commonplace understanding of the world.

One possible explanation for these counterintuitive findings is that leader selection processes are fraught with error. Hence, faulty procedures regularly cause nonleaders to acquire leadership roles. It is also conceivable that, although the right people are in leadership roles, the tests used to measure the characteristics which distinguish this august group from nonleaders are somehow faulty, failing to adequately measure the traits intended. Yet another possible explanation may lie in the failure of investigators to select and measure attributes that truly are critical in differentiating leaders from nonleaders. Also, it may well be that no single trait, by itself, is descriptive of a leader, but rather that combinations of traits cluster in a complementary fashion to distinguish those among us who are leaders.

Finally, an explanation some find most compelling is that, contrary to the leaders-have-certain-traits approach, what characterizes a good leader differs from situation to situation. Invariable leadership traits simply do not exist. On the contrary, different traits may be the necessary ingredients of leadership behavior and temperament when different conditions are operative. What makes for effective military or political leadership in wartime, for instance, may be very different than what makes for effective leadership in these realms during peacetime. Similarly, what makes for effective leadership in government may be very different from what makes for effective leadership in industry or education. Consider, even, our great leaders in history and the diverse traits customarily used to describe them: Abraham Lincoln's humane commitments to freedom and equality, Napoleon Bonaparte's strategic genius, and Winston Churchill's bulldog determination. Each of these men is thought by many to have been a great leader. Yet each was very different from the others. It is conceivable that the times in which each lived, the norms and values which were then most prevalent, and the problems that plagued society during the epoch demanded a different brand of leadership. Perhaps each of these men could only have been successful during his own time.

This way of thinking suggests that leadership is a vastly more complex phenomenon than is implied by the trait approach. It appears that an individual's attributes *in conjunction with situational factors* will determine who is a successful leader in a given circumstance. Thus, while personal attributes are not unimportant in determining who becomes a leader and who is successful in that capacity, they are not the whole of the story. This greatly complicates the process of identifying leadership qualities. For to do so, one must understand the critical parameters of situations and have a means of classifying them into categories. To this, one must add a knowledge of which traits are most likely to result in effective leadership for each of these situation types. Thus far, only one scholar, Fred Fiedler, has fully developed his thinking along these lines. His work reflects a contingency approach to leadership.

The contingency approach: Personality and situation

Rather than asserting that there is one set of optimal leadership characteristics, this contingency approach holds that it is the interaction between a leader's personality and the situation that determines the effectiveness of any leader.[5] The leading proponent of this point of view has unquestionably been Fred Fiedler who, along with his colleagues, has been writing about and investigating this idea since the mid-1950s. Fiedler proposes that a particular personality variable, namely the goals to which an individual gives highest priority, is a central one in determining leader performance. To measure this motivational orientation, the Least Preferred Co-Worker (LPC) Scale has been developed. The instructions for this instrument ask an individual to consider all the people with whom he/she has worked, and then to describe on a series of scales the one person with whom he/she could work *least well*.

By now, behavioral science has seen to it that these scales are a familiar sight to most people. They consist of two adjectives, one at each end, which are opposite (or as close to opposites as possible). The individual leader simply selects a point on each scale that comes closest to describing the one person with whom he/she could work least well. An LPC scale includes the following items:

> pleasant–unpleasant
> friendly–unfriendly
> rejecting–accepting
> tense–relaxed
> distant–close
> cold–warm
> supportive–hostile
> boring–interesting
> quarrelsome–harmonious
> gloomy–cheerful

> open–guarded
> backbiting–loyal
> untrustworthy–trustworthy
> considerate–inconsiderate
> nasty–nice
> agreeable–disagreeable
> insincere–sincere
> kind–unkind

Through proper procecedures, it is possible to use this scale to calculate a total LPC score, which has interesting properties. A high score—that is, more favorable ratings of the least preferred co-worker—indicates that the respondent is *relationship motivated*. Such people "tend to accomplish the task through good interpersonal relations."[6] A low LPC score, in contrast, indicates that the respondent is *task motivated* and is one of a group that is "strongly motivated to accomplish successfully any task to which they have committed themselves. They do this through clear and standardized work procedures and a no-nonsense attitude about getting down to work."[7] Thus, the "high-LPC" leader sees close interpersonal relationships as a requisite for task accomplishment and the "low-LPC" leader opts first for working on the task and only secondarily for good interpersonal relationships.

The second key factor in Fiedler's theory, "situational favorableness," is the extent to which a leader has control and influence in a situation. It is measured using three different indicators: the quality of leader-subordinate relations; the degree of task structure; and the amount of position power available to the leader. Leaders are assumed to have more control and influence if their subordinates support them; they know what needs to be done and how to do it; and they have the means to reward and punish subordinates.[8]

What is the relationship between situational favorableness and a leader's LPC score? Which are the situations in which high- and low-LPC leaders perform best? Fiedler's extensive research on the contingency model has consistently demonstrated that task-motivated (low-LPC) leaders tend to perform most effectively when the situation is either very favorable or very unfavorable. Relationship-motivated (high-LPC) leaders, on the other hand, tend to perform most effectively when the situation is only moderately favorable or unfavorable to the leader.[9] This is depicted in Figure 5-1. The vertical axis denotes performance, the horizontal axis denotes "situational favorableness" as measured by each of its three components. The solid line traces the performance of high-LPC leaders and the broken line the performance of low-LPC leaders under each of eight circumstances.

The validity of the Fiedler model continues to be hotly debated. Critical reviews have identified conceptual and methodological concerns pertaining to the model.[10] But its contribution to the study of leadership cannot be underestimated. Fiedler sought to identify critical personality variables and critical situational variables and examine their interrelationship. This, in and of itself, must be heralded as a tremendous advance.

The implications of Fiedler's theory for managerial functioning are, unfortunately, rather limited. True, it does allow prediction about what type of leaders will perform best in a given job. And it also suggests how work situations might be altered to fit the personality characteristics of a leader.[11] But it provides little advice for managers who might be trying to alter their behavior. This kind of advice seems necessary. Job conditions are not frozen into one form. They change, often for reasons quite beyond a manager's control, and the type of leader who might have performed

Figure 5-1
Schematic representation of the performance of relationship- and task-motivated leaders in different situational-favorableness conditions

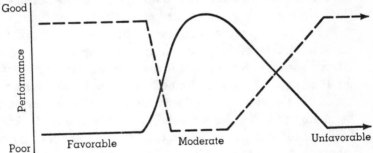

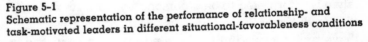

	1	2	3	4	5	6	7	8
Leader-member Relations	Good	Good	Good	Good	Poor	Poor	Poor	Poor
Task structure	High	High	Low	Low	High	High	Low	Low
Leader Position power	Strong	Weak	Strong	Weak	Strong	Weak	Strong	Weak

– – – – – – Task motivated

——————— Relationship motivated

Fiedler, F. E. *A theory of leadership effectiveness.* New York, McGraw Hill, 1967.

well at one point could very well perform inadequately at another if no alteration of leadership behavior occurs. Since the motivational-orientation variable is a personality characteristic, it is considered to have an enduring and stable quality, not easily changed. As Victor Vroom points out, "the possibility that some leaders may have flexible leadership styles or that people can be trained to adapt their behavior to the demands of the situations is rejected as unfeasible."[12]

Recognizing that his views include the idea that a leader's style is unchangeable, Fiedler and two of his associates have developed a training program called *leader match*.[13] It aims at training leaders to diagnose situations and change them to match their own style.[14] The program, which takes three to four hours to complete, consists of a text containing cases and a series of questions about the cases. Readers select answers and move ahead to the next case only if their answers are correct. Before beginning this work, they learn about contingency theory a la Fiedler, and they also complete the LPC scale in order to determine their preferred style, the one to which they must mold and fit situations that they encounter. To Fiedler, manipulating situations to fit a leader's style seems easier than changing a style to fit situations, because style is interpreted to be a personality trait. Implicit in the quotation from Victor Vroom, however, is an alternative: Managers may have preferences, but they are not ice statues whose behavior is frozen into a single, never-varying posture.

In contrast to Fiedler's approach, there is a group of social scientists who, rather than looking to the personality traits of the effective leader, have concentrated on discovering what leaders do: that is, they have examined the actual *behavior patterns* or *styles* of effective and ineffective leaders. If a distinct pattern of behavior could be isolated, then not only would we know what leaders do, but we could create effective leaders by teaching others to do the same things. This approach, which has obvious significance for the development of effective leadership skills, is discussed in the next section.

Leadership style

In 1950, R. F. Bales, a professor at Harvard, developed a comparatively reliable and comprehensive procedure for observing group discussions and recording individual group member's behavior.[15] In examining his data, he consistently found two different types of leadership style. One, he termed *task* and the other he termed *socio-emotional*. The former consisted of behaviors focused on getting the work done, such as timekeeping, clarifying issues, and proposing new ideas. The latter consisted of behaviors focused on keeping the interpersonal functioning of the group optimal and included such acts as arbitrating disputes, making sure others are heard, and providing encouragement. These two foci of leadership behavior—work and people—have figured prominently not only in Bales's schema but in that of others who have approached the study of leadership style from different starting points. Two prominent examples of these are the Ohio State studies and the Managerial Grid.®

The Ohio State studies

Rather than observing ongoing behavior, one group of investigators at Ohio State University decided to study leadership by asking subordinates to describe the behavior of their supervisors. For this purpose, they created a questionnaire, the Leadership Behavior Description Questionnaire (the LBDQ). Analyses of the subordinate's responses to these items revealed that two critical dimensions cut across the whole group. These were similar to the two categories identified by Bales and were labeled *consideration* and *initiating structure*. Consideration includes supervisor behaviors that are people oriented, and initiating structure includes those that are task oriented. Samples of items from the LBDQ are:

Consideration items
Is friendly and approachable
Treats all group members as equals
Gives advance notice of changes
Looks out for the personal welfare of group members

Initiation of structure items
Lets group members know what is expected of them
Encourages the use of uniform procedures
Decides what will be done and how it should be done
Assigns group members to particular tasks
Schedules the work to be done[16]

Identifying the dimensions of leader behavior was not the only goal of the Ohio State studies. These investigations were also concerned with understanding how the two dimensions, consideration and initiating structure, related to employee productivity and morale. Over a long period of time, a very active research program using the LBDQ has provided a tremendous amount of data addressing this question. Generally, the findings indicate that leaders who are rated high on consideration have more satisfied subordinates than have those who are rated low on consideration.[17] Fewer absenses[18] and lower grievance rates[19] also are associated with high consideration scores. However, the relationship between employee effectiveness and the two leadership dimensions is far less clear. It appears that effectiveness is not consistently associated with either behavior style.[20] Rather, the particular job and organizational setting in which the research takes place seems to play an important role in determining the effects of the two leadership styles of performance. This idea and its implications for management practice will be discussed in this chapter's last section, where we present the work of Yale University psychologist, Victor Vroom.

The Managerial Grid®

Yet another way of representing the task versus person orientation in leadership style has been advanced by Robert R. Blake and Jane Srygley Mouton. Their "Managerial Grid"® is a means of representing the two, by now familiar, dimensions of leader behavior: concern for production and concern for people.[21] But, rather than dealing with each dimension separately, Blake and Mouton are interested in the proportion of each concern reflected in a given leader's style. Using a nine-×-nine-point matrix, or grid, it is possible to rate any one leader on both of these dimensions simultaneously with a 1 on a dimension representing a low score and a 9 a high score. The grid is a diagnostic device enabling managers to determine just what their style is.

There are five typical leadership styles. A 1,9 style reflects great concern for output but very little for the people who do the producing. In contrast, a 9,1 style reflects a great concern for people but virtually none for productivity. The 1,1 style is the "dropout style" reflecting concern for neither people nor production—it is indicative of individuals who have essentially dropped out although they are still physically present on the job. The 5,5 style is what Blake and Mouton label the "organization man." This person seeks the middle of the road. He/she does everything in moderation and never sticks his/her neck out too far. The 9,9 style, clearly the most valued by Blake and Mouton, reflects a high concern for both production and people. They claim that this style is "the soundest way to manage to achieve excellence."[22] Unfortunately, although the statement has common-sense plausibility, very little acceptable research evidence exists to support its validity. Neither is there concrete evidence depicting what the consequences of the other styles are on either employee attitudes or effectiveness.

Despite this lack, Blake and Mouton were extremely creative in translating these ideas into action by developing Managerial Grid® management-training programs. These programs, to which thousands of managers have been exposed, include the following learning objectives: (a) understanding one's managerial style in terms of the grid; (b) developing team action skills; (c) creating unobstructed communication within teams; (d) enhancing the use of grid-oriented critiques for problem solving; (e) analyzing one's corporate work culture. Throughout the week-long program, individuals and teams work on projects and problems, critiquing performance using grid-oriented ideas. The experience is aimed at highlighting one's behavioral preferences and providing opportunities for exploration and change.

Summary.   In sum, people-oriented and task-oriented distinctions between leader styles have been popular. Observations of what leaders do, statistical discoveries using questionnaire responses of subordinates, and armchair theorizing have all led to this same conclusion. The practical consequences of these two dimensions of leader behavior and their various combinations for work, are, unfortunately, less than clear. One thing which is indisputable, however, is that these two classes of behavior do not occur in a vacuum, and the situations in which they occur will certainly affect the outcome of any style of leadership. It is hardly surprising, for instance, that leaders who are high on consideration are rated as less effective when the raters are air-crew commanders in combat.[23] Surely in a crisis circumstance, concern over the task will be far more important to subordinates than concern over people. This suggests a contingency approach to leadership, but one that is different from Fiedler's. For, rather than positing that situations will dictate which *leader* is optimum, we are suggesting that situations will dictate which *leader behavior* is optimum. Thus, any one leader can, in fact, match the situational requirements by simply shifting from one bahavior to another as the pressures and demands of a situation change.

It is possible to capture the various modes of thinking presented so far in this chapter in a four-celled table as pictured in Figure 5-2. The trait theorists, those who assert that there is a *stable quality* of leadership that enables effective leadership behavior regardless of circumstance, are depicted in the first cell. The Fiedler point of view, proposing it is a mix of *personality and circumstance* which determines a leader's effectiveness, is depicted in cell 2. In cell 3 fall those who propose that certain *behavior patterns or styles* are what make for effective leadership. Since these are not the direct outgrowth of personality, they are therefore learnable. The final cell—cell 4—represents the belief that there are no unique leadership traits which are always desirable; neither is there a set of leadership behaviors which is invariably successful. Rather, the effectiveness of any leader's behavior is dependent upon the attributes of the immediate situation in which the leader finds him/herself. Therefore, developing a skillful flexibility in oneself and an ability to diagnose organizational circumstance is critical. Let us now consider this point of view.

Figure 5-2
Four perspectives on leadership effectiveness

	Personality	*Behavior or style*
Stable	1	3
Contingent	2	4

The contingency approach: Combining leadership style and situational contingencies

The most ambitious and exhaustive study of leadership as a function of both an individual leader's style and situational contingencies was launched several years ago by a psychologist and management educator, Victor Vroom. Focusing on the decision-making process as a critical aspect of leadership functioning, Vroom and his associate, Phillip Yetton, sought to determine the conditions under which various leadership styles are most effective. Singling out decision making as a key phenomenon seems an apt choice, since it is hard to imagine any other aspect of a manager's job that more pointedly underscores the joys and woes of leadership. Memoirs and biographies of great leaders in which life stories are organized around critical decision points attest to this centrality in the leadership experience. All too often, however, decision making is misconceived of as a solely cognitive process in which logic and problem-solving skill are brought to bear in almost mechanical fashion. Laments may exist, but no one can deny that decision making is a social process, as well. For a manager, decisions are rarely made in isolation—the information brought to you by others as well as their acceptance of a decision are both potentially critical factors in determining success. With this in mind, Vroom and Yetton, focused on the way in which leaders involve their subordinates in decision making. They identified five decision-making strategies ranging from no subordinate involvement whatsoever to full collaboration with subordinates:

1. You solve the problem or make the decision yourself, using the information available to you at the present time. (The first variant on an autocratic process, represented by the symbol AI.)

2. You obtain any necessary information from subordinates, then decide on a solution to the problem yourself. You may or may not tell subordinates the purpose of your questions or give information about the problem or decision you are working on. The input provided by them is clearly in response to your request for specific information. Subordinates do not play a role in the definition of the problem or in generating or evaluating alternative solutions. (The second variant on an autocratic process, represented by the symbol AII.)

3. You share the problem with the relevant subordinates individually, getting their ideas and suggestions without bringing them together as a group. Then you make the decision. This decision may or may not reflect your subordinates' influence. (The first variant on a consultative process, represented by the symbol CI.)

4. You share the problem with your subordinates in a group meeting. In this meeting, you obtain their ideas and suggestions. Then you make the decision, which may or may not reflect your subordinates' influence. (The second variant on a consultative process, represented by the symbol CII.)

5. You share the problem with your subordinates as a group. Together you generate and evaluate alternatives and attempt to reach agreement (consensus) on a solution. Your role is much like that of a moderator, coordinating the discussion, keeping it focused on the problem, and making sure that the critical issues are discussed. You can provide the group with information or ideas that you have, but you do not try to press them to adopt "your" solution and are willing to accept and implement any solution which has the support of the entire group. (A group process, represented by the symbol GII.)[24]

The model that Vroom and Yetton created identifies three general elements which determine a decision's effectiveness in organizations: quality, acceptance, and time consumed in arriving at the decision. They suggest that the importance of these three elements in the effectiveness of organizational decisions is not fixed; rather, it differs from one problem to the next. In this spirit, they posed a series of seven questions for managers to ask themselves in any decision-making situation. Each must be answered with a yes or a no and the yes or no answers become a guide through the branches of a "decision tree." One's exit point from the tree, which will depend on the particular combination of yes's and no's that has been given, indicates which of the decision-making processes (1 through 5 in the above list) is most advisable. Before presenting the tree, let us examine the questions that managers must answer.[25]

1. Does the problem possess a quality requirement? This question suggests the importance of finding a solution which is of high quality. Although it may seem incongruous at first blush, there are many organizational problems for which quality is not really a major consideration if a decision is to be effective. Take, for instance, the problem of selecting cups to be used at the coffee machine, or scheduling lunch hours for staff. Surely you have seen groups in organizations treat problems like these with a seriousness that is all out of proportion to what is required. In instances like these, there often is no technical or rational basis for selecting among alternative courses of action, since the primary goals of the organization can be met equally well whatever solution is arrived at. This state of affairs can be contrasted with others in which some problem solutions are more consequential for organizational goals because they are substantially less costly, more technically sophisticated, or more politically astute, and therefore can be identified as preferable to other solutions. In these cases, a quality requirement does, in fact, exist.

2. *Do you have sufficient information to make a high-quality decision?* Leaders often possess sufficient information to solve a problem without involving subordinates, but not always. Thus, every decision obligates leaders to make an assessment of their knowledge vis-à-vis the problem. Deficiencies in such knowledge can be technical, e.g., not fully understanding complex production processes, equipment operation, or the subtleties of financial analyses, or they can be factual, e.g., not knowing the outcome of past attempts at a solution, EEO regulations, or current cash reserves.

3. *Is the problem structured?* Structured problems are those for which the information needed to solve the problem is apparent, and it is clear who has it and how to go about getting it. Once this information is acquired, the decision itself is rather routine. Alternative solutions and the criteria by which to assess them are known. Unstructured problems, on the other hand, often require new and creative solutions; the type of information needed to make an optimal decision and where to get it are not known.

4. *Is acceptance of the decision by subordinates important for effective implementation?* In a branch of a nationally known bank in New York City, a new computer system was installed. It was designed to increase the accuracy and speed of transactions. However, its effect was quite the opposite. The error rate increased astronomically and the transaction speed was cut in half. Those who designed the system were left scratching their heads—they had brought all their skill and expertise to bear, and yet the plan had failed miserably. A similar event occurred in an internationally known European airline during the early 1970s. In this case, a group of supervisors at one terminal redesigned the operation for handling check-ins. Rather than have counters check in passengers for particular flights, it was decided that each counter would handle check-ins for any flight leaving during set time periods, thereby eliminating long lines and distributing the work load when some flights were more heavily booked than others. The procedure is common nowadays, but at the time, for this airline especially, it was unorthodox.

In operation, despite its apparent logic, the solution failed miserably. Check-in times increased by 32 percent. Staff operating the counters resented the change because they felt it exploited high ability and rewarded lack of ability. Under the old arrangement, when handling a single flight, staff who worked quickly finished quickly—when all the passengers were checked in, they were done. Under the new arrangement, according to the staff, those who worked quickly were punished by having to handle more check-ins than did slower staff. In unidentifiable decrements, they slowed their pace and undermined the well-intended plan.

As these examples illustrate, even technically excellent solutions to problems can fail because of the resistance or opposition of these who must carry them out. These problems are ones which, according to Vroom, possess an "acceptance" requirement. In short, the success or failure of the decision is dependent upon the support of subordinates. Two considerations are paramount in determining whether a decision problem has an acceptance requirement.

a. Are subordinates going to have to execute the decision under conditions in which their initiative, judgment, and thinking will be required in order to make the decision successful?

b. Are subordinates likely to feel strongly about the decision so that they might actively support some alternatives and actively oppose others? Would such opposition take the form of attempts to block the execution of a decision?

Answers of yes to these questions indicate that acceptance is important. If, however, the answers are no, and subordinates will not be involved in the execution of a decision (either because the leader him-or herself will implement the solution, or some other group will do so), or implementation of the decision involves merely a routine process, not initiative or creativity, then subordinate acceptance is not viewed as crucial.

5. *If you were to make the decision by yourself, is it reasonably certain to be accepted by subordinates?* There are some circumstances in which a leader's decision, unilateral as it may be, will be accepted by subordinates. Thus, Vroom suggests, when an acceptance requirement is important, the relationship between thd leader and his/her subordinates must be examined. Specifically, three aspects of that relationship are said to affect the likelihood that subordinates will voluntarily go along with a leader's decision:

a. Do subordinates believe the leader has the right to make the decision because of his/her position?

b. Do subordinates believe the leader has the right to make the decision because of his/her expertise and knowledge?

c. Is the leader admired and his/her approval sought and valued by subordinates?

If the answer to any of these three questions is yes, then it should be less difficult for a leader to gain his/her subordinate's acceptance of a unilateral decision and participation in decision making would not be essential even if an acceptance requirement exists.

6. *Do subordinates share the organizational goals to be obtained in solving this problem?* We frequently make a mistake in believing that the quality of a decision is directly related to the knowledge and expertise of those making the decision. Unfortunately, this is not always so. The degree to which decision makers, subordinates, or others are motivated to use their knowledge and expertise to achieve the organizational goals implicit in the problem may influence the course of their involvement in decision making. There are many situations in organizations in which the goals of individuals are diametrically opposed to those of the organization. And, in these cases, personal goals rather than organizational ones may guide the decision-making process.

Examples of such situations in organizational life are numerous. Decisions about the distributions of pay increases or budget cuts, the allocation of additional work, or the design of evaluation processes all are obvious ones. What is in the best interests of the organization may not at all jibe with what individuals view as being in their best interests. More subtle are the attempts by groups to maintain their own cultures even when doing so is not in the service of the total organization. The resistance by members of an academic department to hiring a senior colleague who would have brought prestige and status to the university as a whole is a good case in point. Here, personal or group goals of maintaining the status quo are in conflict with organizational ones, and this conflict poses a serious threat to the quality of any decision that might be arrived at jointly.

Thus, to answer this question, a leader must assess not only the knowledge or expertise of his/her subordinates, but also their self-interest. To register an affirmative response, the leader must be convinced that there is some common area of interest in which the optimal solution will serve individual and organization alike.

7. *Is conflict among subordinates likely with the preferred solution?* Leaders must assess whether subordinates are likely to differ measurably about the "best" solutions to the problems. Although group members may share a common goal, one which is

consistent with the organization's, they may differ radically in their opinions about the means of accomplishing it.

Sometimes such disagreements stem from the different information individuals possess or think they possess. For example, Smith, from finance, "knows" that the economy is going to take a turn for the worse, whereas Brown, from marketing, "knows" with equal certainty that the economic situation has hit bottom and improvement is only around the corner. Given their conflicting points of view, it is going to be difficult to arrive at short-term decisions about marketing or production strategies.

Such disagreements also arise from the differing self-interest of those involved. The training group of one organization moved a relatively new employee into a job in which his responsibility was to visit operational units (the headquarters of worldwide product groups as well as their smaller manufacturing and marketing companies), selling them on the idea of designing training programs tailored to their needs. His success was determined by how much interest and response he created. A second unit in the group conducted standard training programs. The group's success was determined by the number of such programs and their evaluation by participants. Tailor-made programs, delivered on-site were inconvenient, distracting obstacles to success as they interpreted the meaning of that word. All parties were delighted when they learned that senior management had agreed to an increase in personnel for the training group. Their conflicting self-interest, however, guaranteed that they would disagree about how the additional personnel should be allocated.

On an individual needs basis, the same processes are evident. Take, for example, the following event which occurred in a communications company that had put special emphasis on the goal of increasing international sales within an upcoming business period. Several salespeople were discussing the operational complications of the decision. One possible action was increasing travel to make personal contact with clients. Certainly a reasonable means to the desired end. One of the salespeople, a new, young, unmarried employee, advocated that alternative and embraced the opportunity to "see the world." Another, a 40-year-old veteran with several campaigns like this on his record, supported a more passive advertising approach, followed by a limited number of direct contacts. Subsequently, in private, he voiced concerns about family and other commitments which contributed to making the "aggressive travel" solution aversive and disruptive.

Vroom and Yetton suggest that, when such disagreement is likely to occur, it is critical to choose a decision-making strategy in which subordinates interact. Interaction, they claim, allows the greatest possibility of increasing uniformity and convergence on a common solution.

The model

Vroom and Yetton constructed a model that specifies a set of optimal decision-making strategies for a leader to use when confronted with a decision problem. The model, which is presented as a decision tree (see Figure 5-3) is based upon rules derived from problem-solving and decision-making research.[26] The rules protect two critical aspects of a decision's effectiveness—the quality of the decision and its acceptability.

When dealing with a particular problem, by answering each of the seven questions just reviewed and following them sequentially through the decision tree, a manager obtains a set of effective decision-making alternatives. The first alternative in Figure 5-3 specifies the decision style that maximizes efficiency; it is the quickest alternative that does not jeopardize either the quality or the acceptance of the decision. The second alternative in Figure 5-3 specifies the decision style that maximizes participation of subordinates, although it requires a greater time investment. Therefore, after eliminating the decision-making methods that threaten quality or acceptance of the solution, the model enables the manager to select among decision-making alternatives depending upon his or her needs to be time efficient or to encourage participation among group members.

To fully understand the model, it is best to work a decision problem through it. Consider the following problem:

Because of unforeseen economic problems, you have been charged with the unpleasant task of recommending how your division's budget can be cut by 15 percent for next year. Although this news is not apt to be a total surprise to your five department heads, it is not fully expected either. Each of them has worked for the organization for over 15 years and has experienced ups and downs before.

For some time, however, you have been having trouble with your department heads. They never seem to agree on anything. There is a

Figure 5-3

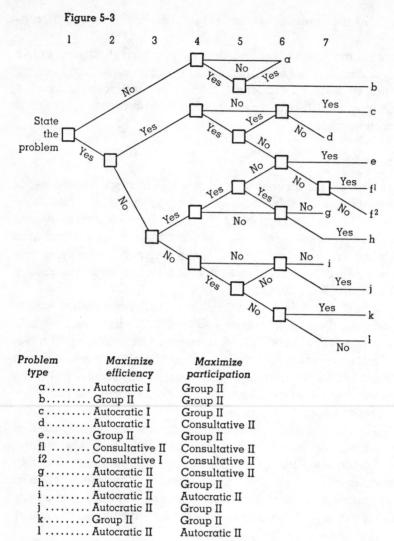

Problem type	Maximize efficiency	Maximize participation
a	Autocratic I	Group II
b	Group II	Group II
c	Autocratic I	Group II
d	Autocratic I	Consultative II
e	Group II	Group II
f1	Consultative II	Consultative II
f2	Consultative I	Consultative II
g	Autocratic II	Consultative II
h	Autocratic II	Group II
i	Autocratic II	Autocratic II
j	Autocratic II	Group II
k	Group II	Group II
l	Autocratic II	Autocratic II

Source: Adapted from Vroom, V. H., & Yetton, P. W. *Leadership and decision-making.* Pittsburgh: University of Pittsburgh Press, 1973.

good deal of bickering among them as to which department within the division should receive priority. At times, the competition among the department heads gets turned on you, and you are accused of favoritism and incompetence. Now, confronted with this problem, you are reluctant to simply hand down a decision about where the cuts should occur, although you know the division inside out and, due to a very effective yearly review process, have more information about the totality than any one of your department heads has.

Answering the seven diagnostic questions and following them through the decision tree we get:

1. Does the problem possess a quality requirement? Answer: Yes, the way in which budget cuts are made will have massive effects on the well-being of your division in the future.
2. Do I have sufficient information to make a high-quality decision? Answer: Yes, I know the division and its subparts well and have access to information from annual review reports. This brings us to:
3. Is acceptance important? Answer: Yes, department heads must execute the budget cuts, whatever they may be, and have the necessary initiative and creativity to redistribute the remaining funds in the most effective way.
4. If I were to make the decision myself, is it reasonably certain that it would be accepted by my subordinates? Answer: No, the department heads are apt to be extremely irate about any decision that I make—neither my role, my perceived expertise as division director, nor their feelings about me is apt to make a unilateral decision acceptable to them.
5. Do subordinates share the organizational goals to be attained in solving this problem? Answer: Yes, despite their power struggles within the division, the department heads all are "old-timers" and committed to the organization.

Following the decision tree, it can readily be seen that there is only one decision-making method that is likely to be effective in this situation regardless of whether efficiency or participation is being maximized. The model recommends a group consensus decision in cutting the division budget.

Research on the Vroom and Yetton model has indicated that there is a fair degree of overlap between the model's recommendations and a manager's actual behavior. A typical manager is said to use an advisable decision method 40 percent of the time.[27] That is, managers seem to have some understanding of the principles the Vroom model embodies, and they use them in daily work life. Nonetheless, it is important to heed some of the warnings made by Kolb, Rubin, and McIntyre about using the Vroom model.[28] Essentially, they warn that (1) managers are not equally skilled in using the different decision-making alternatives; (2) groups are not equally skilled in their use of the decision-making alternatives; and (3) organizational history and norms often dictate which decision-making method is chosen regardless of which

would actually be best in a given situation. These authors therefore stress the importance of training in management development, team building and organizational development to optimally
apply the Vroom model.

The Vroom and Yetton model in perspective

Throughout this chapter, we have been examining the role of
situational and personal variables in the leadership process.
Some approaches have argued that certain personality traits are
invariably desirable for leaders to have. Other approaches have
argued that certain behaviors are desirable regardless of circumstances. The approach of Vroom and Yetton is different. Their
model is concerned with contingencies. And, unlike Fiedler, they
see variability not only in situations but also in the behavior that
can be produced by a given leader. The model, in fact, specifies
that a leader's behavior should be adapted to the demands of a
given situation. But note that, when Vroom and Yetton speak of
leader behavior, they are referring to the process used for decision
making. And when Vroom and Yetton speak of situational elements, they mean the problem attributes reflected in the seven
diagnostic questions. Does this mean their approach is limited to
only this facet of leadership activity? No. They explicitly indicate
in the concluding paragraphs of their book that their approach is
relevant to other aspects of the leadership process as well:

> While we have dealt with only one facet of leadership—the sche-
> ma . . . the research methods employed in this book could prove
> equally relevant to an examination of other aspects of the leader-
> ship process.[29]

This orientation to leadership leaves the door wide open for
training activities. Assuming that all leaders can learn to analyze
situations, one must simply provide them with the tools that will
enable them to deal effectively with the situation at hand. A
leader's response in one circumstance should not predetermine
his/her response in another. They key skill to be acquired is a
flexibility which allows for adaptation to the demands of a particular situation. This is, indeed, a far cry from the implications of
the theoretical points of view epitomizing the other three cells of
our leadership matrix in Figure 5-2.

The forgotten element of leadership

All of the theories thus far presented have focused on the leader and his/her behavior. But leaders do not really exist without followers. With some notable exceptions, little of the thinking about leadership to date has really come to grips with this critical fact.[30] Moreover, regardless of what leaders do, it is only the *perception* of what they do that perpetuates their leadership roles. Leadership is, after all, an interpersonal process.

Consider, for instance, the following scenario:

Ms. Xavier, the head of the special products division of a major company, has had a busy day. In the morning, she called together the people reporting to her, asking them to decide as a group upon a new recruiting strategy for first-line managers. A little later, a memo came from Ms. X's office decreeing that from here on in all sales contracts would have to go through her office for final approval. In the afternoon, she met individually with each member of her top management group, reviewing the current state of their operations and their suggestions for increasing efficiency in making promised deadlines. Soon after, another memo circulated from Ms. X's office outlining a new strategy for making deadlines. And, at the end of the day, there was the top management group, again sitting around the conference table, once more making a decision as a group.

For a subordinate to Ms. Xavier, this sequence of events can have several different consequences. If you implicitly understand Vroom's and Yetton's contingency model of leadership *and* you have the same information as did Ms. X when she diagnosed these problem situations, you may applaud Ms. X, see her as a flexible and skilled leader, and be proud to have her as your superior. If, however, you do not implicitly understand and accept the model's decision rules, your reaction may be quite different. Ms. X may appear inconsistent and confused. Her behavior may feel random and desultory and, in the end, she may appear anything but effective—wishy-washy and erratic may be more like it.

This underscores a very critical point about any theory of how leaders should behave. Regardless of the "rightness" or "wrongness" of a leader's actions as measured on some accuracy scale, follower perceptions of the leader's behavior ultimately determine whether or not the leader is effective. If, to followers, a leader appears inconsistent and weak, even if he or she is following the Vroom and Yetton model with total accuracy, the effectiveness of that objectively arrived at series of behaviors will be severely undermined. A consistent stance, one which violates the rules of the Vroom and Yetton or, for that matter, of any model advocating behavioral contingencies, may be regarded as strong, firm, and leaderlike and, therefore, ultimately be more effective.[31]

This all serves to point out a number of important issues. First, as a manager, one must never forget the interactive part of leadership. Leading implies the involvement of at least two people. Followers are essential if a leader is to lead effectively. The best solutions in the world cannot undo that. Second, at present we have no idea of what the thinking of followers is. Do they share a contingency approach to leadership, seeing various behaviors as appropriate in different circumstances? Or do they have a trait-theory approach—always expecting a leader to be "dominant," "extroverted," "ambitious," and so on? Recent work by Staw suggests the latter.[32] Third, even if the same contingency theory is shared by leader and follower, because of different information and different perspectives, their assessment of a given situation may differ radically. Thus, the leader may be perceived as violating the rules of leadership even when he or she is not.

Conclusions

Taking the ideas that have been presented throughout this chapter, and extracting from them the points that are most useful to managers who are trying to develop and refine their leadership skills, the following set of principles emerges:

1. *The situation in which a leader finds him/herself can have a tremendous effect on the optimal way of handling a leadership problem.* Aspects of the situation, such as time constraints, relationship with subordinates, relationship with superiors, relationship among subordinates, the nature of the task to be accomplished, and the history and norms of the organization all are of particular importance. These vary and, depending upon their current status, can create a very different context for effective leadership activity.

2. *There is no one leadership skill or attribute.* Being an effective leader requires a range of behaviors, some relevant to the task and others relevant to interpersonal acumen. What is critical is the fit between the demands of the situation and the particular behavior that is utilized.

3. *Leadership skills can be learned and attuned to the dictates of a situation.* Regardless of his/her personality type, if a leader has an arsenal of different behaviors, all of which he/she is comfortable with and capable of executing when action is required, the behavior that best fits can be selected and implemented. Here, flexibility and multiple skills are key.

4. *Diagnostic skills are critical if leaders are to match their behavior to the requirements of the situation.* Managers must be well versed in the ways of analyzing situations in order to determine which behavior is "best," and what the pitfalls of alternative behaviors are likely to be. This entails broadening one's own naive diagnostic framework to include aspects of organizations often overlooked.

5. *Leaders must never forget that leadership is an interactive process and followers are their constituents.* This means that, whatever behavior they select, it must be understandable to their followers and make sense to them. To accomplish this, information about the situation may have to be shared. Remember, even if a manager does what is classically correct in textbook terms, he/she may be deemed a weak, ineffective, and/or incompetent leader because followers do not possess important information about changing situational contingencies.

Thus, becoming a good leader entails not only the learning of leadership behavior, but also the learning of the skills with which to assess situations. In addition, sensitivity to the perceptions of subordinates and determining what they see from their vantage points are important. Only when equipped with skills in each of these three areas does a manager have the foundation upon which to excel as a leader.

Notes

1. Pfeffer, J. The ambiguity of leadership. *Academy of Management Review*, January 1977, pp. 104–112. Calder, B. J. An attribution theory of leadership. In

B. M. Staw & J. R. Salancik (Eds.), *New directions in organizational behavior.* Chicago: St. Clair Press, 1976.

2. Gibb, C. A. Leadership. In G. L. Lindzey & E. Aronson (Eds.), *Handbook of social psychology* (Vol. 4). Reading, Mass.: Addison-Wesley, 1969, pp. 205–282. (See pp. 215–227 for references to these investigations.)

3. Ibid.

4. Campbell, J. P., Dunnettee, M. D., Lawler, E. E. III, & Weick, K. E. *Managerial behavior, performance and effectiveness.* New York: McGraw-Hill, 1970; Ghisilli, E. E. *Explorations in managerial talent.* Pacific Palisades, Calif.: Goodyear, 1971.

5. Fiedler, F. E., Chemmers, M. M., & Maher, L. *Improving leadership effectiveness: The leader match concept.* New York. John Wiley & Sons, 1976.

6. Ibid., Summary of high LPC leaders, pp. 6–11.

7. Ibid., Summary of low LPC leaders, pp. 6–11.

8. Fiedler, F. E. *A theory of leadership effectiveness.* New York: McGraw-Hill, 1967.

9. Fiedler, F. E. The leadership game: Matching the man to the situation. *Organizational Dynamics,* Winter 1976, pp. 6–16.

10. Ashour, A. S. The contingency model of leadership effectiveness: An evaluation. *Organizational Behavior and Human Performance,* 1973, 9, 339–355; McMahon, T. The contingency theory: Logic and method revisited. *Personnel Psychology,* 1972, 25, 697–710.

11. Fiedler, *Theory of leadership effectiveness.* (See p. 250 for a discussion of the notion of organizational engineering), Fiedler, F. E., & Chemmers, M. *Leadership and effective management.* Glenview, Ill.: Scott, Foresman, 1974 (see for a discussion of how individuals can change situations to better fit their tendencies).

12. Vroom, V. H. Leadership. In M. D. Dunnette (Ed.), *Handbook of industrial and organizational psychology.* Chicago: Rand McNally, 1975, p. 1536.

13. Fiedler, Chemmers, & Maher, *Improving leadership effectiveness.*

14. Csoka, L. S., & Bons, P. M. Manipulating the situation to fit the leader's style: Two validation studies of leader match. *Journal of Applied Psychology,* 1978, 63, 295–300.

15. Bales, R. F. *Interaction process analysis: A method for the study of small groups.* Reading, Mass.: Addison-Wesley, 1950.

16. Stogdill, R. M. *Manual for the leader behavior description questionnaire — Form XII.* Columbus, O.: Bureau of Business Research, Ohio State University, 1963.

17. Fleishman, E. A., Harris, E. F., & Burtt, H. E. *Leadership and supervision in industry.* Columbus, O.: Bureau of Educational Research, Ohio State University, 1955.

18. Ibid.

19. Fleishman, E. A., & Harris, E. F. Patterns of leadership behavior related to employee grievances and turnover. *Personnel Psychology,* 1962, 15, 43–56.

20. Korman, A. K. "Consideration," "initiating structure" and "organizational criteria": A review. *Personnel Psychology,* 1966, 19, 349–361.

21. Blake, R. R., & Mouton, J. S. *Building a dynamic corporation through good organizational development.* Reading, Mass.: Addison-Wesley, 1969.

22. Ibid., p. 62.

23. Halpin, A. W., & Winer, B. J. A factorial study of the leader behavior descriptions. In R. M. Stogdill & A. E. Coons (Eds.), *Leader behavior: Its description and measurement.* Columbus, O.: Bureau of Business Research, Ohio State University, *Research Monograph* No. 88, 1957.

24. Vroom, V. H., & Yetton, P. W. *Leadership and decision-making.* Pittsburgh: University of Pittsburgh Press, 1973.

25. This section draws largely from Vroom, V. H., Yetton, P. W., & Jago, A. G. *A normative model of leadership styles.* Unpublished manuscript.

26. Vroom & Yetton, *Leadership and decision-making,* pp. 32-35.

27. Vroom, Leadership, p. 1546.

28. Kolb, D. A., Rubin, I. M., & McIntyre, J. M. *Organizational psychology: An experiential approach.* Englewood Cliffs, N.J.: Prentice-Hall, 1971.

29. Vroom & Yetton, *Leadership and decision-making,* p. 209.

30. Graen, G., Dansereau, F., & Minami, J. Dysfunctional leadership styles. *Organizational Behavior and Human Performance,* 1972, *1,* 216-236 House, R. J., & Mitchell, T. R. Path-goal theory of leadership. In K. N. Wexley & G. A. Yukl (Eds.), *Organizational behavior and industrial psychology.* New York: Oxford University Press, 1975.

31. Staw, B. M., & Ross, J. Commitment in an experimenting society: A study of the attribution of leadership from administrative scenarios. *Journal of Applied Psychology,* 1980, *65,* 249-260.

32. Ibid.

6

Influencing People

ON one occasion while this book was being written, the authors were in a conversation with a mutual friend; let's call him Bruce Tracy. Bruce, a product manager for a major food company, was telling us about a troubling experience that he was having with one of his subordinates, Jerry Knott. We listened to the story, discussed the issues with Bruce, and then both of us spontaneously announced that Bruce's tale would form the openings for this chapter, "Influencing People."

Jerry, Bruce said, was filled with the energy of youth as well as with pride in his shiny, new Ivy League M.B.A. Combined with some notable creativity and imaginativeness, these qualities had won him a place on the company's "high potential" list. Unfortunately, Bruce also described Jerry as an abusive snob who was impatient with and impolite to his subordinates. Bruce had been alerted to these issues before Jerry's arrival. In an effort to remain unbiased and fair, Bruce took note of the warning, then tucked it away. A short while after Jerry joined his staff, however, stories traveling through the grapevine reminded him of the issue, and now he was wondering what to do. Jerry's public insults of subordinates could not be allowed to continue. In Bruce's view, although Jerry ultimately produced very good work, which helped his image in the company, he was adversely affecting others'

113

productivity to a degree that nullified his worth. Yet here was a talented person with truly high potential, if his behavior could be changed.

Bruce's dilemma is not uncommon for managers. In order to improve overall organizational functioning, he needed to influence the behavior of one of his subordinates. It was not a simple problem. Bruce had authority. But, in practical terms, when does a manager's authority allow him/her to alter subordinate behavior? Bruce wondered whether the effort would upset Jerry, causing him to complain about Bruce or leave the company. Jerry was on the "high potential" list, and if either of these two things occurred, managers senior to him might become concerned about Bruce's abilities. What if Jerry became angry because of Bruce's effort, and even more punishing of subordinates? What if he withdrew, and became dysfunctionally timid in an exaggerated effort to correct the problem?

We listened to Bruce, told him about our intention to include his story in this book, and then helped him to consider his options. The ideas that we examined during that conversation and many others are included in this chapter. Bruce benefited from that discussion, even if he and Jerry never lived "happily ever after." We believe that reading this chapter will also help managers in Bruce's situation. The chapter describes the types of power that managers can have and the many different ways they can go about using that power to influence people's actions. It also discusses some of the misconceptions people commonly have about the dynamics of power and influence in organizations.

Power

Power is the capacity to influence others to behave in the way you wish them to. The resources of power are many and varied. In organizations, such resources include prestige; skill; information; the ability to gratify or frustrate people's needs for recognition, respect, and affection; and the ability to gratify or frustrate people's desire for money, job assignments, and other organizational benefits. In a classic paper, French and Raven classified these many resources of power into five categories: reward power, coercive power, legitimate power, expert power, and referent power.[1]

1. *Reward power* is the perceived ability to control the rewards that are valued by another. Thus, influence based on this type of power is based on the assumption that the influencer has the ability to bestow benefits on those whom he or she is attempting to influence.
2. *Coercive power* also is based on the perceived ability of the influencer to control the outcomes of the one he/she attempts to influence, but in this case the control is over unpleasant or undesired outcomes. Use of this type of power assumes the possession of ability to enact punishments or sanctions.
3. *Legitimate power* is the power that results from position. Those holding high-status positions are perceived to have the "right" to make certain demands and, because of their position, those subordinate to them are obliged to comply.
4. *Expert power* results from special knowledge regarding a particular task. The possession of such expertise enables the holder to influence others successfully because they feel he or she knows what is best.
5. *Referent power* has its basis in the attractiveness of the influencer to those he/she is trying to influence. An influencer who is liked and admired can influence others successfully because of their desire to be like him/her and do as they believe he or she would in a given situation.

Most managers have a mixture of these five power bases. Nearly all, for instance, have legitimate power. By dint of their titles and positions, they are the bosses, and their employees are the subordinates. The degree of reward, coercive, expert, and referent power is less consistent, varying from manager to manager and situation to situation. Generally speaking, a manager who has all five of these power bases is potentially more influential than one who has fewer than five. If, at the extreme, a manager's power resources are very limited, then he or she may not even have enough influence to get his/her people to do their jobs. Consider, for instance, the situation of Mr. P, a supervisor in an organization with strong labor unions. Because of the negotiated union rules, he has little reward or coercive power, and even his legitimate power is severely curtailed. This leaves only expert and referent power resources. And, alas, Mr. P, a generalist, has less expertise (the tasks are highly technical) than his subordinates. Only referent power remains. And with the particular cast of characters Mr. P supervises, referent power is not an easy commodity to acquire. This clearly is a management situation with no leeway for action.

But, even when a manager has a strong power base, with many resources of power to draw upon, success in influencing others is not guaranteed. A manager must be ready, able, and skillful at utilizing his/her power. Part of this process is the important realization that often power is only in the eye of the beholder. If, for instance, a manager actually has the expertise to help a subordinate, but that subordinate is not aware of it, the manager does not have expert power vis-à-vis that subordinate. Similarly, if a subordinate believes a manager has the power to demote, then that manager possesses coercive power despite the fact that he or she may not, in fact, have this capacity. So, power is, in part, a matter of perception, and the ability to communicate one's resources to subordinates is crucial if these resources are to be useful in influencing others.

Influence strategies

When a manager has power over subordinates, there typically are many different ways he/she can influence them. Take, for example, the situation of Ms. G, a sales manager in a large manufacturing company. She is growing concerned about the apparent hostility between one of her subordinates and the representative of one of the company's major customers. Ms. G, fearing loss of the customer, wishes to influence her subordinates's behavior. She has a variety of methods to choose from. She might attempt to persuade her subordinate to recognize that his actions are potentially harmful. She might appeal to her authority as his boss and order him to be civil and polite. She might offer him a special bonus for going along with her wishes, or she might threaten him with punishment if he does not. Or, without saying anything directly to her subordinate, she might send someone else along on all future meetings with the representative, thereby constraining her subordinate's actions at such meetings.

Influence can take many forms. Managers must make a choice. The discussion that follows is aimed at increasing awareness of the options and of some of the criteria that managers might employ in selecting among them.

Threats and promises

A manager who has control of another's outcomes (reward or coercive power) can use threats and promises in an effort to influence the other. Threats and promises have two ingredients. They contain a fairly explicit direction (e.g., "do this," "don't do that," "vote this way," "keep quiet about this") and a specified consequence of personal relevance to the target of influence. Threats indicate that, if another does not do as you wish, you will punish him/her. Promises, alternatively, indicate that, if another does do as you wish, you will reward him/her. Thus, the essential form of threats and promises is identical, only the desirability of the specified consequence for action (or inaction) differs. But this difference is a very critical one, with far-reaching consequences.

To start, those who threaten tend to be disliked much more than those who promise.[2] This makes a good deal of sense. Someone who threatens is apt to be seen as malevolent, spiteful, and generally more ill intended than someone who promises. And the dislike of threateners can lead to attempts at retaliation. This can take the form of sabotage and other types of hidden attempts to complicate the life of the threatener. In addition, the negative feelings that threats generate also can provoke counterthreats. Simply put, threats involve the risk of commencing a cycle of influence that is marked by ill will and rancor.[3]

Threats and promises also differ in the information they convey. While promises clearly delineate what behavior is desired, threats often are informationally deficient. Most of the time, they tell the target person what he or she must do to avoid punishment, but fail to tell him/her what, precisely, must be done to win approval. Thus, although they may deter unwanted behavior, they do not necessarily encourage wanted behavior.

Finally, because threats are enacted only when someone has failed to comply, in order to implement threats effectively one needs to create and maintain a surveillance system. This can become complicated and costly. Think of your own behavior when you are threatened. Sometimes, with amazing ingenuity and investment of effort, you cleverly find ways of hiding your misbehavior. Other people do the same. People who have not complied with a threat are apt to try to hide evidence of their noncompliance in the hope of avoiding punishment. Without a way of monitoring behavior, threats lose their forcefulness and the threatener, his/her credibility. Promises, however do not require surveillance to be successful. They encourage people to provide evidence of compliance in order to claim their rewards.

All this sounds as if promises are the preferable of the two influence strategies. And there is indeed evidence to this effect; promises have been repeatedly shown to produce more compliance than do threats.[4] But the picture of promises is not all rosy. While better liked, promisers tend to be depicted as weaker than threateners, and there are certainly instances in which perceptions of benevolence are of less value to a manager than are perceptions of potency.[5] Moreover, when the stakes are particularly high, the impetus to cut one's losses by abiding with a threat can be more compelling than the impetus to maximize one's gains by abiding with a promise. Nonetheless, promises generally seem to be more beneficial to the influencer than are threats and, because of the positive feelings they engender, this is especially true in the long run.

Combining threats and promises into a simple statement is a common alternative to using one or the other. Often, the combination is referred to as a "carrot and stick" strategy. Presumably, in combination, the benefits of each remain, while the liabilities are magically canceled. The idea is a useful one, but not always correct. One major adviser to organizations has, on occasion, asked people to think about the carrot and stick strategy and tell him what image comes to mind. A frequent response is a jackass. "And what are the characteristics of a jackass?" he asks. Stubborn, stupid, and lazy is the common response. Just the characteristics that are usually attributed to an unmotivated employee. Perhaps these characteristics are the unintended by-products of management's influence strategy. Although the algebra is unclear, intuition makes it plainly evident that there are times when the carrot and stick approach is seen as demeaning and controlling. By treating people as if they were jackasses, we may inadvertantly cause them to act like them.[6]

Threats. Thus far, we have been acting as if managers have both reward and coercive power at their disposal. If they do and find themselves caught between using a threat or a promise, then it is important to carefully consider the differences between these two influence strategies. But what if you do not have the resources to both threaten and promise? How do you make the most of what you've got? Here are some tips about how to maximize the effectiveness of both threats and promises.

1. Keep the threat private. Often, people do not comply with threats because they do not want to lose face.[7] Eliminating an audience should alleviate this pressure to not comply.
2. Do your best not to instill hostility. Be firm but not inappropriately punitive.
3. Whenever possible, specify not only the behavior that you hope to avert, but also the behavior that you desire to elicit.
4. Be very clear about what compliance entails. When possible, limit it in scope and in time, e.g., "vote yes in the next meeting" rather than "agree with me on important issues." This reduces the extent to which you are jeopardizing the other's autonomy.
5. Always stay within the bounds of what punishment you can administer and are comfortable with administering. It is hoped that you will not have to punish the other but, if you do, you must be ready to carry out your threat.
6. Make sure that the punishment fits the crime. If it is either too small or too large, it lacks credibility.
7. Be clear about the consequences for noncompliance—how, when, and where the punishment will occur and exactly what form it will take.
8. Only demand behavior you can monitor. People try to cover up noncompliance so as to avoid punishment. If you are to be effective, you have to be able to determine whether or not compliance has, in fact, occurred.

Promises. These, obviously, offer a different set of circumstances.

1. Do not offer rewards which will upset others who work in the same setting. People may often draw attention to their good fortune and, if a reward is inequitable, you can inadvertantly create havoc.
2. Remain tough although benevolent. It is important not to be seen as promising out of weakness.
3. Make clear what compliance entails, so that the individual knows exactly when he or she is entitled to the reward. Miscommunication is this regard can have very unfortunate consequences.
4. Promise only what you can deliver. Failing to fulfill a promise is considered very unfair and underhanded—people really feel as though they have been "had."

5. Make sure that the reward fits the favor. As with threats, incongruity reduces credibility. In the case of promises, too big a reward raises the spectre of "there must be more to it than that," which can attenuate compliance.
6. Be clear about the reward—what it is, where and when it will be bestowed.

Threats and promises, influence strategies that derive from the power to control another's outcomes, each can be effective when used wisely. But threats and promises are useful only in influencing overt behavior. What happens when a manager seeks to influence attitudes, opinions, and beliefs so that changes in behavior originate from internal, not from external sources? Here, another set of influence strategies are relevant—all roughly falling under the heading of persuasion.

Persuasion

A manager who tries to influence a subordinate through persuasion does not directly draw upon his or her power to reward or punish the other. There are, in fact, no concrete inducements offered. The appeal in persuasion is to the intelligence, rationality, and ultimate reasonableness of the individual one is trying to influence. Consequently, the influencer must draw upon his or her expert power and/or referent power to persuade another. For, in evaluating a persuasive argument, the perceived knowledge and expertise of the influencer is critical, as is his/her prestige, and the degree to which he or she is held in respect.

Even if the ultimate goal of a persuasive attempt is to influence behavior, persuasion focuses on changing attitudes, beliefs, and values. The assumption underlying persuasive efforts is that, by changing someone's orientation or convictions, one can, indirectly, change that person's behavior, as well. This approach has several implications, all of which render persuasion a far more efficient influence strategy than either threats or promises.

First, the exact behaviors which are desired or undesirable need not be itemized. If a change in heart occurs, one would expect an array of behaviors to change—behaviors which are not even apparently related to one another. An example is useful here. Suppose, for instance, a manager can convince a subordinate that a particular project is not simply an exercise in futility but is actually feasible and, if successful, very important. This change in attitude would then be likely to affect a variety of the subordinate's behaviors, ranging from his or her general mood to his/her promptness in completing assigned work to his/her accuracy in the work that he/she does. These and many other behaviors can be affected by the change in attitude brought about by persuasion.

Second, persuasion, if successful, makes surveillance unnecessary. If a behavior stems from a person's attitudes, not from external inducement, then the energy and motive for sustaining the behavior is always present. Because the motivation comes from within, the person feels good about what he/she is doing and that, in itself, generates additional motivation to continue. The troublesome problem of behavior monitoring is simply not relevant.

Third, because persuasion does not prescribe specific behaviors, and rewards and punishments are not involved, the person being influenced is apt to feel as if he/she has greater freedom to act. Incentives, whether positive, as in promises, or negative, as in threats, create constraints. In contrast, persuasion leaves room for voluntary action, and often is viewed as an influence strategy that displays more respect for individual integrity.

Thus, in a number of ways, persuasion seems a superior influence method when compared to threats and promises. But there are drawbacks, as well. Persuasion takes time. It entails sitting down with someone and trying to convince him/her of your point of view. This can take five minutes, but it may take five days, and the time investment does not result in any greater guarantee of success. Indeed, commonplace wisdom is that people's attitudes, values, and beliefs are often quite fixed and attempts to alter them may prove futile. In addition, some of these attitudes, values, and beliefs are supported by group norms in the work setting, creating an additional obstacle to change. Persuasion, therefore, takes skill. To be effective at persuading another requires attention to the influence process itself: how you are making contact with the other, how you are transmitting your message, and how he or she is likely to react.

Research on persuasion has turned up a number of critical aspects of this influence process which are worth noting.[8] The first concerns the influencer him- or herself. Both the perceived level of expertise the influencer brings to the situation and his/her perceived trustworthiness are of special importance. If, for instance, the influencer is seen as speaking from ignorance or as acting in his/her own self-interest, his/her persuasiveness is severely hampered. Additionally, being dynamic, socially adept, authoritative, and liked have definite benefits for the influencer.

The second aspect of the persuasive process that is of importance is the persuasive message and how it is organized. There is indication, for example, that presenting only your own point of view can backfire. If the person you are trying to influence is not particularly well-disposed toward your point of view, or if you want the persuasive message to have a long-lasting effect, the effectiveness of a one-sided approach is limited. Rather, it is more useful to present both sides of an argument and, when you do so, present your argument last, explicitly stating your conclusions, repeating them often.

Another element of the persuasion process is the way in which the person you are trying to influence is involved in the discussion. There is evidence, for instance, that if someone actively "steps into another's shoes," defending a position that had been unacceptable to him or her, that position is more likely to be accepted. In general, successful persuasion depends more on active participation than on passive listening.

As you can see, even from this brief discussion, persuasion is a complicated process. Some rules of thumb follow.[9] Managers who choose to influence through persuasion might find them useful to keep in mind:

1. Get as much information as you can—know important facts, figures and be as up-to-date as possible on the issues. You must be seen as competent if you are to be influential.
2. Learn as much as you can about the individual you will be trying to influence. This will enable you to engage him or her more easily, and to recognize cues of annoyance, amusement, or enthusiasm. It also will help to know something about the individual's history in the work setting and his/her reactions to other influence attempts.
3. Select a contact situation in which you are either equals or you have a slight power advantage. You might, for instance, invite the person into your office rather than go to his/hers.
4. Try to create some common ground between you and the other. Persuasion is enhanced when there is some apparent similarity with the influencer. The similarity need not relate

to the issue at hand or even be work related. A brief discussion of who is apt to win a major league pennant can, for instance, be effective at creating a sense of similarity and, therefore, greater receptivity to persuasion.

5. Avoid group situations when you know or suspect the prevailing sentiment to be counter to your own. In such a situation, the group members provide support for one another and highlight the fact that to be persuaded is to turn against the others.

6. Listen attentively to what the person says. This not only encourages a dialogue but makes clear that you are open and responsive to his/her feelings and ideas.

7. Call the person by name and make apparent that you are cognizant of his/her uniqueness and individuality. This is particularly important if the individual is your subordinate and likely to feel that you see him/her as merely part of some large, indistinguishable group of employees.

8. Make the person realize that you care about the issue you are discussing and that persuading him/her is something which is important to you personally, not just because of your organizational role.

9. Do not put your best arguments in the middle of your presentation—they will not be well remembered. Put them first if you want to motivate or interest the other, or last if interest already is strong.

10. Remember, present both sides of the argument. And draw conclusions—state them squarely, repeating the major points in your argument.

11. Try not to put the other on the defensive. Do not even ask him/her to defend his/her position.

12. Try to find areas of commonality. When you find some, draw attention to them.

13. When possible, get the person to role-play your position, put him/herself in your place, and otherwise actively participate in stating your ideas and conclusions.

Persuasion, like threats and promises, assumes that the person you are trying to influence would not act in the way you wish without being actively encouraged to do so. But there are circumstances in which exerting such deliberate, overt effort is unnecessary. These are discussed in the following section.

Relationship-based influence

Some managers exude a kind of charismatic aura. Others are successful at building friendships with those in their work settings. In either case, the manager can successfully influence others not because of what he or she can provide for them, or because he or she is so convincing in his/her arguments, but because the others "feel good" about him/her. Influence can be wielded by simply indicating, through suggestion or request, what it is that is desired. The resource of relevance here is referent power. Because of admiration, respect, and/or liking, the individual one tries to influence is only too eager and willing to please.

There is another type of relationship-based influence. It draws upon legitimate power. In becoming members of organizations, most individuals "buy into" the power structure. That is, they implicitly agree to the right of those in higher positions to make some demands and, similarly, they implicitly agree to their obligation to comply with such demands. Consequently, individuals who have designated authority over others are often able to exert influence without the use of threats or promises or persuasive tactics. Their wishes always contain an unspoken appeal to their legitimate authority. To quote Cartwright and Zander, "It is expected that supervisors will supervise, coordinators will coordinate, and leaders will lead."[10]

These two types of relationship-based influence are very different from one another.[11] Charisma or friendship is personal, authority is impersonal; charisma or friendship involves feelings and emotions, authority involves facts; charisma or friendship highlights affective relationships, authority highlights status differences. Consequently, these two types of influence modes do not go hand in hand. More often than not, a manager cannot use both as the whim hits him/her—they are too inconsistent in their bases and their effects. A choice must be made.

The scope and range of these two types of relationship-based influence also differ. Whereas influence through charisma and/or friendship can be effective regardless of whom one wishes to influence, influence through authority can be effective only with those directly below the manager in the organizational hierarchy. On a day-to-day basis, however, most managers need to influence their superiors, their peers, and sometimes those totally outside the organization if they are to do their jobs effectively. Furthermore, influence based on charisma and/or friendship is not limited in the number and types of behaviors that can potentially be affected, but influence based on authority is very limited in this respect. Thus, although all managers enjoy legitimate power and all have the right to make demands, depending upon influence through authority as one's primary influence mode may prove shortsighted.

So far, we have focused on influence methods which require interaction between the influencer and the individual he or she wishes to influence. But there are influence methods which do not involve any interaction whatsoever. These are discussed below. Two types of manipulation strategies, each quite different from the other, are ecological control and roundabout control.

Manipulation

Manipulation is a more indirect method of influence than those that have been discussed so far. The person being influenced is kept unaware that any attempt at influence is being made.

Ecological control. This involves modifying the social or physical environment of another so that the desired behavior occurs.[12] Influence by ecological control is frequently used in work settings. In forming work groups, for example, some managers seeking to motivate lethargic employees place these people on projects with others who are enthusiastic and upbeat. Or, in order to stimulate creativity, managers sometimes resort to a periodic "reshuffling" of their employees into new work teams, thereby preventing a dangerous inbreeding of ideas. Managers also use this type of control in making office assignments; someone who is a chronic time waster because of his/her excessive social activity is put into a relatively isolated area, with limited opportunity for conversation. Finally, managers commonly use this type of control in designing their own work space and in controlling how they, themselves, are treated. Comically, and perhaps unconsciously, but not infrequently, some decide to have chairs in their offices that are lower in height than their own. Others, seeking a different effect, decide to have an informal seating area in which to chat with visitors. A few even rid their offices of desks and have only informal lounge furniture. Look at your own work space. Its design may reflect your effort to subtly influence the behavior of those who enter your office.

Roundabout control. Although it also is a form of influence that occurs without the knowledge or consent of the one being influenced, this is very different in character from ecological control.[13] It involves the use of third parties in the influence process. One common roundabout strategy used in organizations utilizes rumor as a source of influence. By telling someone who you know will pass along the information, it is possible to create pressure on others while disguising your own involvement. A good example of this type of influence is captured in the experience of a 59-year-old vice president of a major communications company. The company was eager for him to leave, and he was eager to go, if he received a satisfactory deal. At one point during the negotiations for a larger early retirement package, he was not pleased with what seemed to be the company's final offer. Shortly after learning the details, he sent a "confidential" memo to the personnel office inquiring about procedures and costs for obtaining a three-year extention of the company's health insurance for his son, who was approaching maturity. Of course, word of this inquiry was passed on and, without saying a word, the vice president was in a better bargaining position. A substantially better offer was made to him within only a few days. By separating himself from the message (of his intent to stay), and by having it delivered by others, the believability of the message was heightened and, therefore, its impact enhanced.

Choosing an influence strategy

We have outlined a number of different strategies for influencing others. But, as a manager, which influence mode is optimal? There is no one answer to this question. In this section we shall briefly outline some of the major considerations that a manager should take into account when making a decision among influences modes.

Who is the target of influence?

The type of influence strategy you embark upon must take account of the power relationship between you and the person you are seeking to influence. You can be weaker than, stronger than, or equal in power to the other. Whichever is the case, it has implications for how you go about exercising influence.[14]

When trying to exert influence upward, threats and promises are most often inappropriate. Threats presume superiority and promises, equality (at the very least), and even if one does have power over the outcomes of a superior, to use it in this manner violates the implicit authority structure. Because of this, threats to superiors often come across as blackmail, and promises as bribes. Both are likely to produce annoyance and even anger, and the influencer is apt to be seen as arrogant and "out of bounds." However, persuasion is an appropriate strategy to use with superiors. It presumes rationality and reasonableness on the part of the other and does not imply that the influencer is in any way the higher in status of the two. For this reason, it is far more likely to be successful than threats and/or promises will be. Finally, when trying to exert influence upward, relationship-based influence is limited to that based on friendship and congeniality; one has no authority over one's superiors.

When attempting to influence one's subordinates, all of the influence modes we have discussed are potentially effective. Thus, the choice among influence strategies involves a decision about which will be most effective in a situation and produce the fewest negative by-products. This issue is examined in subsequent parts of this section.

Last, there is the issue of influencing one's peers. Here, also, it would seem that a threat is an inappropriate tactic. The presumption of superiority inherent in this influence attempt violates the relationship of equal power and is apt to produce an unfavorable reaction. Promises, however, are not as likely to be received so negatively. They convey benevolent intent and tend not to be seen as inappropriate because they are commonly exchanged among friends and equals. Persuasion, with its capacity to communicate respect for the integrity of the other, and relationship-based influence attempts, when based on friendship, also are apt to be effective in equal-power situations.

You may have noticed that no mention has been made of the relative merits of manipulative influence strategies in the discussion so far. That is because both ecological control and roundabout influence can be effective whatever the power relationship between the influencer and the person he/she wishes to influence. Since, by definition, these manipulation tactics do not entail the knowledge or the consent of the person being influenced, considerations of status and violations of appropriateness vis-à-vis relative status are irrelevant.

How likely is the influence attempt to succeed?

To determine whether an influence attempt will succeed requires an assessment of one's own power and an assessment of the other's needs.[15] For, unless an influencer is perceived to have the power to control outcomes that are valued or feared by the other, he/she cannot successfully threaten or promise. Similarly, unless an influencer is believed to have information and expertise, and the other views him or herself as deficient or somewhat less knowledgeable, the influencer cannot successfully persuade. And finally, unless the other has needs for approval from the influencer or desires to maintain a friendship with him/her, or alternatively needs to abide by the "rules of the game," relationship-based influence cannot succeed. Thus, determining the likelihood that an influence attempt will be successful requires an honest appraisal of both self and other and, not to be forgotten, of how the other views you.

In analyzing the likely success of various influence attempts, it is critical to keep in mind that influence often provokes resistance and/or opposition. Because the very nature of influence is to bring about change in the attitudes or behavior of another, one must contend with the fact that the person you are trying to influence is committed to a different viewpoint or course of action and, in changing it, must give something up.

It is useful here to make a distinction between opposition and resistance.[16] *Opposition* occurs when the person being influenced objects to the substance of what he or she is being asked to do. *Resistance*, however, is not based on reactions to the substance of the influence attempt but to the way in which influence is exerted. Consequently, resistance often appears arbitrary, irrational, and occasionally may even seem self-defeating.

Opposition to an influence attempt is dependent upon the degree to which the influence request is at variance with what the person wants to believe or do, and on the degree of commitment the individual has to that particular course of action. Public commitment, for instance, creates more rigid opposition to change than does nonpublic commitment. Research evidence supports these ideas.[17] It also indicates that the importance of the issue at stake is a significant component of opposition to influence—people are far more willing to give up positions that matter little to them than positions about which they care a great deal.

Since opposition results from the substance of an influence attempt, this may suggest that whatever form of influence is used will trigger the same reaction. But this is not so. Kurt Lewin, in discussing influence, concluded that there are three ways to influence someone: (1) by adding new forces on the person; (2) by changing the direction of the current forces; and (3) by reducing the magnitude of forces that oppose change.[18] Lewin strongly suggests that the latter two methods are preferable to the first, because they generate less opposition. Threats, promises, relationship-based influence, and manipulation all can be classified as "adding new forces"—they do not really change the situation of the person being influenced, but only create additional pressure on him/her to comply. Persuasion, however, does not operate this way. Instead, it brings about compliance by changing attitudes and, thus, either changes the direction of oppositional forces or reduces their magnitude, thereby producing less opposition than do the other influence strategies. In short, when what you wish the other to do is apt to be found very objectionable, persuasion is probably your best bet.

Resistance, which results not from the content of the influence attempt, but from its style, is also a major obstacle to success. It takes the form of anger and open rejection of the influence attempt or resentment and unenthusiastic compliance. In general, resistance is aroused when the act of complying can be interpreted as yielding, submitting, losing face, or somehow being defeated.[19] This is most likely to occur when the influence attempt is viewed as illegitimate or coercive.[20] In particular, those influence attempts which violate the requirements of status relationships and those which greatly constrain the freedom of action of the other are resisted. As we already have mentioned, threats and promises can appear to violate status relationships and, thus, are unlikely to be successful in certain types of situations. And, while all influence attempts reduce the individual's freedom to some extent, producing "psychological reactance" and the desire to resist,[21] some influence modes do so more than others. Threats, in particular, have this freedom-inhibiting quality.[22]

Thus, in assessing the likelihood of success of alternative influence strategies, one must attend to a variety of issues: the assessment of one's power, the other's needs, the degree to which opposition is likely, and the type of influence attempt which will arouse the least resistance in that particular situation.

How costly is the influence attempt?

It is possible to calculate the potential costs and benefits likely to accrue to various influence strategies in a given circumstance. Clearly, influence modes that appear to, on balance, produce a net advantage for the influencer are preferable to those that do not. In this vein, Thibaut and Kelley have coined the term *usable power*, meaning only that power which does not result in great cost to the user.[23]

Consider, for instance, Mr. G, a manager who wants one of his subordinates, Ms. K, to stay late one Friday evening and even to come in on Saturday to complete a project report. Even though Mr. G may be reasonably sure that Ms. K would, indeed, comply with his wishes, he has to take into account the fact that Ms. K would be likely to resent his intrusion on her weekend time and consequently be less than cooperative in other areas of work for some indeterminable period of time. If Mr. G has equally important work to be handled in the future, then he may be reluctant to exercise his power in the present situation. The costs of an angry Ms. K are greater than the benefits of pressuring her to put in overtime to complete the report.

In the case of Mr. G and Ms. K, the costs are rather straightforward. But sometimes the costs of influence are more subtle. Take, for example, the reputational consequences that result from an influence episode. Issuing a threat may create the sentiment that you are not such a nice person after all, and, if you have depended upon friendship as a means of influencing others, this may no longer be a viable option for you. Being considered manipulative may have even more negative consequences. In short, one of the costs (or benefits) of an influence attempt is what it communicates about you personally and what it portends for the relationship between you and the person you try to influence. Too often, this is forgotten in the heat of the moment and, not recognizing just how costly these consequences can be, we exercise threats or appeal to our rights as authorities with the aim of influencing another, creating tension and hostile feelings which, in the final analysis, are quite costly indeed.

Yet another cost of influence is the consequence if the attempt fails. This is particularly important when the process is visible and observed by others. Issuing a threat or a promise to which someone does not comply can, for example, make the influencer seem very weak, out of control, and foolish. Failing to persuade someone can cast doubt upon your expertise. And, finally, appealing to your authority as a reason for compliance, if it fails, can, in fact, raise doubts about your status vis-à-vis the other. Thus, in calculating the costs and benefits of various influence modes, it is important to consider what happens if the influence attempt does not succeed.

Finally, and most obviously, some types of influence involve expending one's resources and others do not. Threats require the costs of punishing the other for noncompliance, and promises require the costs of rewarding the other for compliance. Depending upon how much the act of rewarding or punishing the other actually penalizes the influencer, these influence attempts may be judged more or less advantageous. However, not all forms of influence reduce the resources of the influencer. In fact, some can increase them. Effective persuasion can enhance one's expert power, reinforcing the view of you as knowledgeable and informed. Similarly, effectively harnessing the loyalty and admiration of others to influence their behavior certainly does not diminish the influencer's power and, in many instances, can increase it. Thus, the task of assessing the relative costs and benefits one can expect from employing different influence strategies is more complicated than it at first seems.

How does the influence attempt fit into the organizational context?

As a manager, it is essential to keep in mind that the choice of influence method must be contingent upon the setting in which it is to be used. Most organizations have established social systems in which norms exist concerning the influence process. Thus, threats of physical punishment may seem natural and acceptable in some military establishments but be considered outrageous in other organizations. This point is dramatically made by noting the uproar that periodically flares when teachers are given the right to corporally punish unruly children. It is important, as a manager, to be aware of the influence strategies that seem to be generally accepted, and to recognize that going beyond these makes the influence attempt more salient and is also more likely to arouse resistance.

Not only are there norms governing how power and influence are exercised in a given organization, but there also are norms governing how power and influence are exercised within certain organizational groups. One would not expect, for instance, that the same types of influence strategies would be found acceptable by those in all departments and at all levels of any one organization. By and large, the higher the level in the organizational hierarchy and the more professional the group, the more inappropriate coercive tactics will seem to be. But again, lest unfair generalizations be made, we hasten to add that this is likely to differ from organization to organization.

At this point, it is useful to say a word about manipulation as a mode of influence. The word *manipulation* is characteristically considered a bad one, with the assumption that those who engage in this form of influence are evil and those who succumb to it their prey. Nonetheless, manipulation permeates behavior in organizations, and being aware that it can and does occur is important to effective functioning. Whether such behavior is encouraged or discouraged will, in the final analysis, be determined by the degree of trust and openness that exists in the organization generally. Manipulation is an unacceptable influence strategy when trustworthiness and respect for others are valued above all.

In summary, the following points seem important to keep in mind when choosing an influence strategy:

1. *Behave appropriately!* That is, abide by the constraints inherent in the status relationship between you and the person you are trying to influence. Inappropriate influence attempts are sure to be resisted.
2. *Keep the probabilities on your side!* Be conservative in assessing the likely success of various influence modes. The cost of failures is often very steep.
3. *Do not cut off your nose to spite your face!* Exerting influence can be costly in a number of different ways: retaliation, reputational consequences, and the expenditure of resources. Make sure that the costs of the influence mode you choose do not exceed its benefits.
4. *Mind those norms!* Violating the informal rules about what type of influence is acceptable can backfire. Influence is rarely accepted when its form is unacceptable.

This all sounds as though managers should put aside their own values and sense of what is right when attempting to influence others. This, of course, is not so. In fact, the very first consideration necessary in choosing among influence strategies is which of them falls within the range of what *you* consider acceptable. It is only then that these guidelines are useful in narrowing down the field of options. For no influence attempt is truly successful if it costs you your self-respect. In the long run, the use of power in a way which you find personally objectionable will create many more problems than it solves.

Finally, pervading this chapter is the idea that the use of power affects the relationship between the influencer and the person he or she attempts to influence. Depending upon the type of influence strategy chosen and its effectiveness, the relationship is either improved or worsened, but it never remains quite the same. This simple fact should weigh heavily in a manager's use of power and choice of how to go about influencing others.

Notes

1. French, J. R. P., Jr., & Raven, B. The bases of social power. In D. Cartwright & A. Zander (Eds.), *Group dynamics*. New York: Harper & Row, 1968.

2. Heilman, M. E. Threats and promises: Reputational consequences and transfer of credibility. *Journal of Experimental Social Psychology*, 1974, *10*, 310–324.

3. Deutsch, M. *The resolution of conflict: Constructive and destructive processes*. New Haven: Yale University Press, 1973.

4. Heilman, M. E., & Garner, K. A. Counteracting the boomerang: The effects of choice on compliance to threats and promises. *Journal of Personality and Social Psychology*, 1975, *31*, 911–917; Rubin, J. Z., & Lewicki, R. J. A three-factor experimental analysis of promises and threats. *Journal of Applied Social Psychology*, 1973, *3*, 240–257.

5. Heilman, M. E., Threats and promises.

6. Levinson, H. *The great jackass fallacy*. Boston: Division of Research, Harvard Business School, 1973.

7. Brown, B. R. The effects of need to maintain face on the outcome of interpersonal bargaining. *Journal of Experimental Social Psychology*, 1968, *4*, 107–121.

8. McGuire, W. J. The nature of attitudes and attitude change. In G. L. Lindzey & E. Aronson (Eds.), *The handbook of social psychology* (Vol. III). Reading, Mass.: Addison-Wesley, 1969.

9. Many of these are adapted from Zimbardo, P., & Ebbeson, E. B. *Influencing attitudes and changing behavior*. Reading, Mass.: Addison-Wesley, 1970.

10. Cartwright, D., & Zander, A. Power and influence in groups. In D. Cartwright & A. Zander (Eds.), *Group dynamics*. New York: Harper & Row, 1968, p. 221.

11. Hamner, W. C., & Organ, D. W. *Organizational behavior: An applied psychological approach*. Plano, Tex.: Business Publications, 1978.

12. Cartwright & Zander, Power and influence in groups.

13. Bonoma, T. V., & Zaltman, G. *Psychology for management*. Boston: Kent Publishing, 1981.

14. Bonoma, T. V. Conflict, cooperation and trust in three power systems. *Behavioral Science*, 1976, *21*, 495–514.

15. Cartwright & Zander, Power and influence in groups.

16. Cartwright, D. A field theoretical conception of power. In D. Cartwright (Ed.), *Studies in social power*. Ann Arbor: Institute for Social Research, University of Michigan, 1959.

17. Allen, V. L. Situational factors in conformity. In L. Berkowitz (Ed.), *Advances in experimental social psychology* (Vol. 2). New York: Academic Press, 1965.

18. Lewin, K. *Field theory in social science.* New York: Harper & Row, 1951.

19. Heilman, M. E., & Toffler, B. L. Reacting to reactance: An interpersonal interpretation of the need for freedom. *Journal of Experimental Social Psychology*, 1976, *12*, 519–529.

20. Deutsch, *The resolution of conflict.*

21. Brehm, J. W. *A theory of psychological reactance.* New York: Academic Press, 1966; Wicklund, R. A. *Freedom and reactance.* Potomac, Md.: Lawrence Erlbaum Associates, 1974.

22. Heilman & Garner, Counteracting the boomerang.

23. Thibaut, J. W., & Kelley, H. H. *The social psychology of groups.* New York: John Wiley & Sons, 1959.

7

Solving Problems and Making Decisions

Hours of fruitless debate have been spent trying to decide whether individuals or groups are superior at problem solving. "A camel" the individually oriented enthusiasts claim, "is a horse designed by a group." Undaunted despite these barbs, the group advocates retort loudly and proudly, appealing to such concepts as "synergy" and "assembly effect," in the hope of convincing listeners that the whole of a group effort can be greater than the sum of its parts. The debate will no doubt continue in apparent disregard of existing evidence which clearly shows that neither individuals nor groups are superior at problem solving *all of the time*. Their superiority varies, being contingent on such factors as (1) characteristics of the tasks on which people are working, and (2) characteristics of individuals who are doing the work.[1]

Task characteristics

Managerial problems can be classified into at least four different general categories. One involves tasks which require organization members to make *estimates* based on their experience and whatever data are available. Forecasting internal and external reactions to organization changes, and some projections of sales and pricing conditions fall into this category.

135

A second category includes tasks which have an *audit*, or *clerical* quality. Checking or recording figures, invoices, and inventory are all examples of this kind of problem.

A third category of tasks requires people to *generate ideas* or *remember past events*, while a fourth requires *integrating information* and experience from a number of people with different backgrounds and knowledge in order to solve a problem.

Performance on the first three categories of task improves when the input of several people is combined. But the people may be working in isolation and the process of combining their output can be a clerical operation. There is no clear evidence with these tasks that a group effort involving face-to-face interaction yields special benefits. In these instances, two heads are better than one, but the two can be miles apart.[2]

Group efforts, however, are essential for performing tasks which fall into the fourth category. This apparent exception, however, should not be dismissed as an infrequent anomaly. On the contrary, many astute observers of organizational life have argued that these tasks are the very ones which increasingly confront today's manager. William Dyer, for example, has said, "Over the past 15 years, the role of the manager has changed significantly in many organizations. The strong manager capable of almost single-handedly turning around an organization or department, while still a folk hero in the eyes of many, has given way to the recent demands of increasingly complex systems for managers who are able to pull together people of diverse backgrounds, personalities, training and experience and weld them together into an effective working group."[3]

Another well-known behavioral scientist, Edgar Schein, a professor at M.I.T., confirmed Dyer's observation when he remarked that today's manager "cannot any longer safely make decisions by himself; he cannot get enough information digested within his own head to be the integrator and decision maker. Instead he finds himself increasingly having to manage the *process* of decision making, bringing the right people together around the right questions or problems. . . ."[4]

Individual characteristics

If these observations are accurate, then we indeed have a problem because common sense and available research evidence both suggest that diversity of personality, background, and position in a problem-solving group is a double-edged sword. On the one hand, a diversity of personnel improves a group's problem-solving potential by increasing the array of alternative resources which are available. But, simultaneously, the diversity can become a source of interpersonal discomfort and alienation, thereby increasing the difficulty of developing productive social interaction.[5]

The quality of a group's social interaction is critical inasmuch as it affects the actual utilization of intellectual talent and technical ability which members possess.[6] In considering these issues, one group of researchers who clearly have a group bias was forced to conclude, "In general, in the evaluation of the relative quality of the products produced by groups in contrast to the products produced by individuals, the group is superior. The superiority of the group, however, all too frequently, is not as great as would be expected from interactional theory. In many studies the product of the 'best' individual is superior to that of the 'best' group."[7] Thus, although there is a "pooling effect" which sometimes gives the group an advantage over individuals in problem solving, there are also "process losses," which are attributable to ineffective social interaction.[8]

Similar gains and losses occur as *group size* increases: (1) more people increase the probability of at least one person finding a correct solution; and, (2) if the task involves combining people's judgments, then individual judgments made by members of increasingly diverse groups is likely to result in the averaging out of errors. But size also increases the likelihood of creating social obstacles: (1) lapses in adherence to an orderly structure of working arrangements become more critical in larger groups; (2) the likelihood of subgroups forming with inconsistent goals is greater; (3) for some people, feelings of inhibition increase with group size, resulting in (4) wider differences in individual rates of participation.[9]

Thus, if, on occasion, managers need diverse, talented personnel as an aid to problem solving, then they also need an understanding of how group process can facilitate or hinder problem-solving efforts as well as skills in managing the process problems that arise. In both this chapter and the next we will examine several measures which might help managers deal with these problems. But first we will review some of the ways in which group process can either facilitate or hinder organizational problem solving and decision making.

Group process in problem solving and decision making

Groups, like individuals, experience periods of relative stability. These are times when efforts produce results which are both satisfying and consistent with organizational aims. Unfortunately, these periods are often short-lived. As Figure 7-1 illustrates, it is common to find that disruptive events inside and outside of the group interfere with the smooth, efficient operation of so-called normal work procedures. The resulting losses in performance and outcome as well as personal discomfort and stress become forces which press for a solution to the problem in order that some relative stability might be reestablished (see Figure 7-1).

Human beings are *human* however, and their responses on these occasions, regardless of whether they act alone or collectively, are influenced by many factors, a great number of which have little, if anything, to do with the objective character of the problem that they are facing. The point is made very nicely by Miller and Starr in their book, *The Structure of Human Decisions.* They comment: "The effect of these psychological and sociological factors leads individuals to make decisions and to take actions without recourse to maximization of utility in the classical economic sense. Alternatively phrased, it can be said that these factors cause people to act irrationally—but it should be noted that this is simply a matter of definition, rationality having been defined as maximization of economic utility."[10]

For some people, it is unpleasant to admit that the world of organization problem solving and decision making is not an orderly place. They subscribe to the idealized view that individuals and groups act mechanically, dealing only with objective facts. In this idealized world, a group selects the solution which optimizes its outcomes after examining the costs and benefits of every available alternative. Even a casual observation of behavior in organizations however, suggests that this idealized approach, which is called *optimization,* occurs only occasionally.[11]

In 1969, Ross Stagner published an article in the *Journal of Applied Psychology* reporting data that he collected from vice presidents of 125 firms identified by *Fortune* magazine as America's largest and most successful. Twenty-eight percent of them said that, in making high-level decision, only a *rough* estimate of

Figure 7-1
A model of group problem-solving responses

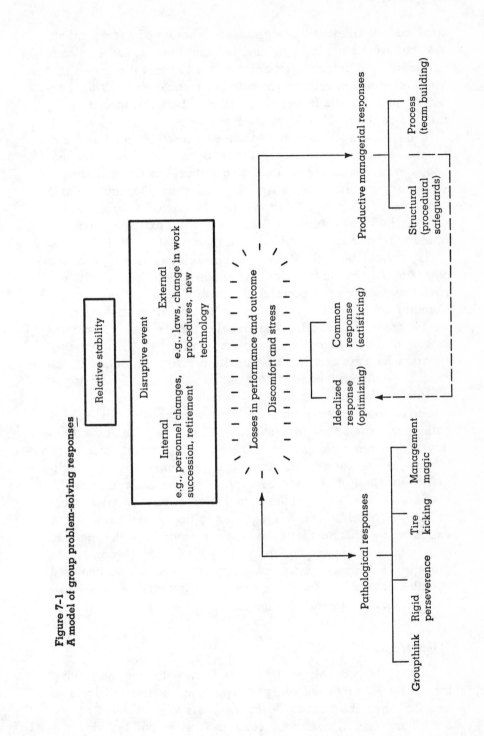

costs and marginal profits were used. Whereas 65 percent admitted that issues of company image often outweighed economic considerations in making decisions, and 50 percent reported that tradition and past policy were major influences on decision making.[12] Clearly, organizational functioning is not as mechanically rational as the idealized approach suggests.

In considering these same issues, Herbert Simon, a world-renowned authority on organization dynamics, concluded that people make decisions by *satisficing* rather than by optimizing.[13] When they satisfice, decision makers select an alternative that is "good enough." It is a solution that is expected to produce outcomes which are an improvement over what exists, but without introducing any serious risks. When they satisfice, decision makers do not compare all alternative possibilities, one against the other, as they would do if they were optimizing. Rather, alternatives are compared in pairs until one that *satisfices* is hit upon. Constrained in this way, the process is less informative than desirable or necessay. Satisficing runs the risk of causing premature closure of a problem-solving effort by limiting (1) the number of criteria which are employed to test alternative possibilities; (2) the number of alternatives which are examined; and (3) the testing of alternatives against agreed upon priorities.[14]

Under stress, group problem solving and decision making may suffer from worse than *satisficing*. As Figure 7-1 illustrates there are times when a group's response to organizationally disruptive circumstances seems pathological in the sense that it is self-defeating. Contrary to their best interests, groups, and individuals as well, often act as if they are (1) sheltering themselves from disquieting information, and/or (2) engaging in behavior which supports the illusion that problems are being solved, when, in fact, nothing is happening. Four such pathological responses are presented in Figure 7-1. One of the most thoroughly documented is called *groupthink*; the three others are *rigid perseverence*, *tire kicking*, and *management magic*.

Groupthink

This is a term developed by a Yale University professor, Irving Janis.[15] He used it to describe group problem solving and decision making when the interaction of members is dominated by extraordinary social pressure to conform to some point of view despite personal opinion or contradictory evidence.

In order to illustrate this process of groupthink, Janis analyzed four historically important incidents of group problem solving and decision making: (1) the policy of appeasement developed by Chamberlain and his advisers despite evidence that it would not produce the results that they desired; (2) the decision to pursue the war deep into North Korean territory made by President Truman and his advisers despite evidences that it would produce a Chinese Communist military response; (3) the approval of the Bay of Pigs invasion by President Kennedy and his advisers despite information that it would fail; (4) the escalation of the war in Vietnam by President Johnson and his advisers despite intelligence reports forecasting its failure and other adverse political consequences.

In each of these instances, Janis discerned that certain conditions within the group heightened the pressure to conform. Among them were:

1. High cohesiveness.
2. Insulation of the group from other sources of influence.
3. An absence of fixed problem-solving and decision-making procedures which would encourage thorough analysis and exploration of issues.
4. Directive leadership centered in one or more influential people.
5. Stress without any hope of finding better solutions.

Eight symptoms of groupthink accompany the resulting pressure to conform:

1. The illusion of invulnerability.
2. A tendency to rationalize inconsistent information.
3. Strong belief in the group's moral position.
4. Stereotyping of outgroups.
5. Intolerance of dissent.
6. A tendency for members to strictly censor themselves.
7. Pretense of a solid front.
8. Mindguards—people who protect the group from contradictory information.

In the end, the pressures to conform result in an ineffective process of problem solving and decision making. Consequently, the solutions which are generated not only fail to relieve the disruptive problem, but they often result in escalating costs. The ineffectiveness of the process is hallmarked by:

1. An incomplete assessment of available alternatives.
2. A failure to examine risks associated with the preferred alternative.
3. A limited search for relevant information.
4. A bias in processing information so as to give false support to the preferred alternative.
5. A failure to reappraise alternatives in light of new information.
6. An absence of contingency plans.

Groupthink is a dramatic instance of a more common and pervasive event in group life. Members of groups are nearly always under some subtle pressure to abide by a group's unwritten traditions, rules, values, customs, and standards. An inevitable and natural product of social interaction, these social norms, as they are called, become a frame of reference for group members—a window on the world which profoundly influences individual thought, feeling, and behavior.[16]

A classic and dramatic illustration of the power of social norms in organization life occurred during the late 1920s and early 1930s at the Hawthorne plant of the Western Electric Company.[17] At that time, a group of researchers was concerned with investigating the effects of lighting on work performance. Their expectation was quite reasonable: Adequate lighting will improve performance, inadequate lighting will hinder it. Using what appeard to be a well-designed, even if standard, research procedure, they selected a small number of people to be their experimental group. These people were to experience altered levels of illumination and then their work performance was to be compared to that of others—the control group—who experienced no change in the levels of illumination at their work sites.

When the lighting was raised and lowered for the experimental group, a surprising thing occurred: Performance improved regardless of the level of illumination! The investigators were determined to pursue the anomalous result. Over the next five years, additional data were collected as this group experienced altered rest periods, pay plans, work breaks, and work weeks. By and large, their performance was unrelated to these changes. *Norms*, not structural change regulated work behavior. Special status and treatment by the company, combined with hours of social interaction, resulted in a cohesive group that was favorably disposed toward company interests. Group norms about appropriate levels of output developed and were informally enforced, causing steady improvement in work performance.

The Hawthorne experience illustrates one way in which social norms produce organizational benefits. In this case, a cohesive group rewarded its members for higher productivity. If the group had been disinclined to support organization goals and instead rewarded lower productivity (or punished productivity), the opposite results could have easily occurred. Indeed, there are many examples of social norms and the social pressures which fuel them adversely affecting organization performance, including problem solving and decision making.[18]

Concern about these negative consequences of social norms was particularly strong during the 1950s when W. H. Whyte, Jr. wrote *The Organization Man*.[19] In it, Whyte expresses concerns about conformity and tries to explore how group life may smother individual initiative and creativity. His concerns are well supported by behavioral science research.

There are times when groups will not tolerate deviance from their view of the world. Initially, deviants become the center of attention in a group as members try to persuade them to depart from their errant ways. If their efforts at influencing fail, however, then the deviant will be abandoned, ostracized, even physically cast out of the group. Of course, norms do not apply equally to all members. Leaders and group stars, for example, are often allowed greater latitude in their behavior than are other members, but even they are not allowed to wander too far from the group's position.[20]

For organization life, it is particularly important to note that this process of social influence is especially likely to be successful in turbulent environments when (1) issues are unclear, (2) group members feel incompetent and unqualified to make independent judgments, and (3) the group seems reliable. Groups which have been successful and those which have been able to provide their members with the rewards that members desire are also most likely to be in a position to influence members' behavior. Also, in the absence of clear-cut, concrete facts—when the issues under consideration involve highly subjective considerations—group members are increasingly likely to be persuaded by nonrational forces such as their liking of other group members and the status of the communicators.[21] Time and again, the role of these nonrational forces of social influence can be observed in problem-solving groups when apparently successful, prestigious authorities persuade others to accept their views, even when they are wrong. Of course, there are occasions when people harbor private doubts but publicly conform nevertheless in order to gain social approval from important and/or liked others, or to avoid their disapproval. In the extreme, the results of social influence processes like these can be disastrous as Irving Janis's book, *Victims of Groupthink,* so cited above, well illustrates.

Rigid perseverence

This is a label which applies when groups unquestioningly insist on using a solution for a problem because it has "worked in the past." Common expressions in organization life symbolize this pathological response to problem solving. At meetings, it is not uncommon to hear organization members defend a solution by saying, "This is the way it's always done," or "Tried and proven ways are best." Using a variant of this theme, people sometimes try to solve problems without making any changes.[22] They claim that the solution is to "Redouble our efforts" or to "Do more of what we've been doing, only harder." Sometimes this approach is appropriate. But often, organizational problems arise just because of what people *have been doing,* and if they do it twice as hard, the organization will sink twice as fast.

The headquarters of a retail chain contacted an organization consultant. Four problems were identified by them as particularly irksome: (1) they, i.e., the executives, get in each other's way; (2) there was no sense of teamwork or unified effort, despite generally positive interpersonal feelings; (3) subordinates complained about conflicting decisions from above; (4) although the chain of command was clear in principle, it did not seem to operate efficiently or decisively during crisis.

In the course of interviewing each member of the top management group, the consultant noted that, without exception, they said, "If you want to get ahead in this organization, you've got to get into the field as often as possible." The universal acceptance of this idea, combined with the axiomatic quality with which it was imbued, puzzled the consultant.

One day, while the consultant was on the premises, the "old man" visited. The old man was the business' creator. Possibly curious about the consultant-stranger who was mucking about in **his** organization, the old man asked to have lunch with the consultant. During lunch, in an effort to make conversation, the consultant casually asked, "How has this place changed since its early days?" To which the old man replied, "Well, for one thing, in the early days, if you wanted to get ahead and make things happen, you had to get into the field, but that's not true now." Flabbergasted, the consultant questioned the old man about his claim. "In the old days," the old man explained, "we had a couple of stores, not too far apart. Now we have more'n a dozen spread over a couple thousand square miles. You try to get around to them all, all of the time, and it's just going to foul things up right here in this office."

Without any awareness of what was happening, the members of this group were rigidly persevering in behavior that had outlived its usefulness. Conditions had changed, but those changes had not been registered in the minds of the managers, neither had they been transformed into new styles of problem solving.

Tire kicking

This form of pathological problem-solving behavior in organizations is described in a book titled *Making Organizations Work*, by Trevor Owen, formerly a senior manager with Imperial Chemical Industries, Ltd., now managing director of Remploy.[23]

People who buy secondhand cars know what tire kicking is all about. Not wanting to appear uninformed or inexpert, buyers of secondhand cars frequently walk over to a car and gracefully kick its tires, emiting loud positive and negative sounding grunts in the vain hope of creating an impression of great knowledge.

Managers often do the very same thing when confronted with the task of solving a problem. Owen offers two examples: "Beginners" he observes, "find some abstruse figure showing the cost of, say, nuts and bolts in a comprehensive expenditure proposal for the siting of a new factory which will cost millions to build, and ask with an anxious frown on their foreheads who the supplier of the nuts and bolts is to be. . . ." Showing consternation at the response, the beginners then sit quietly for the rest of the meeting" trying to decide by listening to the conversation of the others which way the voting is going to go so that they can be on the side of the angels."[24] When they ask their question and show consternation at the response, these beginners are tire kicking.

Senior executives do the same when "they breeze into the room, ask a whole series of searching questions of doubtful relevance to which they know that the answers can not be immediately available, refer the matter back for further consideration and rush on to repeat a similar process at the next meeting."[25] If the scene is familiar, you have witnessed tire kicking, an all too frequent substitute for real problem solving.

Management magic

Another pathological response to disruptive events is also discussed by Trevor Owen.[26] The label alludes to a familiar magician's trick, the one in which the magician uses a cloth to cover a bowl containing goldfish. When he/she removes the cloth, the goldfish and the bowl have wonderously disappeared. Then, he/she goes into the audience, reaches into someone's pocket or handbag, plucks out and wiggling wet goldfish and hands it to its new owner who feels disgusted, if not nauseated, as the magician struts away to thunderous applause.

In "solving" problems, managers often perform the same stunt. Faced with a problem, they cover it up and, lo and behold, when the cloth is removed, someone else—who feels quite nauseated—finds this wriggling, wet thing resting squarely in his/her lap, as the manager takes his/her undeserved bows.

Owen tells the story of the CEO of a holding company which grouped together five small companies in a new industrial field. Two professional bodies were struggling to be recognized as the appropriate one for technical staff in this area. The CEO was a council member of one of these groups, but was not convinced about its appropriateness as the representative. As fate would have it, that group decided to launch an aggressive recruitment drive. CEOs were asked to enroll their managers or to identify a local executive to act as a recruiting officer and liaison for the group. The CEO of this holding company was in an awkward position. Confronted with these perplexing and problematic developments, he resorted to management magic. Rather than solve the problem of which group should be the representative, he decided to send each of the five executives who reported to him a copy of the recruiting letter, telling them that they could do as they pleased. They now had the goldfish in their laps and sat about, wondering what to do.

Productive managerial responses

Satisficing, groupthink, rigid perseverence, tire kicking, and management magic are all observable consequences of group efforts at problem solving and decision making. But they are not the only consequences. Groups also offer many benefits for organizational efforts at problem solving and decision making: (1) Although they may use more total work hours to solve a problem, groups tend to *check more* and *reject errors* more often than individuals because of the greater number of perspectives and inputs which they can muster if there are open channels of communication as well as social norms which permit deviancy, critique, and review. (2) Group-member interaction is capable of *stimulating new thoughts and ideas*, if participation is allowed and errors are not punished. (3) If cooperation, trust, and respect for other members' ability is high, then a fruitful *division of labor* is sometimes possible. (4) Commitments to *private prejudices* may be reduced in a group if its social atmosphere is supportive, thereby lessening members' needs to be defensive. (5) Groups can change *individual knowledge* and *skill* through direct tuition, feedback, and modeling, if individuals are not confined to narrow role definitions. (6) Groups can reward members for higher (or lower) task performance.[27]

There are, of course, no guarantees that the benefits of group problem solving and decision making will actually occur. They require work at developing proper structure and process. Ineffective social interaction undermines performance and is potentially dangerous. But, just as the benefits of group problem solving are not guaranteed, neither are its dangers. Organizational problem-solving groups are not hopelessly at the mercy of pathological responses; neither are they limited to *satisficing* as a strategy of problem solving and decision making.

Two courses of action are identified in Figure 7-1 as being available to managers who want to deal with ineffective social interaction in problem-solving and decision-making groups. One, a *structural* approach, involves techniques which try to *avoid* the dangers of social interaction by employing procedures to regulate the problem-solving and decision-making behavior of group members. (Two of these, the Nominal Group Technique and Delphi, are discussed in this chapter.) The second course of action is *process* oriented and it involves direct attempts to diagnose and remedy the dysfunctional social interaction of group members. It will be discussed in the next chapter, "Building Work Teams."

Nominal Group and Delphi techniques are both designed for use in situations where a number of people with diverse backgrounds and knowledge must pool their views in order to develop a satisfactory solution to a problem. Both techniques are highly structured, and, for that reason, they are thought of as means of avoiding some of the common dangers of group problem solving and decision making. Procedures for carrying out each of these techniques are detailed in a book by Andre L. Delbecq, Andrew H. Van de Ven, and David Gustafson, titled *Group Techniques for Program Planning.*[28] Here, we will provide a summary of each.

Nominal group technique (NGT)

In its most orthodox form, NGT is a six-step process.

Step one begins with the presentation of the "nominal" question to the group. This is the central focus of the meeting, its *raison d'être*. It is the problem for which the group hopes to develop a solution. Therefore, any widespread disagreement among group members about which problems are primary may require attention before any one problem can be addressed using NGT. If a question can be formed, then members are asked to "silently" generate their responses in writing. Examples of questions might be "What conditions are obstructing coordination between the school system and relevant community agencies?" "Discounting initial costs, what currently untapped markets provide the easiest opportunities for entry by this company?"

Step two is simply a round-robin recording of the ideas in a way which ensures that everyone will be heard. *Step three* involves "serial discussion for clarification." During this period, each of the ideas is discussed in turn, and members are urged to raise questions of clarification and offer comments reflecting their agreement or disagreement. Debate, however, is entirely discouraged.

In *step four* members vote, expressing their views about each idea's importance. A common procedure is to have members rank (or rate) five items from the entire list. While this approach protects the group from the obvious problems of majority rule and from control by a few loud members or powerful authorities, it is not without its own problems. Rank ordering produces oddities. The average ranks of the following votes, for example, are all equivalent, although they clearly represent very different group views:

Item one: 1, 1, 1, 5, 5, 5.

Item two: 3, 3, 3, 3, 3, 3.

Item three: 2, 2, 3, 3, 4, 4.

NGT makes an effort to deal with this problem in *step five* which involves a "discussion of the preliminary vote." The purposes of the discussion are to (1) "examine inconsistent voting patterns," and (2) "provide for the opportunity to rediscuss items which are perceived as receiving too many or too few votes." During this time, leaders are encouraged to (1) "define the task of this discussion as clarification, not social pressure," and (2) "ensure that the discussion is brief, so as not to disturb perceptions of items not discussed." But, of course, as we have seen, social pressures in groups are both subtle and profound, and there is no guarantee that they will be eliminated here or in step three.

Following the discussion, in *step six*, members make their final vote in order to determine the outcome of the meeting.

Delphi

NGT and Delphi have a great deal in common. Both implicitly require consensus about some central question, i.e., the problem statement. They both begin with private, individual—rather than public—efforts at idea generation. Both provide opportunity for a clerical listing of ideas and, subsequently, a time for them to be clarified and evaluated. And both use rank ordering or rating to reach a final decision. Unlike those in NGT, however, participants in a Delphi process do not meet face-to-face. Communication is carried out by means of questionnaires and reported summaries of questionnaire results.

Delphi has been used to:

1. Forecast consequences of innovation.
2. Inform people about advances in technology and science.
3. Assess strengths and weaknesses of systems and procedures.
4. Identify organizational and community problems.
5. Clarify group positions on issues.

Delbecq, Van de Ven, and Gustafson indentify ten steps in the Delphi process:

1. Develop the question. As with NGT or any problem-solving effort, the first step is critical. The aim is to identify the issue about which decision makers need information, i.e., the problem for which a solution is needed.
2. Select and contact respondents. People who have relevant

information, are motivated to participate, and may profit from the experience must be identified.

3. Establish sample size. Because Delphi does not require face-to-face interaction, it can manage larger groups than most other approaches to problem solving. When it is essential to involve large groupings of diverse people, this feature is a distinct advantage of Delphi.

4. Questionnaire One. This step is comparable to step one in NGT. One or more questions are distributed to respondents in a written questionnaire, and they are given the opportunity to provide their ideas anonymously.

5. Analysis. Responses are examined and integrated into meaningful categories by decision makers and any outside staff that they might be using.

6. Questionnaire Two. Here, respondents are asked to respond to the summary of ideas that questionnaire one produced. They can clarify, ask for clarification, and argue for or against the ideas. In addition, they rank or rate several of the items in terms of their importance.

7. Analysis. The voting is tallied and the comments are summarized.

8. Questionnaire Three. Respondents review the tallies and the comments. Thus, a kind of quasi-dialogue is maintained. On this occasion, respondents are asked for the final vote.

9. Analysis of voting on questionnaire three.

10. Final Report. A report describing the entire process and its results is prepared and distributed to the decision makers and all of the participants.

Delphi takes time. It requires the participation of people who are prepared to do all the reading and writing involved, and who can clearly express their ideas in writing. Although NGT and Delphi may allow groups to avoid some of the pitfalls of ineffective social interaction when problem solving involves judgment, forecasting, and census taking, it is not clear that they can achieve the creative integration of complex ideas which some tasks require and which does occur in well-trained, maturely functioning teams. Therefore, these structural approaches may be excellent managerial aids for solving some kinds of problems, especially when there is neither the time nor the need to build a team. Short-lived ad hoc task forces, for example, might benefit greatly from these approaches, as might socially ineffective groups facing deadlines.

But these approaches offer no remedy for some of the most critical problems that plague work groups: those which require a creative integration of knowledge and information from different specialties. In order to deal with these issues, managers are compelled to face the problem of building teams.

Notes

1. For summaries of the literature on this subject, see Collins, B. E., & Guetzkow, H. *A social psychology of group processes for decision making.* New York: John Wiley & Sons, 1964; Davis, J. H. *Group performance.* Reading, Mass.: Addison-Wesley, 1969, chap. 2; Hackman, J. R., & Morris, C. G. Group tasks, group interaction process, and group performance effectiveness: A review and proposed integration. In L. Berkowitz (Ed.), *Advances in experimental social psychology* (Vol. 8). New York: Academic Press, 1975. Porter, L. W., Lawler, E. E. III, Hackman, J. R. *Behavior in organizations.* New York: McGraw-Hill, 1975, chap. 14. Of historical interest are Stroop, J. B. Is the judgment of the group better than that of the average member of the group? *Journal of Experimental Psychology,* 1932, *15,* 550–560; Thorndike, R. L. On what type of task will a group do well? *Journal of Abnormal and Social Psychology,* 1938, *33,* 409–413; Watson, G. B. Do groups think more efficiently than individuals? *Journal of Abnormal and Social Psychology,* 1928, *23,* 328–336.

2. Collins & Guetzkow, *Social psychology of group processes,* Davis, *Group performance.*

3. Dyer, W. G. *Team building: Issues and alternatives.* Reading, Mass.: Addison-Wesley, 1977, p. xi.

4. Schein, E. Increasing organizational effectiveness through better human resoure planning and development. *Sloan Management Review,* Fall 1977, *1,* (19), 1–20.

5. Hoffman, L. R. Homogeneity of member personality and its effects on group problem solving. *Journal of Abnormal and Social Psychology,* 1959, *58,* 27–32; Hoffman, L. R., & Maier, N. R. F. Quality and acceptance of problem solutions by members of homogeneous and heterogeneous groups. *Journal of Abnormal and Social Psychology,* 1961, *62,* 401–407.

6. Hackman & Morris, Group tasks, group interaction processes, and group performance effectiveness, pp. 24–27.

7. Lorge, I., Fox, D., Davitz, J., & Brenner, M. A survey of studies contrasting the quality of group performance and individual performance, 1920–1957. *Psychological Bulletin,* 1958, *55,* 337–372.

8. Steiner, I. D. *Group process and productivity.* New York: Academic Press, 1972.

9. Davis, *Group performance,* chap. 4.

10. Miller, D. W., & Starr, M. K. *The structure of human decisions.* Englewood Cliffs, N.J.: Prentice-Hall, 1967, pp. 24–25.

11. Simon, H. A. *Administrative behavior: A study of decision-making processes in administrative organization* (3rd ed.). New York: Free Press, 1976.

12. Stagner, R. Corporate decision making: An empirical study. *Journal of Applied Psychology,* 1969, *53,* 1–13.

13. Simon, *Administrative behavior*.
14. Janis, I. L., & Mann, L. *Decision making: A psychological analysis of conflict, choice and commitment*. New York: Free Press, 1977.
15. Janis, I. L. *Victims of groupthink*. Boston: Houghton Mifflin, 1972.
16. Asch, S. E. Studies of independence and conformity: I. A minority of one against a unanimous majority. *Psychological Monographs*, 1956, *70*(9, Whole No. 416); Kelley, H. H. Two functions of reference groups. In G. E. Swanson, T. M. Newcomb, & E. L. Hartley (Eds.), *Readings in Social Psychology*. New York: Holt, Rinehart & Winston, 1952; Mayo, E. *The human problems of an industrial civilization*. New York: Macmillan, 1933; Newcomb, T. M. *Personality and social change*. New York: Dryden, 1943; Sherif, M. *The psychology of social norms*. New York: Harper & Row, 1936.
17. Mayo, *Human problems*.
18. Schacter, S., Ellertson, N., McBride, D., & Gregory, D. An experimental study of cohesiveness and productivity. *Human Relations*, 1951, *4*, 229–238.
19. Whyte, W. H., Jr. *The organization man*. New York: Simon & Schuster, 1956.
20. Schacter, S. Deviation, rejection, and communication. In D. Cartwright & A. Zanda (Eds.), *Group dynamics* (2nd ed.). New York: Row Peterson, 1960.
21. Cartwright & Zanda, *Group dynamics*, Pts. 2 and 3.
22. For a discussion of routine and innovative solutions, see Harvey, E., & Mills, R. Patterns of organizational adaptation: A political perspective. In M. N. Zald (Ed.), *Power in organizations*. Nashville, Tenn.: Vanderbilt University Press, 1970.
23. Owen, T. *Making organizations work*. London: Martinus Nijhoff, 1978.
24. Ibid., p. 93.
25. Ibid., p. 93.
26. Ibid.
27. Blau, P. M., and Scott, N. R. *Formal organizations: A comparative approach*. San Francisco: Chandler, 1962; Collins & Guetzkow, *Social psychology of group processes*; Davis, *Group performance*, Steiner, *Group process and productivity*.
28. Delbecq, A. L., Van de Ven, A. H., & Gustafson, D. *Group techniques for program planning*. Glenview, Ill.: Scott, Foresman, 1975.

8

Building Work Teams

In their classic book, *The Managerial Grid*, Robert R. Blake and Jane S. Mouton say that "true team action is . . . like a football situation where division of effort is meshed into a single coordinated result; where the whole is more, and different, than the sum of its individual parts."[1] Although not all organization tasks need this kind of synergy, true *team* tasks do. For these tasks, success is precluded unless each member's performance is *coordinated to and integrated with that of every other member.*

When successful organization output only requires individual efforts to be pooled, there is no need to build a team. The sports analogy to this kind of organization task is team golf, not football. In team golf, each person is critical to the group's success, but the separate performances are simply pooled, and the group's output is a mechanical composite of these individual activities. It does not represent a coordinated endeavor in which separate efforts are integrated, one building upon the other, in order to form an outcome which is something more than the averaging or collating of individual member behavior.

Consider the following example:

Following the oil crisis in 1974, the senior executive group of one company revised the portfolios of its members. One member of that group received responsibility for reviewing plans and recommending policy aimed at dealing with developing problems in business areas that used petroleum.

In considering his task, the executive recognized that, although he had competence in the area, he needed additional aid. The situation was fluid, and he was not able to assess potentially critical, rapidly changing conditions in several of the important geographic, product, and financial markets.

His solution was to organize a group composed of the presidents of major product divisions that were likely to be directly affected by these events. Prior to that, all problems of petroleum policy and planning were resolved separately, by the division heads, or by a division head and a member of the senior executive group who was responsible for overseeing that division's activities. On this occasion, however, the senior executive reasoned that recent world events rendered this usual procedure unreasonable and ineffective. Resource availability, costs, and consumer markets were all changing too rapidly and on too wide-spread a basis. The expertise and perspective of people from different technical, business, and geographic backgrounds were needed in order to (1) provide information, (2) assess information, (3) formulate multifaceted, companywide guidelines and policy, and (4) create an emergency task force in the event of any future crises.

Initially, the results were disappointing. Division heads had different priorities and perspectives, and they used meetings as a forum to argue for their own interests. They were not using the time to identify or solve common problems. Rather, they were trying to convince the senior executive of their positions' validity. Discussions were disjointed as people shifted topics in order to present problems that *they* were facing. Similarly, the information that people shared tended to be narrowly focused around their own concerns.

It seems reasonable to speculate that members of this group were behaving in accordance with established practices, i.e., social norms. Acting as a frame of reference, these norms affected each member's view of his/her role, the role of the senior executive, and the group's primary task. Feeding these norms were each head's own interests. Despite the objective change in circumstance, and the changes in the senior executive's view of the group, these dysfunctional behaviors persisted.

During their fourth meeting, after several discussions with a consultant, the senior executive suspended work on substantive matters and turned the group's attention to its own functioning. In a very difficult session, he described what he saw happening and discussed his view of the group's goal as well as his original image of how it might function. He identified the common problems that he saw and tried to illustrate how these problems were affecting success in individual product areas. Finally, he inquired how they might go about changing the "team's" functioning and what obstacles to change existed.

Although some difficulties continued, after this meeting, the team's work behavior changed. Groups of common problems were identified, members worked at sharing and assessing relevant information, and plans, which had an interdivisional rather than a separate product focus, were developed for securing raw materials and allocating resources.

This senior executive's approach to team building is not intended to be a superlative example of "how to do it." As a case example, however, these events are important because they illustrate how team productivity is determined by members' task abilities *and* by their ability to relate to each other—to coordinate and integrate their efforts. Each of the division heads was skilled and knowledgeable. But, for a time, human forces, not technical or business skills inhibited the development of the kind of interaction upon which task success depended.

In this team, at least four common obstacles to effective team functioning may have existed.

Maturity.   The group was new. Unless special procedures are used to hasten the process, groups ordinarily require some time to develop and stabilize their own working style.

History.   Social norms, rooted in past practice, adversely influenced group members' current behavior.

Mixed motives.   Team members' motives are almost never purely cooperative. In varying degrees, members may desire team success, but at the same time, each may also desire to have his/her own interests satisfied. Football players want to be stars, so that their contracts are secured; division heads also want to be stars, so that their promotions are secured.

Obstrusive individual characteristics.   Despite good intention, some people talk too much, argue too often, intimidate others, wander from the topic, become obsessed unnecessarily over detail, acquiesce too soon, stubbornly resist, and generally behave in a very human fashion, complete with neurotic and nonneurotic foibles which obstruct group functioning.

Other obstacles to effective functioning can also be identified, including leadership skill, goal clarity, and role clarity, but our aim is not to provide an exhaustive list of causes. Rather, it is to illustrate that the productivity of teams is not a simple function of team members' task abilities. Neither is productivity guaranteed because all team members have an interest in attaining the team's task goal. Successful team performance requires attention to the human forces which regulate social interaction.[2]

Managers who are responsible for organizational efforts which are analogous to team golf avoid this added burden. They are simply faced with the problem of supervising individuals, trying to elicit from them the best possible performance. But managers, like the one in the case example, who are responsible for organization efforts which are analogous to football, face this problem foursquare. They must facilitate the coordination and integration of individual efforts by diagnosing and changing social interaction. These managers, like the coaches of sports teams, must work to minimize dysfunctional social process and produce an "effective work group."

The effective work group: An ideal

There are several views within the behavioral sciences of what social and psychological conditions characterize an effective work group. Some authorities state very firmly that effective teams invariably possess a single set of characteristics. Chris Argyris takes this position in several of his books, most notably in *Management and Organization Development: The Path from X.A. to Y.B.*[3] Rensis Likert makes a similar claim in his book *New Patterns of Management.*[4] Each of these men argues that work effectiveness is favored in a particular kind of social organization. Argyris calls it "Type B," and Likert, "System 4." While differences exist in their views, both depict forms of social organization which tend to be participative and democratically led, exhibiting a concern for both socio-emotional *and* task needs. Argyris and Likert contrast these organization forms with a more bureaucratic, centrally controlled, authoritarian form which is almost exclusively concerned with task needs.

One of the earliest proponents of a position similar to the one that these men espouse was the late Douglas McGregor, from M.I.T.[5] A summary of his conclusions about the characteristics of an effective work group follows:

> Working in an informal atmosphere people are involved and interested, there is little boredom or tension.
>
> There is much task-relevant discussion.
>
> The group's task is discussed and developed so that it is understood and members are committed to it.
>
> People build on one another's comments and there is a tolerance of ideas.
>
> If disagreements occur, they are not suppressed. Yet conflict is not used as a means of controlling the group.
>
> Generally, solutions are formulated and reformulated until consensus is reached and people are in general (even if not complete) agreement.
>
> Criticism occurs, but of ideas, not of people.
>
> Feelings and ideas are legitimate issues for discussion. There are few "hidden agendas."
>
> Job assignments are clear.
>
> There is an authority of knowledge, not role, and "leadership" shifts as task needs change.
>
> The group reflects on both its process and procedure and tries to solve obtrusive problems in its functioning.

In general, McGregor, Argyris, and Likert all subscribe to the view that leadership style (and the values and assumptions which guide it) affects group process as well as individual motivation, ultimately having effects on productivity. As a consequence of their research and observation, they have identified a preferred leadership style and a desirable group process. Other scholars considering the same problem have arrived at different conclusions.[6] Some of these were discussed in Chapter 5 of this book, "Leading People."

In that chapter, we discussed work by Vroom, Fiedler, and others, which argues for a contingency model of leadership behavior. They say that circumstance determines what leadership style is most likely to produce an effective work group. Their research findings suggest that there is no universally unvarying *best* approach. Others, looking at group participation and cohesiveness—two issues which are related to leadership and central to team building—have made similar claims: neither is *always* desirable.

Participation

Kurt Lewin, a distinguished psychologist who invented the concept of "group dynamics," once offered a distinction between two forms of motivation. *Induced* motivation, he suggested, is what happens when someone holds a gun to your head and says, "Do it!" Conforming behavior may follow, but so will feelings of resentment and resistance. Consequently, the behavior is not likely to continue if either the inducement or surveillance is removed. The "gun" can be a piece of hardware or it can be a managerial weapon. Promotions, pay raises, performance evaluations, vacation time, and dismissal are all potential "guns" for inducing employees to behave in some desired manner.[7]

Own motivation is different. It emanates from within, and external controls are not required in order to maintain the desired behavior. On some occasions, when employees have an opportunity to participate in organizational problem solving and decision making, *own* motivational forces are generated and individual commitment to group goal attainment is heightened. Without claiming that it is paramount over economic and political causes, it seems certain that an implicit, even if indiscriminate recognition of this principle is evident in the recent flurry of concern about worker participation, autonomous work groups, and industrial democracy.[8] Although no one can clearly identify all of the conditions which regulate the benefits of participation, it is clear that participation is not beneficial all of the time.[9]

The organizational investigation of this approach to management was started in 1939, when Kurt Lewin visited the Harwood Manufacturing Corporation, located in Virginia. Over the next several years, a number of organization issues were investigated. One such investigation has become a classic study of participative management, reported in 1948 by Lester Coch, Harwood's personnel manager, and John R. P. French, Jr., a psychologist.[10]

During the years following Lewin's initial visit changes in Harwood's production procedures were causing turnover, reduced efficiency, and increased hostility toward management. Ordinary management efforts to remedy these problems using monetary incentives and layoffs calibrated to worker efficiency were of no avail. In an effort to investigate why people resisted the change and what might be done to overcome the resistance, three different kinds of work groups were created. In one, job changes continued to occur in the usual way. In a second, workers had an opportunity to influence how the change occurred through representatives selected by the entire group. In the third work group, every member had an opportunity to directly influence the plans for changes.

After the changes, the first group's productivity dropped markedly, their grievances continued, and approximately 17 percent left the company. In the other two groups, productivity dropped immediately after the change, but recovered rapidly and surpassed prechange levels. The number of grievances decreased and no resignations occurred during the first 40 days. Neither were there any substantial numbers of resignations attributable to these changes thereafter. Subsequently, when members of the first group were given an opportunity to participate, their behavior also changed and resembled that of the other two groups.

Over the past three decades, several other studies have illustrated the benefits of participation.[11] But there have also been exceptions. In fact, John R. P. French, Jr., one of the original investigators, coauthored a subsequent report in which participation did not yield expected benefits.[12] Several conditions, which define the limits of participation, were suggested in this report:

1. The issues under consideration cannot be trivial. They must be regarded as important by the employees who are being asked to participate. Belaboring the obvious fails to produce benefits and may, in fact, be counterproductive.

2. The content of the decision which employees are participating in making must be directly relevant to some condition that they recognize as needing change.

3. Participation must be considered legitimate by employees who are being asked to join in the effort. For various reasons, employees draw psychological boundaries around themselves and may neither expect nor desire involvement in some decision.

4. Negative feeling about the management of change should be minimal, and employees must recognize that the opportunity to participate is genuine, not sham democracy.

Lyman Porter, Edward Lawler, and J. Richard Hackman, in their excellent book, *Behavior in Organizations*, identify other conditions under which participation works:

1. "The topic of participation must be relevant to the work itself . . . task-irrelevant participation may serve to direct attention and motivation of group members *away from* work issues and thereby lower productivity."[13]

2. Changes in work behavior which might result from participation must have clear-cut benefits for the individual. If participation leads to an understanding that "hard work doesn't pay," people will not work any harder regardless of their involvement in decision making.

3. Participation can only have an effect on productivity when productivity can be controlled by employees. When it is primarily determined by workers' skills or remote environmental conditions, there is no reason to expect participation to yield any benefit.[14]

Cohesiveness

Early research on cohesiveness supported commonsense assumptions by illustrating some of the obvious organizational benefits of creating cohesive teams. Later, people recognized that, like participation, cohesiveness had its limitations. It was no panacea for curing organization ills.[15]

A group is cohesive when membership is an attractive commodity to its members. Alternatively, cohesiveness can be defined as the degree to which members desire to remain in a group. When group cohesiveness is high—that is, when members are very attracted to the group and want very much to be a part of it—this can cause members to experience an increased motivation to contribute to the group's effectiveness, advance its objectives, and participate in its activities. Increased cohesiveness also tends to discourage splintering and subgroup formation. All of this works toward increasing the likelihood of team goal attainment.

In one of the most authoritative compendia of group-dynamics research and theory, Dorwin Cartwright and Alvin Zander, two social psychologists, discussed four interdependent conditions which affect individual attraction for a group, hence affecting cohesiveness:[16]

1. *Individual motives* for joining a group vary. People join groups in order to satisfy needs for such things as affiliation, recognition, security, and money.

2. The *incentives* which groups offer likewise vary. Because of their task, structure, process, and place in an organization,

groups offer different levels and kinds of prestige, chances for social interaction, and work opportunities. These group characteristics may or may not be suited to satisfying member needs.

3. Regardless of what actually is available, individual member beliefs about the rewards and costs of membership will also affect attraction for the group.

4. Individual understanding of alternatives which are available in other groups will affect attraction for a group.

Using these ideas, people have tried to raise group cohesiveness by doing such things as (1) selecting members with compatible or mutually rewarding interests, attitudes, and values;[17] (2) heightening awareness of similarity among members;[18] (3) identifying common enemies;[19] (4) underscoring cooperative interests;[20] (5) emphasizing the prestige of the group in relation to other groups in an organization;[21] (6) minimizing diversity of hierarchical positions;[22] and (7) reducing competition for rewards.[23]

Cohesiveness can be double-edged, however. It may cause uniformly high productivity among group members because cohesiveness increases a group's ability to influence member behavior. But it may also cause uniformly low productivity among members, and has been observed to do so.[24] Members of cohesive groups are loyal to the group, and that can produce cooperation and helping. But these same feelings can also produce a country club atmosphere, causing group members to concentrate on enjoying the interaction itself without any concern for working on the team task, or can result in a total absorption in working on removing interpersonal obstacles which endanger continued cohesiveness.[25] Finally, cohesive groups may develop extremely rigid, impermeable boundaries. In these instances, an extreme we-they image of the world can develop, disrupting intergroup relations.[26]

Most people with experience in organizations have witnessed this adverse consequence of cohesiveness. For example, after a series of successes, a regional management team in one company became very insulated. New members and strangers were made to feel unwelcome. In-group jokes and other symbols developed. Loyalty to the senior manager became so extreme that no one was acceptable as a replacement. In turn, the senior manager's loyalty to group members was so unshakable that he protected and shielded them, always placing their needs and interests before any others.

Thus, while team building often employs and almost always

results in increased cohesiveness, care must be taken to insure that the cohesiveness is accompanied by social norms which support work effectiveness and that cohesiveness is tempered in a way which prevents a harmful we-they ideology from developing.

Team building

In 1975, J. Richard Hackman and Charles G. Morris, two of the world's leading authorities on small-group process and organization behavior published a chapter in that year's volume of *Advances in Experimental Social Psychology*. The chapter was concerned with "Group tasks, group interaction process, and group performance effectiveness." After reviewing the relevant literature, they proposed "that a major portion of the variation in measured group performance is proximally controlled by three general 'summary variables': *(a)* the *effort* brought to bear on the task by group members; *(b)* the *task performance strategies* used by the group in carrying out the task; and *(c)* the *knowledge and skills* of group members which are effectively brought to bear on the task." More importantly, they added that "each of the summary variables can be substantially affected (both positively and negatively) by what happens in the *group interaction process.*"[27]

In the pages that follow, we will first describe how group interaction process might affect member effort, task performance strategy, and member knowledge and skill. Then we will consider four alternative approaches to managing ineffective group-interaction processes. Unlike the structural approaches that were discussed in the last chapter, which are designed to sidestep group interaction process problems, these four approaches are directly aimed at diagnosing and altering process itself.

Group-interaction processes affect each of the three "summary variables" in very different ways:

Member effort.   (1) Interaction processes can enhance or hinder the coordination of individual endeavor. (2) Interaction processes can raise or lower the level of effort to which group members commit themselves.

Task performance strategies.   Groups frequently concentrate their efforts on the substance of their task, on the *what* of their work. Rarely do they actively attend to *how* they are working. (1)

Interaction processes can facilitate or hinder group efforts by encouraging or discouraging the use of preexisting strategies of behavior which may or may not be appropriate to current task demands. (2) Interaction processes can benefit or block a group's effort to reformulate its task performance strategy in order to bring it more into line with task demands.

Member knowledge and skills. (1) Interaction processes will cause member knowledge and skills to have varying levels of impact on group performance. These variances may or may not be consistent with the levels of task-relevant abilities which members process. (2) Interaction processes may aid or obstruct members' opportunities to develop additional knowledge and skill, and opportunities to apply them to the group's work.

Because group interaction affects all three of these critical mediators of group performance, it seems safe to conclude that improvements in interaction processes are likely to produce improvements in performance. The conclusion is not unwarranted, but it should not be overinterpreted either. Group interaction does not have an exclusive effect on these mediators of group performance. In fact, after examining the available evidence, Hackman and Morris speculated that *member effort* is most likely to be responsive to changes in task design; and *member knowledge and skill* are most likely to be responsive to changes in group composition. Nonetheless, it is very clear that group interaction processes are also an important means of changing member effort, task performance strategies, and member knowledge and skill, the central mediators of group performance.

The evidence is clear, but its implication for practice is not readily observable in organizational life. Crises, deadlines, and other organization pressures all conspire to divert a group's attention from its interaction processes, despite their centrality as an influence on group performance. When groups are given a task, a solution orientation descends and concern with *what* understandably replaces attention to *how*. Yet, successful *team* efforts require a division of attention between task and process. Consequently, monitoring group process and remedying its dysfunctional aspects is a management task. Over the years, methods have developed which can aid managers in performing this part of their job.

Michael Beer, in a thorough review of the ideas and practice of organization development, divides methods of team building into four categories. First, there are approaches that emphasize goal-setting and problem solving. Here, a work group's task is of central concern. The group's team-building effort is aimed at identifying problems that interfere with attainment of desired team goals and then formulating action plans for overcoming obstacles.[28]

The second category of the four created by Beer incorporates approaches to team building that focus on developing interpersonal skills. On the surface, the assumption underlying this category of tactics seems straightforward enough. People who are interpersonally competent are more likely to be effective team members than those who are not, and the more effective a team's members, the more effective will be the team. Managers who accept the argument as valid are still faced with the enormous problem of deciding how to increase interpersonal effectiveness.

The third category of team-building approaches sidesteps this issue by focusing on team members' roles, rather than on interpersonal behavior. The aim is to clarify understanding and form some agreement about the job roles of individual group members. In the second category, concern was with such behaviors as communication, conflict management, and decision making. Here, it is with more task-related behaviors, such as delegation and information sharing.

The fourth category that Beer identifies is wholly composed of an approach developed by Robert R. Blake and Jane S. Mouton. It uses their *Managerial Grid,*® which this book described in the chapter titled, "Leading People," as a framework for team self-analysis and action planning.

The distinction among techniques of team building offered by Beer is useful, but it is not singular. Alternative schemes exist and, as Richard N. Woodman and John J. Sherwood, two professors of management, say in an article they published in the *Psychological Bulletin,* "These categories are not mutually exclusive and in practice are often integrated or mixed."[29] For these reasons, the four examples of team-building techniques that we have elected to include in the following sections reflect what practitioners are actually doing, and they do not exactly parallel Beer's categories. Each of the four to be discussed contains a mixture of Beer's first three categories. (As noted above, the Blake and Mouton Managerial Grid, a highly specialized approach, is discussed elsewhere in this book.) The four that we discuss here are: team feedback, process planning, process consultation, and role negotiation.

Team feedback

There is no single approach to team building. One general characteristic of several approaches, however, is that they rely on some form of data feedback to a team. This is captured in a generic model of a six-step, "team-building cycle" offered by William G. Dyer in his book, *Team Building: Issues and Alternatives*.[30]

Team building, he points out, often begins because (1) one or more group members senses a problem: production may be down; grievances, complaints, conflicts, and turnover may all be increasing; job responsibilities and decisions made about various problems may be unclear or poorly communicated; vendors, as well as consumers of the team's output, and subordinates may all be complaining about ambiguous, confused, and mixed messages; apathy, low morale, and general antagonism for the team's senior manager and/or the entire organization may be apparent and growing; meetings may be unproductive, leaving organizational problems unresolved; and, when solutions are developed, follow-through may be totally lacking.

Gathering data about the problem is the next step in the cycle (2). This may be done through questionnaires, interviews, or what Dyer calls "open data sharing," which involves a public discussion of the issues by group members. Questions which might be asked vary, but in the main, they focus on four areas: *(a)* an individual member's perception of the problem(s), *(b)* obstacles to team effectiveness, *(c)* team strengths, and *(d)* possible solutions. These data are then fed back to team members for their consideration.

The next step (3), diagnosis, involves the team in an effort to order the problems in terms of some priority. A second part of this step is for members to organize and assess information which might reveal some causes of problem conditions.

During the next step, planning (4), a team develops alternative solutions to the problems of team functioning which have been identified, taking into account the team's assessment of causes. After examining a group of alternative possibilities, the team then selects one and plans for its (5) implementation, setting responsibilities and deadlines, and also arranges for some (6) follow-up evaluation.

There is a danger that this description of the team-building cycle will wrongly persuade readers to believe that team building occurs only after a problem has been recognized, and for that reason it is a passive, reactive tactic. There are, in fact, prophylactic team-building procedures, and some believe that they are useful devices for both maintaining team effectiveness and forestalling the development of serious problems.

Post-meeting-reaction forms (PMRFs) are one such device. One management team which heads a division of a company in the pharmaceutical industry sets aside about two hours after a meeting, on a quarterly basis, in order to complete and to discuss a PMRF. The four or five questions which appear on this form vary. At first they were selected by an outside consultant. Subsequently, they were submitted by members of the team to a staff aide who prepared a single sheet of material for the team which summarized the data.

The questions remain simple and straightforward, and have included such items as:

Is every one participating or have the meetings been dominated by a few people?

Have ideas been explored, or have they been quickly evaluated and dropped?

Have people been building on each others' comments?

Have you had the kind and level of influence that you would like to have on this group's decision making?

Have you had all the information you need to make informed decisions?

In what ways have conflicts been handled productively and in what ways have they been handled unproductively?

Are we providing adequate support for dissenting ideas?

Are people taking sufficient responsibility for summarizing, clarifying, keeping time, and making sure that we follow problem-solving steps?

What adjectives characterize the tone of the team's feelings.

Has the group been taking enough time to explore its own process?

Work with newly formed teams also has been aimed at preventing poor team development. Dyer comments, that "The major tasks facing the new team are basically the same as the one [sic] that has worked together—that is, they must build a relationship, establish a facilitative emotional climate, and work out methods for (1) setting goals, (2) solving problems, (3) making decisions, (4) insuring follow-through and completion of tasks, (5) developing collaboration of effort, (6) establishing lines of open communication, and (7) insuring an appropriate support system that will let people feel accepted and yet keep issues open for discussion and disagreement."[31]

As an aid to managing these tasks, Dyer describes a four-stage workshop for members of new teams. First, members work on clarifying individual feelings of commitment to the team's work. This is done in order to avoid problems which might subsequently arise because individual members hold different priorities that might eventually be reflected in unexpected differences in commitments of effort and time to team endeavors.

Second, members share fantasied expectations of the best and the worst outcomes which might be experienced by the team. Third, they work on clarifying the team's objectives in as concrete and precise language as possible. And fourth, they work on developing operating guidelines. That is, they discuss such things as how decisions will be made; how communication channels will be kept open; how conflicts will be managed; how follow-through will be insured; and how division of labor will occur.

An alternative to this is a procedure used by this book's authors and called "barrier analysis." In this instance, a new team lists key areas of group interaction. Dyer's list, which is quoted above, is an example, (e.g., "setting goals," "solving problems," etc.). In public view, next to each of these key areas, the team describes some ideal state. Members then discuss and list ordinary *barriers* to attaining these ideal states. These are barriers which members have regularly encountered in other groups. Finally, a fourth list is developed in which *operating plans* are identified for each of the *key areas* which can enhance progress toward the *ideal state* by avoiding the *barriers*. An example of a form used in such analysis is given in Figure 8-1.

Preliminary process planning

Variations of the appproaches used with newly formed teams can also be used with established working groups. Unfortunately, when groups have a past they also have social habits—that is, customary ways of working together which tend to be followed without question.[32] Often, this indiscriminate, unconscious application of past behavioral strategies to current tasks causes diffi-

Figure 8-1
Barrier analysis

Key areas	Ideal state	Barriers	Operating plan
1.			
2.			
3.			

culty because the fit is inappropriate and/or the strategy has always been less effective than desirable.

Hackman and Morris observe that "Probably the most
straightforward process consultative technique for helping members consider and possibly revise their norms about performance
strategy is simply to provide the group with a 'preliminary group
task'. . . . [This] would require members to discuss task performance strategies they plan to use on the main task—and to
consider revising or replacing them if warranted by the discussion."[33]

An implication of their comment is that managers might profit
by taking the time that is needed before beginning work to have a
team consider *how* it will work, given current task demands.[34]
This preliminary process planning might be facilitated by using
some of the procedures described for helping newly formed teams.

Process consultation

This difficult and hard-to-define approach to team building requires the service of an outside party—someone who is outside
the team, but not necessarily outside the organization. Edgar
Schein, who developed the concept of process consultation, contrasts it with two other consulting styles: the purchase model and
the doctor-patient model. In the former, some manager "defines a
need—something he wishes to know or some activity he wishes
carried out—and if he doesn't feel the organization itself has the
time or capability, he will look to a consultant to fill the need."[35] In
the case of the doctor-patient model, management contracts with

an outside party to examine the organization's corpus and prescribe a remedy for whatever ills might be found.

Schein objects to these models. In neither instance do they produce joint agreement on diagnosis. Moreover, in the case of the first model, action is predicted on the perilous assumption that the client has conducted a diagnosis and the conclusion arrived at is a proper one. And, in the second model's case, the client is subordinated and excluded from the process of diagnosis and action planning, creating an unhealthy dependency.

Process consultation is the alternative Schein proposes. He defines it as a set of activities "which help the client to perceive, understand, and act upon process events which occur in the client's environment." The definition betrays a bias: "The important elements to study in an organization are the human processes which occur. . . . Improvement in organizational effectiveness will occur through effective problem finding in the human process area, which in turn will depend upon the ability of managers to learn diagnostic skills through exposure to P-C [process consultation]."[36]

Process consultants work with teams on real tasks. The consultant's jobs are to "establish a helping relationship, know what kinds of process to examine, and intervene in a way that causes improvement in organization process."[37] In effect, process consultants observe process events and share their observations with teams in a manner which allows the team to develop insight into and understanding of how process is affecting performance. Armed with this knowledge, the team is then aided in its effort to improve functioning by the process consultant.

For Schein, the areas of process most critical for performance are: (1) communication, (2) member roles and functions in groups, (3) group problem solving and decision making, (4) group norms and group growth, (5) leadership and authority, and (6) intergroup cooperation and competition.

Role negotiation

This approach to team building was developed by Roger Harrison.[38] It contrasts sharply with other approaches we have discussed. Some of these approaches, as Harrison points out, subtly subscribe to a humanistic, egalitarian organizational behavior philosophy. They place development of people on a par with task efficiency, and are particularly concerned with the role of individual team members' feelings and attitudes. In varying degrees, they work toward openness of communication, cooperation based on mutual trust, and participation decision making. Implicitly, the approaches seem to be assuming that people work effectively if they can be taught to treat one another with trust, openness, acceptance, and understanding.

Harrison claims that this organizational-behavior philosophy and the management techniques that it spawned neglect the realities of power, coercion, and competitiveness in organizations. Arguing that most people prefer a fairly negotiated settlement to an unresolved conflict, Harrison proposes that groups use role negotiation to remedy ineffective interaction processes. In using role negotiation, participants must take significant risk, and they must be specific about what changes in behavior, responsibility, and authority they wish from others.

The first phase of this process is called *contract setting*. A summary of the conditions of the contract which Harrison proposes follows.

It is not legitimate to inquire about feelings.

Members must be clear and explicit about what they want from others.

Expectations and demands are not adequately communicated until they are in writing and acknowledged as understood by both sender and receiver.

Change occurs as a consequence of bargaining and negotiations. People agree to exchanges. There must be a quid pro quo.

Threats and pressure are legitimate components of the process.

During the second phase of role negotiation, called *diagnosis*, each member lists for each other person those things that she/he would like the other to do more of or do better, do less or stop doing, keep on doing. A period of clarification follows during which hostile expression is discouraged.

The period of *negotiation* which comes next has several parts. First, team members examine the lists which have been created for themselves and for the others. Next, each indicates (1) for others, one or more issues on which she/he would particularly like to see change (or commitment to no change); and (2) for him/herself, issues on which change might be possible. Finally, team members bargain and form agreements. These might involve two, three, or more people and are of the sort, "if you do X, I (we) will do Y."

During a *follow-up* phase, conformity to the agreements is examined and new agreements may be renegotiated. Harrison's aim is to have the team take over the approach, thereby eliminating dependency on him. In evaluating the success of role negotiation he says, "I do not claim any unusual success in freeing clients from dependence on my services. What I do find is that there is less backsliding between visits . . . than when I have applied more interpersonally oriented change interventions. The agreements obtained through Role Negotiation seem to have more 'teeth' in them than those which rely on the softer processes of interpersonal trust and openness."[39]

Conclusions

No precise formula exists to help managers decide when to use one or the other of these four approaches discussed, or indeed, whether to use team building at all. At least one review of the literature on team building pessimistically concludes, "Although there is general support for the finding that team building elicits positive affective responses from participants, the linkage between team building and improved work group performance remains largely unsubstantiated."[40] Others are more optimistic, however, and there are some guidelines which can be offered. In the last chapter ("Solving Problems and Making Decisions"), we talked about when it might be more advisable to use structural approaches than to use process approaches. And in the beginning of this chapter, we discussed the task demands which might indicate the need for building a team. A view similar to ours emerges in an article titled, "Improving the performance effectiveness of groups through a task-contingent selection of intervention strategies."[41] The author of that article, D. M. Herold, suggests that decisions about intervention strategies should rest on an analysis of both the technical and social demands created by a team's task. He proposes that technical demands can be simple (e.g., lifting a weight) or complex (e.g., determining where to move tankers filled with crude oil in order to optimize net profits). Similarly, social demands can be simple (as in team golf where little or no interaction is required for team success), or complex (as in planning a highly flexible, worldwide petroleum policy). This viewpoint can be schematized in a four-part table (Figure 8-2).

Figure 8-2
Demands of group tasks

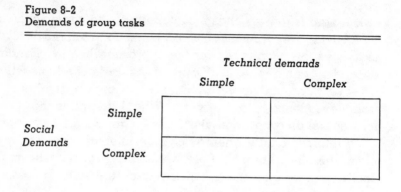

In order to be successful, Herold argues, interventions must fit the technical and social demands of a task. In an analysis of seven intervention efforts, he finds confirmation of his views. When the intervention was inconsistent with technical and social demands, performance not only failed to improve, it worsened. In terms of this chapter's interests, we can say that socially complex team-building interventions should not be employed when task demands only require simple social processes.

A more specific list of circumstances which define when team building might be effective was offered by J. W. Lewis III, who also considered successful and unsuccessful team-building efforts.[42] His work suggests that team building is indicated when:

1. Communication and interaction among team members is inadequate for organizational needs.
2. People imagine themselves to be or want to be an integrated team.
3. Important face-to-face interaction and coordination is either required by supervisors or necessary to complete a task.
4. Change in managerial and team-member activity is possible.
5. Benefits of changing in the direction of increased *team* effectiveness outweigh costs of the transition.
6. The senior manager is comfortable sharing leadership.
7. Interdependence among functions and among managers exists and is necessary for organizational and goal attainment.

8. The environment is turbulent.
9. The organization is fluid and developing.
10. A basis for collaboration, not competition exists.
11. Physical proximity of members allows meetings to occur.
12. Organization conditions are such that managers are dependent on subordinates to make operating decisions.
13. Channels do not exist for exchanging necessary information.
14. Organization adaption requires integration of specialities and frequent use of ad hoc task forces.

Notes

1. Blake, R. R., & Mouton, J. S. *The managerial grid*. Houston, Tex.: Gulf Publishing, 1964.
2. Collins, B. E., & Guetzkow, H. *A social psychology of group processes for decision making*. New York: John Wiley & Sons, 1964; Hackman, J. R., & Morris, C. G. Group tasks, group interaction process, and group performance effectiveness: A review and proposed integration. In L. Berkowitz (Ed.), *Advances in experimental social psychology* (Vol. 8). New York: Academic Press, 1975; Lawler, E. E. III, & Commann, C. *What makes work group successful?* In A. J. Morrow (Ed.), *The failure of success*. New York: AMACOM, 1972.
3. Argyris, C. *Management and organization development: The path from X.A. to Y.B.* New York: McGraw-Hill, 1971.
4. Likert, R. *New patterns of management*. New York: McGraw-Hill, 1961; Likert, R. *The human organization: Its management and value*. New York: McGraw-Hill, 1967.
5. McGregor, D. *The human side of enterprise*. New York: McGraw-Hill, 1960, pp. 228-229.
6. Burns, T., & Stalker, G. M. *The management of innovation*. London: Tavistock, 1961; Fiedler, F. E. *Leadership*. New York: General Learning Press, 1971; Vroom, V. H., & Yetton, P. W. *Leadership and decision-making*. Pittsburgh: University of Pittsburgh Press, 1973.
7. Lewin, K. *Field theory in social science*. New York: Harper & Row, 1951, chap. 10; Lewin, K. Group decision and social change. In E. E. Maccoby, T. M. Newcomb & E. L. Hartley, (Eds.), *Readings in social psychology*. New York: Holt, Rinehart & Winston, 1958; Lewin, K., Lippitt, R. & White, R. K. Patterns of aggressive behavior in experimentally created "social climates." *Journal of Social Psychology*, 1939, *20*, 217-299.
8. Blumberg, P. *Industrial democracy: The sociology of participation*. New York: Schocken, 1973; Foy, N., & Gadon, H. Worker participation: Contrasts in three countries. *Harvard Business Review*, May-June 1976, pp. 358-373; Hartman, H. Codetermination in West Germany. *Industrial Relations*, 1970, *9*, 137-147; Herbert, P. G. *Autonomous group functioning*. London: Tavistock, 1962; Hunnius, G., Garson, G. D., & Case, J. *Worker control: A reader on labor and social change*. New York: Random House, 1973; Marrow, A. J., Bowers, D. G., & Seashore, S. E. *Management by participation*. New York: Harper & Row, 1967.
9. Lawler, E. E. III, & Hackman, J. R. The impact of employee participation in the development of pay incentive plans: A field experiment. *Journal of Applied Psychology*, 1969, *53*, 467-471; Lowin, A. Participative decision making: A model, literature critique, and prescription for research. *Organization Behavior and Human Performance*, 1968, *3*, 68-106; Scheflen, K., Lawler, E. E. III,

& Hackman, J. R. Long-term impact of employee participation in the development of incentive plans: A field experiment revisited. *Journal of Applied Psychology,* 1971, *65,* 182–186; Schultz, G. P. Worker participation on production problems. *Personnel,* 1951, *28,* 24–29; Strauss, G., & Rosenstein, E. Worker participation: A critical review. *Industrial Relations,* 1970, *9,* 197–214; Vroom, V. H. Some personality determinants of the effects of participation. Englewood Cliffs, N.J.; Prentice-Hall, 1960.

10. Coch, L., & French, J. R. P. Overcoming resistance to change. *Human Relations,* 1948, *1,* 512–532.

11. French, J. R. P., Ross, I. C., Kirby, S., Nelson, J. R., & Smyth, P. Employee participation in a program of industrial changes. *Personnel Management by participation.* New York: Harper & Row, 1967.

12. French, Jr., J. R. P., Israel, J., & As, D. An experiment in participation in a Norwegian factory. *Human Relations,* 1960, *13,* 3–19.

13. Porter, L. W., Lawler, E. E. III, & Hackman, J. R. *Behavior in organizations.* New York: McGraw-Hill, 1975, p. 419.

14. Ibid.

15. See Cartwright, D. & Zander, A. *Group dynamics: Research and theory* (3rd ed.). New York: Harper & Row, 1968, for a review of this literature. Studies which illustrates the harmful consequences of cohesiveness are Schacter, S., Ellertson, N., McBride, D., & Gregory, D. An experimental study of cohesiveness and productivity. *Human Relations,* 1951, *4,* 229–238; Seashore, S. *Group cohesiveness in the industrial work group.* Ann Arbor, Mich.: Institute for Social Research, University of Michigan, 1954.

16. Cartwright & Zander, *Group dynamics,* p. 96.

17. Byrne, D. Interpersonal attractiveness and attitude similarity. *Journal of Abnormal and Social Psychology,* 1961, *62,* 713–715; Dittes, J. Attractiveness of a group as a function of self-esteem and acceptance by the group. *Journal of Abnormal and Social Psychology,* 1959, *59,* 77–82; Homans, G. *The human group.* New York: Harcourt Brace Jovanovich, 1950; Loth, A. J., & Loth, S. E. Group cohesiveness as interpersonal attraction: A review of relationships and consequent variables. *Psychological Bulletin,* 1965, *64,* 259–309; Hornstein, H. A. *Cruelty and kindness.* Englewood Cliffs, N.J.: Prentice-Hall, 1976; Thibaut, J. W., & Kelley, H. H. *The social psychology of groups.* New York: John Wiley & Sons, 1959.

18. Back, K. Influence through social communication. *Journal of Abnormal and Social Psychology,* 1951, *46,* 9–23.

19. Sherif, M., & Sherif, C. *Groups in harmony and tension.* New York: Harper & Row, 1953; Pepitone, A., Reichling, G. Group cohesiveness and the expression of hostility. *Human Relations,* 1955, *8,* 327–337.

20. Deutsch, M. An experimental study of the effects of cooperation and competition upon group process. *Human Relations,* 1949, *2,* 199–232; Sherif & Sherif, *Groups in harmony and tension.*

21. Myers, A. E. Team competition, success and adjustment of group members. *Journal of Abnormal and Social Psychology,* 1962, *65,* 325–332; Thibaut & Kelley, *Social psychology of groups.*

22. Exline, R. V., & Ziller, R. C. Status congruency and interpersonal conflict in decision making groups. *Human Relations,* 1959, *12,* 147–162; Kelley, H. H. Communication in experimentally created hierarchies. *Human Relations,* 1951, *4,* 39–56.

23. Deutsch, Experimental study of effects of cooperation and competition.

24. Schacter et al., Experimental study of cohesiveness and productivity.

25. Davis, J. H. *Group performance.* Reading, Mass.: Addison-Wesley, 1969, pp. 78–82.

26. Janis, I. L. *Victims of groupthink: A psychological study of foreign policy decisions and fiascos.* Boston: Houghton Mifflin, 1972; Alderfer, C. P. Boundary

relations and organization diagnosis. In Meltzer, H. and Wickert, F. R. (Eds.), *Humanizing organizational behavior.* Springfield, Ill.: Charles C Thomas, 1976.

27. Hackman & Morris, Group tasks, group interaction process, and group performance effectiveness, p. 18, italics added.

28. Beer, M. The technology of organization development. In M. D. Dunnette (Ed.), *Handbook of industrial and organizational psychology.* Chicago: Rand McNally, 1976.

29. Woodman, R. W., & Sherwood, J. J. The role of team development in organizational effectiveness: A critical review. *Psychological Bulletin*, 1980, *88*(1), 166–186.

30. Dyer, W. G. *Team building: Issues and alternatives.* Reading, Mass.: Addison-Wesley, 1977.

31. Ibid., p. 73.

32. Maier, N. R. F. *Problem-solving discussions and conferences: Leadership methods and skills.* New York: McGraw-Hill, 1963; Weick, K. E. *The social psychology of organizing.* Reading, Mass.: Addison-Wesley, 1969.

33. Hackman & Morris, Group tasks, group interaction process, and group performance effectiveness, p. 33.

34. In this regard, there is a study showing the benefits of process planning: Kaplan, R. E. *Managing interpersonal relations in task groups: A study of two contrasting strategies.* Technical Report no. 2. New Haven: Administrative Sciences, Yale University, 1973.

35. Schein, E. *Process consultation: Its role in organization development.* Reading, Mass.: Addison-Wesley, 1969, p. 5.

36. Ibid., p. 9.

37. Ibid., p. 7.

38. Harrison, R. Role negotiation: A rough-minded approach to team development. In W. W. Burke, & H. A. Hornstein (Eds.), *The social technology of organization development.* Washington, D.C.: NTL Learning Resources, 1971.

39. Ibid., p. 92.

40. Woodman & Sherwood, Role of team development in organizational effectiveness, p. 185.

41. Herold, D. M. Improving the performance effectiveness of groups through a task-contingent selection of intervention strategies. *Academy of Management Review*, April 1978, *3*(3), 315–325.

42. Lewis, J. W. III. Management team development: Will it work for you? *Personnel*, July–August 1975.

9

Managing Conflict

THE following story has two endings.

In an attempt to facilitate the flow of work during peak periods, a textile firm created a task force composed of representatives from the sales, production, and purchasing departments. By sharing information about client purchases, delivery priorities, production schedules, and vendor arrangements, the company hoped that this group would develop solutions to problems which were causing increasingly costly production bottlenecks and late deliveries, as well as over- and under-stocked inventories.

Ending one. The meetings ended unsuccessfully when the purchasing representatives walked out after they were accused of being "tight-assed" and "myopic" by the production and sales people. In private, seething with anger, one purchasing representative hissed that the salespeople were "glory hunters" who neither understood nor gave a damn about costs. The production people, he said despairingly, were a "bottomless well. All they know is more, more, more."

Ending two. The meetings ended successfully, but lasted longer than expected. After each of the representatives spent some time explaining his or her priorities and the reasons for them, they all agreed

177

upon schemes for partitioning production schedules and for developing a more direct linkage between sales and purchasing. Although the
representatives had not changed their own priorities, these schemes
seemed to optimally satisfy each group's goals.

The sales, production, and purchasing departments of this organization were in conflict. They had different interests and preferred different solutions to a common problem. As is the case
with most organization conflicts, this one had two different potential endings—one was destructive and the other constructive.[1]

Conflict in organizations is not all bad. Its consequences can be
either organizationally beneficial or costly. A manager's skill in
conflict management may play a major role in determining which
of these two possibilities occurs.

Benefits and costs[2]

Conflict can be *energizing*. It causes people to feel aroused and
to "stretch" themselves by seeking new achievements. But it can
also be *debilitating*. The aggravation and upset that often accompany conflict can cause mental and physical fatigue, by absorb-
ing all of one's attention in frustrating, stress-producing concerns.
These are times when people "take the problems home with them"
in a way that prevents relief and relaxation.

Conflict occasionally acts as a *safety valve* for larger issues
which are too dangerous to confront. In this way, small conflicts
prevent larger ones from occurring by allowing protagonists to
"blow off steam." But small conflicts can also *escalate* and *spiral*
despite people's earnest desire to keep them limited and contained. As each affront begets retaliation, the stakes mount, causing opponents to feel that they must get even, otherwise they risk
losing face or appearing weak.

Conflicts often have *diagnostic value*. Like body temperature,
conflict signals that something is wrong. By being alert to the cue
potential of conflict, managers may uncover organization problems sooner than otherwise might be the case. But conflict can
also *obscure issues*. People who are in destructive conflicts tend to
drag in an increasing number and array of issues. When this
occurs, an added problem is that information is often distorted
because of exaggeration, deception, and omission. In the midst of
this maelstrom, underlying causes are frequently forgotten and
lost.

Conflict is potentially a stimulant for the generation of totally new *creative solutions* to organization problems. By alerting protagonists to other points of view, conflict may force them to examine old problems from entirely fresh perspectives which integrate various organization interests. But conflict also *obscures alternative solutions* to organization problems. Often, as people become more embroiled in a dispute, their positions harden. Their way becomes the only acceptable alternative. This rigidly narrow focus heightens competitive feelings and increases the likelihood of destructive rather than constructive solutions.

Conflict in organizations is inevitable. It cannot be legislated out of existence by organization rules and management memoranda. Its effects at work (and at home or in any other social setting) do not disappear because people diplomatically avoid discussing the issues. Conflicts require management. They require overt action which is aimed at enhancing their benefits and limiting their costs. To effectively utilize conflict for constructive ends, managers must understand the anatomy and dynamics of conflict, and possess skill in the techniques of conflict management.

The anatomy of conflict

Some conflicts are like a game of checkers. They provide no opportunity for cooperation. Imagine, for example, that a disagreement exists between two departments in a firm. Let us call them purchasing and production. Further, this imaginary disagreement has only two classes of solutions, class A and class B. Table 9-1 illustrates this set of circumstances.

Table 9-1

Outcome for purchasing	Solutions	Outcome for production
+10	Class A	−10
−10	Class B	+10

If class A solutions occur, then purchasing will receive 10 "benefits" (whatever they may be: prestige, budget, personnel, space, power), and production will lose 10 benefits. If class B solutions occur, however, the outcomes will reverse, purchasing will lose 10 "benefits" and production will receive that amount. This is a pure *win-lose* situation and, not surprisingly, there is clear evidence that circumstances like these produce heated and often mutually destructive competition.

Not all organization problems are win-lose, however. Some, in fact, provide an easy opportunity for cooperation. These problems can be thought of as including classes of solutions which yield only benefits and never costs to both parties. An example of these pure *win-win* situations is presented in Table 9-2. Here, the pressures toward a destructive, competitive resolution of the problem are far less than in the win-lose situation. Purchasing and production both prefer class C solutions, where they will receive 8 and 6 "benefits," respectively.

Table 9-2

Outcome for purchasing	Solutions	Outcome for production
+8	Class C	+6
+4	Class D	+3

Perhaps the most interesting and possibly the most common situation in organizations and social life, however, is a *mixed* one containing both win-win and win-lose alternatives. This offers the opportunity for either cooperation (class C and D solutions) or competition (class A and B solutions).[3]

Which way is such a situation likely to turn? What causes situations like this one to move in a cooperative or competitive direction? The research evidence is clear. Whether conflict in a mixed situation takes a cooperative or competitive turn will greatly depend on the quality of six dynamic characteristics of any social conflict. And it is by altering the quality of these, using techniques that will be described in this chapter, that managers can affect the constructiveness or destructiveness of conflict.

Dynamics of conflict

People in conflict have different interests and prefer different alternative solutions to a problem. In mixed situations particularly, the course of conflict will be greatly affected by each of the following conditions: (1) definition of the *goal* to be achieved; (2) perception of the *other*; (3) view of the *other's action*; (4) perception

of *problem size;* (5) *communication* between the conflicting parties; and (6) internal *group dynamics.*

A fundamentally critical characteristic of these determiners of
the course of conflict is that, once they take a constructive or destructive tilt, they tend to have self-reinforcing intra- and interpersonal consequences. Thus, troublesome self-stimulating competitive spirals are born, and, unless these are skillfully altered using
techniques of conflict management, they are capable of thrusting
opponents, despite their best intentions, into organizationally
hazardous, mutually destructive struggles. Let us examine how
each of the six points listed affects the dynamics of conflict.

Definition of the goal.   There was once an experiment in which
two people were told that they were each operating a trucking
company. Their "garages" were at either ends of a one-lane path
and their destinations were at the opposite ends. The profit that
they were to actually receive for participating in this experiment
was to be determined by how quickly they passed between their
garage and their destination on each of several trips. Longer trips
meant greater operating expense and lower profit. In fact, if trips
took long enough, and costs really mounted, they would lose
money from their cash reserves. The problem, of course, was that
each of the people preferred to move his or her truck first across
the one-lane path.

Half of these "trucking company operators" were told that this
was a "problem-solving situation." The other half heard it labeled
a "game of chicken." These labels, not a rational analysis of the
objective economic incentives that were involved, eventually determined how people behaved.

Trucking-company operators who heard this conflict labeled a
problem-solving situation thought of it in terms of potential win-
win goals and were able to develop equitable solutions which
allowed each of them to earn money. When the situation was
labeled a game of chicken, however, people thought in terms of
win-lose solutions. The goal was not simply to do well for oneself.
It was to beat the other, to do better regardless of the cost to
oneself. These people were unable to resolve their differences
about crossing the one-lane path, and, consequently, they lost
money.[4]

Organization life is certainly much more complicated than this
simple experiment. Without question, the costs involved are ordinarily much greater. Nevertheless, every reader has probably

witnessed a number of tragically puzzling exchanges just like the one described, in which people define success in terms of *doing better than the other*. Sometimes they pursue this goal with fanatic zeal, even to a point at which gain is forsaken and the individuals involved prefer solutions for which they suffer some costs because they believe that the other's costs will be still greater.[5]

Two project heads in a major consulting firm, for example, who were bitterly competing for a promotion both requested additional budget money so that an operations researcher might be hired for their project team. After reviewing the case, senior management determined that efficient use of the money would occur if one person was hired and his/her time was divided between the projects. Both of the managers privately acknowledged to an outside consultant that, before they would help provide operations research help for the other guy, they would do without the benefit of an in-house, full-time person and transfer funds from elsewhere to pay for an external operations research consultant.

As so often happens in organizations, their goal was defined in *competitive* terms—their principal aim was to outdo the other, regardless of their own costs. Because of that, an objectively mixed situation was transformed in their minds into a pure win-lose conflict.

People in conflict have an alternative. Despite a difference of interests, their goals can be defined cooperatively—finding a solution which optimizes everyone's (including the organization's) interests. This definition of the goal is frequently evident in quarrels between friends, allies, and lovers. In these instances, the principal aim is not to come out ahead of the other; rather, it is to find the best possible solution for everyone involved.

Perception of the other.   War is an extreme example of social conflict. For that reason, it provides clear examples of how competitive orientations distort the views that human beings in conflict hold of one another. In order to distinguish enemies from the rest of humanity, *they* are given special derogatory labels. *They* are gooks, huns, nips, and slopeheads. In their dealings with other human beings, our enemies are not at all like we are. *They* cheat, steal, rape, and have no love for children. *They* are fanatic, while we are heroic. *Their* sacrifices are barbaric, ours are noble. When *they* attack us from hiding, they are sneaky. Our stealth, however, is an example of cunning. The devil rules in *their* land; God rules in ours.

Organization life can be cruel, but it is rarely as cruel as war. Yet competitively oriented conflict in organizations contains many examples of perceptual distortion which are similar to these in kind, even if not in degree. *They* are seen as greedy, narrow-minded, myopic, lazy, and lacking in true organization commitment. *They* cannot be trusted, do not want to cooperate, stick to rules for rule's sake, and "ass kiss" the bosses. We, on the other hand, are creative risk takers who are trustworthy, cooperative, and properly loyal.[6]

When individuals and groups within organizations are in a competitively oriented conflict where the goal is to defeat the other, each side tends to focus on and exaggerate their differences from the other group, while minimizing their similarities. As time passes, these stereotypes grow until *the other* becomes the devil incarnate and *we* emerge as saintly and pure.

When both sides are cooperatively oriented to the conflict, however, and are aiming at finding the solution which optimizes everyone's interests, then similarities are emphasized and differences are minimized. Allies, friends, and lovers in conflict again provide examples. Our friends may be misguided and in error, but they are not evil. Their goals and priorities may be unwise, but they are not illegitimate. Their ways may not be ours, but they are not bizarre or barbaric.

These positive and negative views of others nurture the cooperative and competitive orientations to conflict that spawned them, creating spirals which steer the conflict in either constructive or destructive directions.

View of the other's action.   There is a story about the chance meeting of two businesspeople in a railway station in Eastern Europe. For years, the two were fierce competitors. "Where are you going?" one asked the other. "To Minsk," the other replied trying to run off. "To Minsk!" the first one shouted. "To Minsk. Ahhh! You say that you are going to Minsk so that I should think you are going to Pinsk. You liar! You *are* going to Minsk."

In competitive relationships, every behavior is suspect. Smiles are smirks. Innocent remarks are insidious deceptions. It happens in organizations as well as in railway stations in Eastern Europe. Late one night you are leaving your office. As you pass by the office of your arch enemy you see that he/she is still working. Which of the following thoughts is most likely to pass through your mind? (1) "Good old so and so. Such a dedicated, hard worker", or (2) "That so and so, always doing the extra bit just to get Brownie points." Very likely the second, or some variation on that general theme. But if a friend was working late one evening, a thought more like the first might be the one which occurs to you.

Even when a difference of interests arises, if both sides are able to maintain a cooperative, problem-solving orientation, then they are more likely to view each other's behavior as benevolently rather than malevolently intended.[7] Cooperative orientation dampens suspicion and breeds greater willingness to grant the benefit of the doubt. When competitive orientations prevail, however, every action is regarded with suspicion and a vigilant, defensive posture is assumed, which has paradoxical consequences. It frequently provides opponents with behavioral evidence that justifies their initial suspicion, causing a deepening mistrust and a heightening competitive spiral.

Perception of problem size.   A group of line managers was once asked to discuss quality-control procedures in their section and make recommendations to senior management. As the discussion progressed, it was clear that two schools of thought existed. Some of the people felt that adequate controls could be established at reasonable cost by monitoring only at a few selected, crucial points, and by the development of an employee education program to encourage informal self-monitoring at every stage of production. The other people felt that adequate controls could be realized only if a much more extensive, sophisticated, and costly monitoring system was installed.

For a time, the discussion was fruitful as people tried to find an alternative which would optimize the benefits of each group's proposals. Then, two managers whose groups were directly competitive for both budget and personnel emerged as spokespersons for the two different points of view. Without anyone realizing what was happening, the conversation became an argument about the relationship between quality control and consumer needs. The managers fought about what quality-control approaches would serve consumers best. The argument drifted into a difference of opinion about the handling of morale problems. Then they heatedly discussed the race of personnel who might be hired for new quality-control positions (in the system which might be created if they ever finished fighting and returned to the problem).

Like Topsy, the problem grew, and the network of issues that emerged masked the group's original concern. Conflicts in which the sides are cooperatively oriented are often characterized by their obvious attempt to limit problem size so that a solution can be found. Competitive orientations produce a very different consequence, however. Problem size escalates rapidly, involving a greater number of broad, ill-defined issues.[8] As the number, irrelevance, and abstractness of the issues involved mount, the difference of interests that caused the conflict originally is lost. All this heightens each side's sense of difference with the other. It intensifies competitive orientation, raising the likelihood of a destructive, rather than constructive, course of conflict.

Communication. When people view conflict as a situation that requires problem solving, rather than as a win-lose struggle, communication tends to be open. Information that is essential for problem solving tends not to be withheld. Constraints which might exist because of fear about one's vulnerability and mistrust of the other's motives are kept to a minimum by the recognition that everyone's aim is to find some win-win alternative.

Under the burden of competitive orientations, however, channels of communication sag and frequently break altogether.[9] Because self-interest is primary and defense is essential, critical information is often withheld, and distortion of information can be extreme. On occasion, deceit occurs as people deliberately distort information. Although people do not like to recognize that they engage in these behaviors, even casual observation makes it clear that they happen at all levels of organization life. How often have you heard, or even said, "He'll (she'll) have to find that out on their own" (when the necessary information could have been shared), or "Give 'em only what they ask for" (and, by deliberate omission, important information is withheld)?

Internal group dynamics. A group of young doctors at a major metropolitan hospital felt that they were in a win-lose struggle with the older physicians and the hospital administration. They wanted to rid the hospital of the "old, outdated fools" or "get killed trying."

In order to plan their strategy and support one another, they ate lunch together every day, occupying one table in the cafeteria, *their table*. At administrative meetings and staff conferences, they tried to enter and leave as a group, and made it a point never to publicly disagree with members of their group, which they called *the cutting edge*. It was a complimentary title which referred to their self-perceived avant-garde posture and their intent to lop off the old folk who were "diseasing" the system. The group eventually recognized an informal leader, its most vociferous and fanatic member. He proceeded to take control of the lunch meetings, verbally punishing people who were at all flippant or in disagreement with group opinion.

These events typify what happens to internal group dynamics during win-lose struggles. *Loyalty demands increase and dissent is minimized* as the group seeks to establish a solid front. The pressure for conformity crushes any creative thinking that might veer away from the group's position. *Task needs dominate member needs.* Winning is what matters. Team relationships, morale, and individual feelings of commitment are all expendable. In the service of the task, *structure centralizes* and is rigidified. Finally, *symbols develop* which are used to praise the ingroup and derogate the outgroup.[10]

Once again, these outcomes support the competitive orientation which originally gave birth to them, setting up a spiral which, unchecked, can lead to mutually destructive consequences. Techniques of conflict management must deal with these internal group dynamics as well as with the other dynamics of conflict by transforming competitive, destructive forces into cooperative, constructive ones.

Techniques of conflict management

For ease of communication, the techniques of conflict management which have been selected for discussion here have been put into two categories: structural approaches and process (or tactical) approaches. Structural approaches include techniques which manipulate the formal organizational structure, particularly reporting relationships, in order to manage conflict. Process or tactical approaches, on the other hand, are a group of techniques that focus directly on the dynamics of conflict in order to create a more cooperative, constructive relationship between the parties so that they can manage themselves.

Some rules can be very loosely applied in order to determine when to use structural or process (tactical) approaches to conflict management: (1) Use structural approaches when there is no particular need to have a constructive working relationship between the parties. This involves treating symptoms but not dynamic causes. (2) Use structural approaches as a means of cooling the situation before using process (tactical) approaches. (3) Use tactical approaches when the interpersonal relationships involved are critical for organization success and the personal/professional development of the parties is important. A clear shortcoming of the process (tactical) approaches is that they require time. Whether they require more time than would be lost in the course of a bitter dispute is an issue that each manager must decide as he/she chooses among the alternative approaches to conflict management.

Structural approaches to managing conflict[11]

Imagine the situation that is depicted in Figure 9-1. A and B, two people from different organizational units, are in conflict. This might be occurring in a university where A and B are responsible for coordinating and developing courses in "organizational behavior" for their respective departments. Alternatively, it might be occurring in a hospital, in which case A and B might be concerned with developing and coordinating the training of interns. Or it might be occurring in an industrial setting. Here, A and B might be the representatives from production and purchasing who were discussed in the case example with which this chapter begins.

Assuming that the conflict between A and B causes costly delays, suboptimum decisions to be made, and considerable discomfort for other staff, what might be done to manage the problem without having A and B actually work directly on developing a more collaborative relationship? Two paths of action are commonly identified as options: One calls for *higher executive involvement*, and the other requires *separating the units* involved, A and B in this case.

Figure 9-1

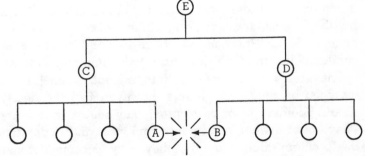

Higher executive involvement.   Insofar as our diagram is concerned, A and B are subordinate to two levels of executives. Their immediate superiors are C and D and E, the person to whom C and D report. Available evidence suggests that, if a structural approach is to be taken, it is best to bring the conflict to the crossover point, that is, to the first executive to whom both units report—in this case, E.

This approach works best when the crossover executive is able to communicate that he/she does not regard the conflict as a personal failure, but rather sees it as reflecting inherent dilemmas and ambiguous goals or policies. When this condition can be met, at least three resulting benefits can be identified: (1) it brings to bear the broader understanding and responsibility which the higher executive theoretically posses; (2) it aborts the spiral which leads to escalating conflict and/or organizationally suboptimum compromise agreements; (3) it satisfies an executive's need to be informed.

Of course, there are shortcomings to this approach, but before examining these, let us consider a structural alternative to higher executive involvement.

Separating units.   A course of action that is costly in terms of money and personnel involves installing a permanent separate unit to coordinate decision making and information flow between A and B. In order to be successful, this unit must be seen by both A and B has having a balanced view of the issues, relevant technical expertise, and power to make certain that decisions are carried out. One benefit of this approach is that it does not involve superiors in issues that may be time consuming and emotionally draining.

Separating units and higher executive involvement have a common characteristic and, because of it, a common shortcoming. Both involve the use of third-party judgments as a means of managing conflict. These judgments may minimize the noise of battle, but they do not create working alliances between embittered opponents. In fact, they may worsen the win-lose character of the conflict. After third parties share their judgments, one side frequently feels victorious, as if their cause was just and God marched on their side. Losers, however, feel the decision was unfair. Their suspicion of the previously neutral third party grows. They doubt his/her competence, motives, and understanding of the problem. Consequently, they may become defensive and guarded, as they lurk in some organization alleyway for their turn to deal with the other group and even, perhaps, with the third party.[12]

Process (tactical) approaches to managing conflict

Structural approaches to managing conflict frequently fail because they do not deal with the dynamics of conflict. The competitive orientations which prevail and each side's dedication to a win-lose struggle often remain unchanged as the structure is altered and third parties pronounce their judgments. Managers who choose to take a process (tactical) approach are more concerned with altering the dynamics of conflict than they are with substituting third-party judgments for those which might be collaboratively developed by the conflicting organizational units. They aim at transforming competitive orientations into cooperative ones. They strive to develop a problem-solving orientation in the conflict and recognition that win-win goals exist. They want to heighten the sense of similarity and lower feelings of suspicion. They try to develop an acceptance of the legitimacy of each side's interests. They work to keep open channels of communication, trying to increase information flow while limiting distorting influences.[13]

A number of alternative ways of producing these effects are identified below. Some managers find them self-evident and easy to employ as they assist their subordinates or peers in working through a conflict. Other managers feel less comfortable with these approaches and less skillful in their use. While it would be inappropriate for us to identify any specific educational opportunities here, it is important to say that, with appropriate training, it is often possible to develop these skills in managing conflict. The listing that follows should provide managers with useful guidelines for action, but it is not intended to be a substitute for additional training in this area.

Working on channels of communication. Provide a neutral site for meetings. One of the common consequences of competitively oriented, destructive conflicts is that the parties refuse to enter the *other's* territory. The result is that they break off contact and isolate themselves physically from one another, eliminating any opportunity for information flow. As the *ambiguity that replaces information grows, it stimulates the development of myth, suspicion, and animosity.* Neutral ground permits contact.

Structure the agenda. Discussions which labor under competitive orientations "jump from heated issue to heated issue."[14] As problem size and angry feelings both grow, problem-solving capacities decline. Work to (a) identify the issues at stake (if possible, establish a priorities from most to least workable); (b) ask questions to stimulate information sharing and maintain a listing of areas of agreement and disagreement; (c) identify the *full range* of solutions before allowing argument on each one.

Working on perception of goals.   Point out win-lose orientations and stress potential win-win solutions. Emphasize the idea that problem solving, not punishment, is the goal. If the people in conflict are themselves unable to, introduce and highlight neglected alternative solutions.

Emphasize superordinate goals. If the parties recognize that they share a common fate it may have a binding effect. For example, "If we are going to get (or keep) this contract, we must solve the problem." Or, "Our competitors seem to be able to produce and deliver this on time at the right price. I wonder what we can do to meet that competition." Or, "If this doesn't get solved with lower costs and better service, headquarters is going to put all our heads on the block."[15]

Change the reward structure. Competitively oriented opponents are defining success as "defeating the other." Managers are often in a position to indicate that reward (in the sense of praise or positive evaluation) is contingent on arriving at a solution which optimizes outcomes to all sides and to the organization. Thus, winning—in the sense of defeating the other—is not a win at all.

Minimize loss of face by introducing win-win alternatives. Even when competitively oriented opponents recognize the wisdom of a solution, they will often resist making a suggestion because it looks like surrender. For the same reason, they may even resist accepting a suggestion if it is offered by the other.

Working with misperception of the other and the other's behavior.   Encourage each side to step into the other's shoes. Competitively oriented conflicts cause opponents to hold a mirror-image view of one another. Each thinks that he/she is thrice blessed, while the other is the devil incarnate. A three-step process that has occasionally been useful is (1) to have each side write down their perceptions of themselves and of the other; (2) exchange these views; and (3) discuss the mirror images which has been generated.[16] Some examples of these management techniques can be found in Burke and Hornstein, *The Social Technology of Organization Development* and Fordyce and Weil, *Managing with People.*[17]

Crystalize differences as well as similarities. In competitively oriented conflicts, mistrust feeds upon ambiguity and produces animosity.

Differences of interest will always exist. They are an inevitable consequence of social life. But the conflicts that result can be lively rather than deadly. They can be constructive rather than destructive. Their course at work and at home depends upon whether we as citizens, family members, and managers can identify and transform competitive orientations into cooperative ones.

Notes

1. The viewpoint being developed here most clearly reflects ideas presented in Deutsch, M. *The resolution of conflict: Constructive and destructive processes.* New Haven: Yale University Press, 1973.

2. For more on this subject, see Deutsch, *Resolution of conflict,* Coser, L. *The functions of social conflict.* Glencoe, Ill.: Free Press, 1956.

3. Deutsch, *Resolution of conflict;* Luce, R. D., & Raiffa, H. *Games and decisions: Introduction and critical survey.* New York: John Wiley & Sons, 1957; Rapoport, A. *Fights, games, and debates.* Ann Arbor, Mich.: University of Michigan Press, 1960; Shubik, M. (Ed.). *Game theory and related approaches to social behavior.* New York: John Wiley & Sons, 1964.

4. Deutsch, M., & Lewicki, P. R. "Locking-in" effects during a game of children. *Journal of Conflict Resolution,* 1970, *14,* 367–378.

5. Brown, B. R. The effects of need to maintain face on the outcomes of interpersonal bargaining. *Journal of Experimental Social Psychology,* 1968, *4,* 107–121; Blake, R. R., Shepard, H. A., & Mouton, J. S. *Managing intergroup conflict in industry.* Houston, Tex.: Gulf Publishing, 1964; Deutsch, M. The effect of multinational orientation upon trust and suspicion. *Human Relations,* 1960, *13,* 123–139; Sherif, M., Harvey, O. J., White, B. J., Hood, W. R., & Sherif, C. W. *Intergroup conflict and cooperation: The Robber's Cave experiment.* Norman, Okla.: University Book Exchange, 1961.

6. Blake, R. R., & Mouton, J. S. Comprehension of owned outgroup positions under intergroup competition. *Journal of Conflict Resolution,* 1961, *5,* 304–310; Deutsch, *Resolution of conflict;* Gottheil, E. Changes in social perception contingent upon competing or cooperating. *Sociometry,* 1955, *18,* 132–137; Sherif, et al., *Intergroup conflict and cooperation.*

7. Deutsch, Effect of multinational orientation upon trust and suspicion; Deutsch, M. Cooperation and trust: Some theoretical notes. In M. Jones (Ed.), *Nebraska symposium on motivation.* Lincoln: University of Nebraska Press, 1962.

8. Deutsch, M., Canavan, D., & Rubin, J. The effects of size of conflict and sex of experimenter upon interpersonal bargaining. *Journal of Experimental Social Psychology,* 1971, *7,* 258–267; Fisher, R. Fractionating conflict. In R. Fiske (Ed.), *International conflict and behavioral service: The Craigville papers.* New York: Basic Books, 1964.

9.   Blake & Mouton, Comprehension of owned outgroup positions; Blake, R. R., & Mouton, J. S. Loyalty of representative to ingroup positions during intergroup competition. *Sociometry*, 1961, *24*, 177-183; Blake, R. R., & Mouton, J. S. Overevaluation of own group's product in intergroup competition. *Journal of Abnormal and Social Psychology*, 1962, *64*, 237-238; Deutsch, M., & Krauss, R. M. Studies of interpersonal bargaining. *Journal of Conflict Resolution*, 1962, *6*, 52-76; Krauss, R., & Deutsch, M. Communication in interpersonal bargaining. *Journal of Personality and Social Psychology*, 1966, *4*, 572-577.

10. Sherif, *Intergroup conflict and cooperation*.

11. Walton, R. E. Third-party roles in interdepartmental conflict. *Industrial Relations*, 1967, 7(1), 29-43.

12. Blake, Shepard, & Mouton, *Managing intergroup conflict in industry*.

13. The proposals which follow are drawn from several sources, principally Blake, Shepard, & Mouton, *Managing intergroup conflict in industry;* Deutsch, *Resolution of conflict;* Walton, R. E. Leadership strategies for achieving membership consensus during negotiations. *Proceedings of the 18th Meeting of Industrial Relations Research Association, 1975;* Walton, R. E. *Interpersonal peacemaking: Confrontations and third-party consultation.* Reading, Mass.: Addison-Wesley, 1969; Walton, R. E., & McKensie, R. B. *A behavioral theory of labor negotiations.* New York: McGraw-Hill, 1965.

14. Burton, J. *Conflict and communication.* New York: Macmillan, 1969.

15. Sherif, et al., *Intergroups conflict and cooperation*.

16. Burke, W. W., & Hornstein, H. A. *The social technology of organization development.* Fairfax, Va.: NTL Learning Resources, 1972, Section III; Johnson, D. W. Use of role reversal in intergroup competition. *Journal of Personality and Social Psychology*, 1967, *7*, 135-141.

17. Burke & Hornstein, *Social technology of organization development;* Fordyce, J. K., & Weil, R. *Managing with people: A manager's handbook of organization development* (2nd ed.). Reading, Mass.: Addison-Wesley, 1979.

10

De-Stereotyping

CHRIS and Sandy are awaiting job interviews. Both are 28-years-old. Both grew up in large urban communities. Both attended Ivy League colleges. Both have recently received M.B.A.s at renowned universities and ranked high in their classes. Both hope to take on managerial responsibilities in a corporate setting. But there is a difference: Chris is female and Sandy is male.

Who will get the job? What would happen if, instead of differing in sex, one of these candidates were 50 instead of 28-years-old? Or black rather than white? These questions are pertinent to society's current demand that personnel selection not be influenced by traits extraneous to the job itself. Title VII of the Civil Rights Act of 1964 forbids discrimination based on race, national origin, religion, or sex. Individuals of ages 45–65 were extended such protection in the Age Discrimination Employment Act of 1967.

The fact of occupational discrimination and bias is undebatable. The culprit: societal stereotypes. Stereotypes influence selection for employment and the manner in which particular individuals are treated when on the job. They also affect the way in which such individuals regard themselves and their accomplishments. How this happens and what can be done about it are the concerns of this chapter.

Stereotypes

One outcome of the person-categorization process described earlier is the formation of stereotypes. The categories of sex, race, and ethnic origin tend to be very salient ones. And it is cognitively efficient to assume that such categories provide information about a host of other characteristics and personal traits. In this way, a new schema need not be freshly created each time a person comes into contact with someone else. Once formed, stereotypes enable an individual to "know what to expect" from certain others and enable that individual to "make sense of what he/she sees."

This all sounds as if stereotyping is a work-saving cognitive enterprise which serves to simplify and organize the complex world we encounter. And, indeed, it is. The problem is that stereotypes often are *overgeneralizations* and are either inaccurate or do not apply to the individual in question. In these cases, stereotypes become the basis for faulty reasoning leading to biased feelings and actions, putting others at a disadvantage not because of who they are or what they have done, but because of the group they belong to.

What, exactly, is a stereotype? It is a set of attributes tagged to a group and imputed to its individual members simply because they belong to that group.[1] Thus, individuals who attach stereotypes to blacks (i.e., are racially biased) will believe certain attributes to be possessed by a significant portion of blacks (e.g., superstitiousness and laziness) and certain others to be lacking in a significant portion of blacks (e.g., intelligence and dominance). The more traits included in the stereotype and the larger the proportion of the group assumed to be characterized by stereotyped attributes, the more bias exists.[2]

The transmission of stereotypes

Societal stereotypes are widely shared and accepted within our culture. They originate in simple experience and subtle input. In short, they are learned. Our "teachers" are an abundant variety of commonplace sources. A few are described below.

History.   Despite our rhetoric about democracy, our history as a nation is chock full of examples of unequal treatment of those in particular groups. After all, it was only a little more than 50 years ago that women gained the right to vote. Quotas designed to keep individuals of certain national origins and religious backgrounds out of schools, work organizations, and communities have, until very recently, been enforced. Even today, racial desegregation is still an issue. These factors in our past (and present) provide a backdrop for societal stereotypes, lending a certain legitimacy to their existence.

Socialization. In the course of growing up, each of us learns and becomes imbued with the predominating attitudes and values of our parents and our teachers. We are told, directly and indirectly, about right and wrong, good and bad, wisdom and foolishness. Also conveyed are attitudes and beliefs about people. Stereotypes are among these. They are communicated through humor (e.g., Polish jokes), through children's stories (e.g., the story of Little Black Sambo), and even through language (e.g., "that is woman's work").

The Media. Newspapers, magazines, movies, and radio are all sources of stereotype transmission, but above them all stands television, which seems particularly potent. Television, which reaches 95 percent of the homes in America, is watched by an incredible diversity of people, and it is watched a great deal. Some have estimated that, in the preschool years, an American child spends more time watching television that he/she will spend in the classroom during four years of college. What do children see on TV? Up until the early 1960s "Amos 'n' Andy" was a favorite. The portrayals in "Amos 'n' Andy" supported prevailing stereotypes about blacks—stupidity, laziness, dishonesty, and looseness of morals. And even today, Flip Wilson's "Geraldine" character embraces the stereotypically loose morality so often associated with black women. Commercials, too, present stereotypic portraits. In a study reported in the mid-1970s, 199 randomly selected weekday television commercials were studied to determine how they depicted males and females.[3] Results indicated that males were far more frequently cast as knowledgeable or expert: 70 percent of the males were portrayed as authorities, whereas only 14 percent of the women were so portrayed. Furthermore, only 11 percent of the characters shown in occupational settings were women. Thus, television, an immensely powerful force in our lives, transmits prevailing stereotypes, reinforcing the information about others acquired from other sources.

Thus, stereotypes are transmitted through multiple sources. They are learned quite early in one's life and often have the status of "truths." That is, we are surprised to learn anyone else does not share our beliefs and, since we tend to associate with people who do, there is little impetus to examine our beliefs critically.

The maintenance of stereotypes

Not only are stereotypes widely shared, they also are extremely rigid. That is, they are enormously resistant to change. It is almost as if people have an investment in maintaining their stereotypic belief systems whether they are accurate or not. And perhaps they do. Stereotypes serve a variety of functions for individuals.[4] But one thing is clear. Eradication of such beliefs requires fundamental alterations in one's approach to the world, rendering it far more complex and less predictable than before.

But how can stereotypic beliefs persist even if they are inaccurate? There are a number of mechanisms that act to maintain them.

Seeing what you're looking for.   Beliefs determine what information we let in and what information we screen out. If, for example, someone believes blacks to be lazy, there will be a tendency to attend more heavily to the one black who is, in fact, lazy than to the nine who are hardworking. Similarly, the one woman who quits work because she gets married will serve to support the conviction that women are unstable members of the work force, although there may be many others who continue to work despite marriage or pregnancy. We seem to attend to events so we can say, "I told you so." We attend to events that confirm our stereotypes, and remember those events more clearly. Consequently, we build a case for our beliefs by accumulating supportive evidence and rejecting conflicting evidence. As in other cases of selective perception, we see what we want to see.

Virtue or vice, it depends.   Identical behavior on the part of two people, one a member of a stereotyped group and one not, is seen differently. So, for instance, Abraham Lincoln is considered wise and sensible for his thrift, but thrifty Jews are seen as stingy and uncharitable. Similarly, forceful behavior in a man is seen as strong whereas the same behavior in a woman is seen as pushy, aggressive, and even "bitchy." Consider the following list:[5]

The family picture is on HIS desk; ah, a solid, responsible family man.	The family picture is on HER desk; Hm . . . her family will come before her career.
HIS desk is cluttered; he's obviously a hard worker and a busy man.	HER desk is cluttered; She's obviously a disorganized scatterbrain.
HE'S talking with co-workers; he must be discussing the latest deal.	SHE'S talking with co-workers; she must be gossiping.
HE'S not at his desk; he must be at a meeting.	SHE'S not at her desk; she must be in the ladies' room.
HE'S not in the office; he must be meeting customers.	SHE'S not in the office; she must be out shopping.
HE'S getting married; he'll become more settled and mature.	SHE'S getting married; she'll get pregnant and leave.

Thus, stereotypic beliefs have a way of coloring what we see. In so doing, they maintain themselves, guarding against contradictory information.

Shifting the ground.   Consider the following scenario.

Mr. X: Women shouldn't be promoted into the managerial ranks of M.C. Industries because they can't be trusted to stay with the company—if they're not married, they'll quit when they get married; if they are married, they'll get pregnant and leave.

Mr. Y: But data from the personnel office indicate that women are actually slightly *less* likely to leave M.C. than men who hold equivalent jobs.

Mr. X: That's why we can't hire women in the higher ranks—they never leave, and it's hard to get rid of them, even when they do poor work.

Mr. Y: But our efficiency manager found that women are somewhat more productive than men, and make fewer errors in their work.

Mr. X: That's the problem with women—they're uncreative, plodding workers.[6]

This hypothetical conversation between Mr. X and Mr. Y illustrates yet another mechanism used to maintain stereotypic beliefs—that of shifting the ground so as to reinterpret contradictory information to conform to one's beliefs. It seems as though almost any fact or figure can be assimilated and even taken as evidence for one's point of view. This fluidity, which defies logic and even rationality, nonetheless enables a recasting of facts so as to support stereotypic beliefs.

Yes, but. . . . In an experimental program in Washington, D.C., women police officers were put on patrol with male partners.[7] Research evaluating the program indicated that many of the men with women partners were satisfied with them. Nonetheless, they were no more likely than were their fellow officers who had not worked with women to approve of the hiring of large numbers of women police. It seems that these officers were, in effect, saying "My partner is okay, but she is an exception. Women in general are not effective police officers."

When undeniable evidence of information contradictory to one's stereotypic beliefs is encountered, that is, the beliefs cannot be reinterpreted because the leaps of logic required are too great, they are ultimately protected by labeling the contradictory evidence an "exception." Gordon Allport, in his book, *The Nature of Prejudice*, terms this the "refencing" device because it enables a quick patching up of a potential break in the protective barrier surrounding the stereotypic belief.[8] By admitting that there are exceptions, the stereotyped belief is kept intact—the contrary evidence does not cause a modification of the stereotype. In essence, by acknowledging the case as an exception, the rule is not jeopardized.

Making it happen. As part of a research study conducted in the late 60s, elementary school teachers were led to believe that some children in their classes were going to show improved scores on IQ tests.[9] They were told that these children were "intellectual bloomers who will show unusual intellectual gains during the academic year." In fact, the information given to the teachers did not correspond to reality; the children in this high-potential group were randomly selected. Eight months later, however, this group of children, who had been no different from the others except in the eyes of their teachers, showed a higher average intellectual gain than did the others. The labeled children actually fulfilled their teachers' expectations of them. What happened?

Evidently, the behavior of the teachers was such that it *created the situation they expected.* This important finding, uncovered by Harvard University psychologist Robert Rosenthal and colleagues, is consistent with the notion of "self-fulfilling prophecy," first proposed by Robert Merton, the sociologist, in 1948.[10] Exactly how the teachers behaved so as to confirm their expectations about the so-called gifted group is as yet unclear, although there is some evidence that the teachers called upon these children more often than the others.[11]

Stereotypes carry with them expectations about behavior. Thus, a manager is apt to expect black subordinates to be lazy. Consequently, he/she may oversupervise them with the ultimate effect of reducing their initiative. The manager's behavior has the circular effect of causing these subordinates to affirm the manager's original expectation, whether it was, in fact, true or false. In other words, the manager creates the behavior he/she expects by acting as if it were there all along.

A cleverly designed research investigation provides evidence for the impact of self-fulfilling prophecies in maintaining racial stereotypes.[12] First, the researchers gathered evidence which established that black job applicants were treated more curtly, less warmly, and received shorter interviews than did white applicants who behaved in an identical manner. Then, in a deliberate turnabout, white interviewees were treated as blacks typically were. The results indicated that, when they were treated as the blacks had been treated, these white interviewees were more nervous and performed less adequately. Thus, the behavior typically directed at blacks in such situations seemed to elicit less effective interviewing skills, regardless of the race of the interviewee. In effect, the interviewer's behavior brought on the very behavior that he/she anticipated from blacks in the first place.

There is little doubt that the self-fulfilling prophecy helps to maintain stereotypic beliefs. In a sense, people provide themselves with their own supporting data via this process. After all, there is little reason to revise or even to question one's beliefs when such ample evidence of their "accuracy" is so abundantly available.

In summary, there are many tactics which we use to bolster our stereotypic beliefs. The information we select to attend to, our interpretations of it, and the way we treat others so as to ensure that their behavior fits with our ideas of what they are like, all are examples of such tactics. The consequence is that stereotypes are

obstinately resistant to change. They tenaciously persist in the
face of contrary evidence, and even personal experience has little
impact on their existence.

The content of stereotypes

What are the prevailing stereotypes concerning black, female,
and older workers? These groups have been singled out for brief
examination here because they are of current interest, and because there is at least some research which documents the
stereotyping of persons in these groups. However, the principles
discussed throughout this chapter apply to a host of other subgroups as well. We shall return to this point at the end of the
chapter.

Blacks.   There seems to be a common conception of blacks as
lazy, superstitious, ignorant, unpredictable, temperamental, untrustworthy, hedonistic, passive, and submissive. On the positive
side, blacks are often viewed as interpersonally sensitive, as
happy-go-lucky, and as warm and outgoing.

Older workers.   The stereotype of the older worker is, it seems,
very negative with respect to performance capacity and potential
for development.[13] That is, older workers are seen as unproductive, inefficient, unmotivated, uncreative, and illogical as compared to younger workers. They also are seen as rigid, dogmatic,
and not easily adaptable to new ideas. On the positive side, the
older worker is viewed as solid, dependable, and trustworth—a
truly stable member of the work force.

Women.   A great deal of work has been done attempting to
capture the cultural stereotypes about women.[14] With respect to
work behaviors, women are seen as indecisive, illogical, soft,
weak, passive, unambitious, and generally ineffective. Positive
traits are assumed to be neatness, loyalty, concern for others, and
interpersonal acuity.

The lack-of-fit model

How do stereotypes have detrimental effects on acceptance,
participation and advancement in the work world? To understand

how stereotypes operate, it is critical to recognize the role that the perception of *person-job fit* plays in the process.

Expectations of how successful or unsuccessful an individual will be when working at a particular job are determined by the degree to which there is believed to be a fit between the individual's attributes and the characteristics necessary to do the job. That is:

$$\left.\frac{\text{Perception of individual's attributes}}{\substack{\text{Perception of} \\ \text{job-required attributes}}}\right\} \text{Person-job fit} \rightarrow \text{Performance expectations}$$

If, for example, someone is believed to be high in verbal but low in quantitative ability, we would not expect him/her to be successful at a job thought to require sophisticated mathematical skills, there is a poor fit between the person's qualities and those required to do the job well. But it is likely that we would predict success for this same person when the job is thought to require writing and communication skills; here, the perceived fit between person and job is a good one. So, an assessment of a good person-job fit leads to expectations of success and an assessment of a poor person-job fit leads to expectations of failure.

$$\left.\frac{\text{Perception of individual's attributes}}{\substack{\text{Perception of} \\ \text{job-required attributes}}}\right\} \begin{array}{l} \text{Poor person-job fit} \rightarrow \text{Expectation of failure} \\ \text{Good person-job fit} \rightarrow \text{Expectation of success} \end{array}$$

Note that the components of the fit ratio both are *perceptions*, not actualities. This is a very important point. Thus, the fit assessment of any person may be inaccurate due to either the inaccuracy of the attributes assumed to characterize him/her or the inaccuracy of the attributes deemed essential to perform the job. Whether accurate or not, however, the corresponding performance expectations and their behavioral consequences ensue.

When one considers the attributes believed to be necessary to be a successful manager, the role of greatest power and status within work organizations, the problem for those in the stereotyped groups we have identified is immediately obvious. Consider, for a moment, what some of those attributes are: forcefulness, aggressiveness, emotional stability, decisiveness, confidence, competitiveness, self-reliance, desirousness of responsibility, objectiveness, and rationality.

Return for a moment to the stereotypes presented in the preceding section, it is clear that the attributes believed to characterize members of the stereotyped groups listed are different from, and in many cases inconsistent with, those believed to characterize successful managers. Taking a leadership role, making hard-nosed decisions, and competing for scarce resources simply are not activities that are consistent with a view of blacks as happy-go-lucky and passive or a view of older workers as rigid and dogmatic. Although for different reasons, there is a distinct *lack of fit* between the perceptions of those in each of these groups and that of the job of manager. This perception of a poor person-job fit prompts expectations of failure.

Performance expectations have many consequences, both for thought and for action. Their influence can be felt when people seek entry to organizations and when they already are on the job. They affect whether or not an individual is chosen for employment and how his/her work is evaluated and rewarded, as shown schematically below:

Performance expectations → Selection decisions

Performance expectations → Performance appraisal and reward allocation

Expectations of failure no doubt create a definite bias toward negativity. To continue with our example, individuals in the stereotyped groups we have identified are apt to be judged inappropriate for managerial roles, and their performance in them is apt to be devalued. Thus, expectations of failure can function as a barrier to the acquisition of employment in such roles and, if employment occurs, to the fair distribution of performance rewards. In short, the perception of poor person-job fit and the negative performance expectations it creates provide the underpinnings for organizational discrimination. Figure 10-1 captures the process we have just described.

To explicate further how the lack-of-fit model operates, it is useful to take an example of one stereotype and discuss the varieties of organizational discrimination that result and the conditions that regulate their occurrence. After all, to do something constructive toward reducing stereotype-based organizational discrimination it is essential to understand its dynamics. For purposes of

Figure 10-1
**The lack-of-fit formulation and organizational
discrimination**

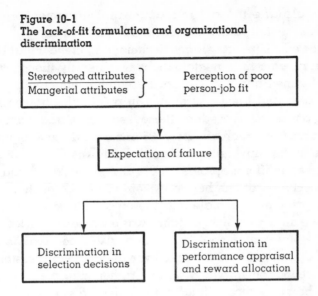

illustration, we will focus upon the discriminatory consequences
of stereotypes pertaining to women in our society.

Sex discrimination

Sex-typing of jobs

Not only is there concurrence about the attributes of women in
our culture, but there also is concurrence about the gender-related
attributes required for various jobs. Such sex-typing of jobs has its
origins in the traditional view that paid work—especially if it is
important, demanding, and lucrative—is a man's domain. Wom-
en's lack of mobility, their failure to maintain career continuity,
and their seemingly lesser ambition with regard to livelihood all
have served to reinforce that image throughout the years. Now,
when these factors no longer weigh so heavily in women's life
plans, the view of work as primarily a man's activity remains.

There have, of course, always been some positions and occupations that are considered female in sex-type: librarian, nurse, secretary, and elementary school teacher, to name a few. By and
large, such jobs are believed to require the skills and talents that
society attributes to women—nurturing, social sensitivity, and
service. Occupations of higher status, however, apparently are
the province of men. They not only have fewer women in the

ranks, but also are thought to require an achievement-oriented aggressiveness that rarely is associated with women.

Evidence exists in many forms documenting the fact that being successful at work in high-status jobs is generally thought to be reserved for men and not women. Research conducted by Feldman-Summers and Kiesler is a case in point.[15] In the course of designing a research procedure, these researchers administered a pretest survey to approximately 85 male and female undergraduates at the University of Kansas. Each was shown descriptions of several different professionals and was asked to indicate how successful he or she believed them to be. For each subject, half were presented as male and the other half as female. The results were dramatic. In no instance was a woman expected to be more successful than a man! The authors also report that, in later work, they were unable to find even a single professionally oriented occupation in which women rather than men were expected to be more successful. This is indeed a very compelling indication that success at high-status work is generally associated with men more than with women.

To bring this point a bit closer to organizational life, it is useful to consider the work of Virginia Schein. In a series of studies she asked 300 male managers[16] and 167 female managers[17] to describe either women, men, or successful middle managers. She found that "men" and "successful middle managers" were described in very similar terms, whereas "women" were described quite differently. Apparently, those attributes thought to characterize a successful manager are not at all those typically ascribed to women. Thus, not only are most managers men, but good management is also thought to be a manly business.

The sex-typing of jobs is very much a fact of life. Many jobs are seen as either predominantly masculine or predominantly feminine, entailing tasks that require skills and attributes associated primarily with one sex or the other. And, with few exceptions, the jobs that carry with them power, prestige, and authority in our culture are cast as male rather than female in type.

Discrimination in selection process

In the brief vignette presented at the start of this chapter, we posed a simple question: which of the two job candidates will be hired? There is ample research evidence indicating that, in general, the man will be hired rather than the woman.

A long list of studies demonstrates that women are given less favorable evaluations than men when the candidates have equivalent or identical qualifications.[18] In one study, for instance, 100 personnel directors were asked to reply to letters from job applicants expressing interest in an accounting job.[19] The letters were signed by either a male or a female. Results indicated that the women received far fewer replies and the replies they did receive were much less positive and upbeat than were those received by the men. And this general finding is not limited only to accounting jobs. In another investigation, the lower acceptance rates and poorest evaluations for managerial positions were of female applicants.[20] Furthermore, discrimination at selection time seems not to be limited to preferential evaluation and acceptance of male over female candidates, but also involves higher starting salaries[21] and higher entry level, as well.[22]

In many of the studies documenting discrimination in hiring decisions, information about the perceived characteristics of the applicants also has been obtained. In one case, for instance, female applicants were found to be less decisive, informed, competitive, motivated, logical, and assertive than were the male applicants.[23] And female applicants were rated as friendlier, warmer, and more emotional than males. This occurred despite the fact that the applicants were identical except for gender. So, as one would expect given the lack-of-fit formulation, sex stereotypes seem to be potent determinants of a woman applicant's perceived attributes.

Also consistent with the lack-of-fit formulation is the fact that women job candidates are not *always* treated unfairly on the basis of their sex. There is evidence, for instance, that when clear, uncontestable information is provided contrary to the stereotype of women, an individual woman is not discriminated against.[24] Furthermore, the literature confirms that it is only when the job in question can be typecast as "masculine" that females are found to be less acceptable than males.[25] A particularly interesting example of this is the finding that female candidates are evaluated more favorably than are males when the predominant sex of subordinates is to be female, and just the opposite is true when the predominant sex of subordinates is to be male.[26] Finally, there is evidence that attractive women (who also are seen as more feminine) are seen as less qualified and employable for managerial positions than are unattractive women.[27] Perceptions of lack of person-job fit are no doubt heightened by the enhanced femininity of the attractive women, causing more unfavorable evaluations.

Discrimination in performance appraisal and reward allocation

It would seem that, once a woman gains entry to an organization, she would be "home free". After all, she now has the opportunity to demonstrate her competence, energy and commitment. But, once again, negative expectations about her performance capability can stand in her way. Decisions about promotion, employee utilization, and training opportunities all are likely to be affected. Two critical aspects of the performance evaluation process are considered separately below.

Performance evaluation. Is the same work product evaluated similarly regardless of the sex of its originator? This was the question raised by Phillip Goldberg in a study reported in 1968. He found the answer to be no. Participants in his study were shown to rate the identical article more highly when they believed it to be written by a male rather than by a female.[28] What followed this report was a slew of investigations—some published and others unpublished—testifying to the universality of this effect. In many different settings, with a wide range of types of work, the identical work performance was found to be rated lower when the person who produced it was female as compared to male. Clearly, the expectation that women are unlikely to succeed at certain jobs gets in the way of unbiased evaluation of their performance.

But, again, there are exceptions and limiting conditions. When definitive information about the quality of work is provided, the tendency toward bias disappears.[29] It seems that, in these instances, stereotypes are precluded from predominating in the impression-formation process. Consequently, the perceived lack of fit and performance expectations that are a product of such stereotyping do not occur, and discrimination in performance evaluation is thus averted.

Causal explanations of success. Even when successful performance is acknowledged, interpretation of why that success occurred can differ in very dramatic ways. There is evidence, for instance, showing that, when equally successful, a woman is viewed as less skilled than a man.[30] Rather, her success is attributed to hard work, to good luck, or to factors outside the work setting. Because success is unexpected, it is interpreted as an exception occurring for out-of-the-ordinary reasons and unlikely to occur again.

The consequences of such underestimations of the skill of successful members of stereotyped groups can be quite profound. Consider the story of Mary Cunningham, the 29-year-old executive who had skyrocketed to become vice president for strategic planning at the Bendix corporation in late 1980. She resigned soon after. Prompting her resignation were rumors of her "relationship" with Bendix chairman William Agee. It was this relationship, not her talent, the gossip said, that accounted for her rapid and dramatic rise through the company's ranks. Cunningham, the rumors would have us believe, was not really a success because of her ability, but because of some extraneous event that gave her an edge over others. If Ms. Cunningham had been a *Mr.* rather than a *Ms.*, would people have talked so about a "relationship"? Probably not. Cunningham would more likely have been seen as a "whiz kid."

Empirical evidence supports the general principle underlying this real-life example.[31] The types of causal attributions typically made when women are successful detrimentally affect the degree to which certain types of organizational rewards are seen as appropriate. A promotion, for instance, is not seen as an appropriate action when success is believed not to be skill-derived. Furthermore, if an organizational reward is to be given in such circumstances, the scope and magnitude of the reward that is viewed as preferable is quite limited.

Self-directed discrimination

So far, we have only discussed the negative consequences of stereotyping when directed toward *others*. But members of stereotyped groups have grown up in the same society as those others and, consequently, share the same stereotypes—only, in this case, they are *self-stereotypes*. These self-stereotypes and the negative performance expectations they create also have detrimental consequences. They lead to self-limiting behavior, both before and after entry into the organization.

There are data which suggest, for instance, that women *choose* to pursue lower-status careers even when the opportunity to do otherwise is available to them. Thus, women who enter professions are disproportionately represented in those specializations considered lowest in status: juvenile, divorce, or welfare law rather than corporate law; pediatrics, dermatology, or psychiatry rather than surgery or neurology, etc.[32] Women's perceptions of the positions in which they will be successful are, no doubt, an important factor here. Careers in which work with children or families, or giving nurturant support are the central activities are consistent with societal views of women and their strengths, and therefore lead to expectations of success. But these careers also tend to be those that are lowest in status whatever the professional category. Thus, if they accept societal stereotypes, women are caught in a bind.

There also is evidence that women consistently devalue themselves and their contributions to the work setting.[33] They, too, have a tendency to explain away their successes as due to a lucky break or an easy task rather than to their own ability. Responsibility for failure, however, tends to be accepted.[34] This is a likely consequence of the negative performance expectations women carry with them into work settings, for it is an unexpected performance outcome that is rejected or denied and an expected one that is accepted as one's doing.[35] Attributing responsibility in this fashion, because it dismisses favorable information, perpetuates a self-fulfilling cycle of negative self-regard. No doubt there are costly consequences. Women's willingness to take risks, their desire to be visible, and their general presentation of themselves all are likely to be affected in a manner that hinders career progress.

De-stereotyping

If stereotypes lie at the core of organizational discrimination, it follows that changing stereotypes should reduce discriminatory practices. But it also should be possible to reduce discimination by altering elements of situations that regulate the extent to which stereotypes are called into play. How this might be done is considered below.

Changing stereotypes

Given the tenacity of stereotypes, how does one go about changing them? Changing the attitudes and beliefs of an individual who has accepted societal stereotypes is no easy task. As

Rosen and Jerdee have pointed out with regard to sex stereotypes, there are many potential motivations for holding on to them.[36] They suggest, for example, that past costly experiences, perception of potential threat, commitment to traditional values, and needs for clarity in a complex world all are potential reasons for the maintenance of stereotypes about women. These and perhaps other motivators, also act to support stereotypes about blacks and older workers. Depending upon which of these motivators supports stereotypic belief systems, the most effective change strategy would differ.

For the most part, the organizational programs that have been developed in recent years have been built upon the implicit assumption that the basis of stereotypes is ignorance—ignorance of what those in the stereotyped group are really like and ignorance that one harbors a stereotype. Consequently, their focus in on the raising of awareness about stereotypic conceptions and on the transmitting of information about the realities of prejudice and discrimination. Human-relations training and other types of workshops on sex bias have, for instance, become commonplace. A host of exercises have been developed for use by individuals and by groups to facilitate exploration of personal and societal prejudices and misconceptions.[37] Techniques such as role playing have been utilized to encourage men and women to experience the other's dilemma. Additionally, educational programs have become widespread. To fill in the presumed knowledge gap, facts, theories, and research findings are presented and discussed.

Unfortunately, the effects of these programs are rarely assessed systematically so no conclusions about their effectiveness can be drawn. It is likely, however, that such programs are successful only when an individuals' stereotypes have been sustained as a convenience or when they simply have never been put to the test. In these cases, forcing people to confront their stereotypes and come to grips with the consequences may be sufficient to bring about change. But when stereotyped views are deeply rooted in value systems, such programs are doomed to failure. Awareness, by itself, has little impact on value-laden convictions.

Thus, changing an individual's stereotypes can be a very complicated process. Moreover, it is likely to be an expensive one. The training and development activities needed to accomplish such a change, if indeed it can be accomplished, are not realistic organizational possibilities in terms of the money and time that would be

required. What, then, can be done to limit the negative consequences of such stereotypes?

Changing the situation

Although stereotypes have roots in socialization processes and
often are firmly entrenched at a very early age, measures can be
taken to limit some of the unjust consequences of these stereotypes without actually changing them. Here, the issue is not the
elimination of a stereotypic belief system but the *control of its
consequences.* The aim is not to eliminate prejudice but to control
discrimination. Accomplishing this requires an understanding of
environmental factors that facilitate or hinder the saliency of
stereotypes and, thus, the degree to which they are used in employment settings. Two such factors will be briefly considered
here. Both can influence the extent to which stereotypic attitudes
are assumed to characterize one specific individual.

Information. Stereotypes are most likely to be employed when
little other information about the individual is available or when
ambiguity exists. Specific, concrete information is often more
compelling in a given circumstance than are stereotypes. This
theme was evident throughout the discussion of sex discrimination in this chapter. This has been further demonstrated in a recent study in which it was shown that not only the clear-cut nature
of such information but also its job relevance undermines stereotyped views.[38]

This suggests that particular care needs to be taken to obtain as
much concrete information about those in stereotyped groups as
possible. In soliciting employees, attention should be paid to past
experience and performance, and information should be acquired
from as many sources as possible. If, for example, it is known that
person X has repeatedly succeeded in the past, has succeeded
admirably in a range of work situations, and/or has been judged
to be greatly talented by many different evaluators using a variety
of evaluative methods, person X's potential and ability are very
difficult to discount. Also, it is essential to create concrete standards for judging job applicants—standards that are directly relevant to job performance. This may entail the development of a
new testing procedure (perhaps including an actual job sample) or
a new interview format, or may be accomplished simply by establishing a new way of looking at old procedures. Being concrete,

such standards preclude distortion; being job relevant, they preclude the "X looks good, but can he/she do the job" complaint. By structuring the richness and the specificity of the information obtained about the job applicant, the biasing effects of stereotypes can be mitigated.

This principle also is relevant for performance appraisal. Again, creating as objective standards as possible is essential for counteracting stereotypic judgments. But of equal importance is the thorough and detailed review of all information available about individual performance. For, when there is a review of just the broad picture, the gaps will tend to be filled with stereotypic notions. Whereas others may be given the benefit of the doubt, the member of a stereotyped group will be judged on the basis of assumptions that may not at all apply to him or her.

There are ways in which managers might use information to check their own prejudices. But information also can be useful in fighting off the biases that those in stereotyped groups direct at themselves. Here, the issue is feedback. If feedback is clear, concrete, and unambiguous, it can undermine stereotypes in the self-evaluation process. Putting it in quantitative form, such as percentages, number of units, etc. is a good idea so that there is an unambiguous index of performance effectiveness. And providing it often so it cannot be discounted as a one-time event also should work toward this end. Unassailable evidence of repeated success should supercede stereotypes, ultimately decreasing the extent of self-limiting perceptions and behavior among those members of a stereotyped group who truly are valuable to the organization.

Tokenism. In her book, *Men and Women of the Corporation*, Rosabeth Kanter claims that the proportional representation of women in work settings not only influences women's feelings and attitudes, but also influences the way in which they are treated by others.[39] When there is a great disproportion in the size of the minority and majority groups, Kanter believes there is cause for concern. Tokens (the members of the small minority) are isolated from the informal social networks, they are viewed as alien and different, and their characteristics are distorted to fit stereotyped conceptions. Since the publication of her book, Kanter has extended this idea to the concept of tokenism more broadly, including any group that constitutes such a minority. According to Kanter, tokenism is deadly, fostering reliance on stereotypes no

matter what the personal characteristics of the individuals in·
volved.

This idea has been extended to selection situations as well.
Thus, it has been shown that the treatment of the same woman
differed depending upon the composition of the applicant pool in
which she was considered.[40] When women had 25 percent or less
representation in the applicant pool, the target woman was
judged to have less potential, to be less likely to advance in the
company, and was offered a lower starting salary. These data
make evident just how detrimental token representation can be in
organizations.

The implications of these ideas for managerial behavior are
rather direct. Whenever possible, those in stereotyped groups
should be clustered rather than isolated in work settings. When a
number of individuals from the same group are to be brought into
positions where there are few others of their sex, ethnic group, or
age, they should be put together where possible rather than dis-
persed. By simply avoiding numerical scarcity and thereby providing evidence of the variety and differences among people belonging to the group, for treatment of any one of them is apt to be
less influenced by stereotypes. Reacting to them all as if they
were the same becomes implausible in this situation.

How the work group is composed has also been shown to have
effects on how members of stereotyped groups view themselves.
There is, for instance, evidence that women's tendencies to reject
responsibility for success and accept responsibility for failure are
only evident when their co-workers are men.[41] This suggests that
having others around who also are members of a stereotyped
group enables individuals to overcome their own detrimental
self-stereotypes. Thus, by eliminating the solo role so often held
by these individuals in organizations, a variety of discriminatory
consequences may be avoided.

These are only two examples of situational factors that can
regulate the degree to which stereotypical attitudes are brought to
bear in personnel decisions about any one individual. When situations require it, readers can create others using the principles, if
not the particulars, we have discussed. Remember, however, that
these strategies serve only to limit discrimination, not to do away
with its source.

Before leaving this section, it is important to point out that,
referring to Figure 10-1, it is the perceived lack of fit of the
stereotyped attributes *with a given type of job* that goes on to

result in discrimination. This suggests that another avenue for combating discrimination lies in altering conceptions of the attributes needed to perform certain jobs. Take the job of manager, for instance. What people typically assume are the characteristics required to be a good manager are not necessarily identical to what it takes to do the job well. The interpersonal skills and sensitivity needed to build teams, manage conflict, coach subordinates, and handle problems of career development are usually ignored, for example. It happens that these characteristics, which are indeed necessary if one is to function effectively as a manager, are ones which often are attributed to women and blacks. It is conceivable, therefore, that, if such aspects of the managerial role were to be highlighted, then the perceived "fit" of those in these groups would be greatly enhanced. Not because stereotypes are altered, but because they now become an asset rather than a liability when such an individual is considered for personnel action.

Concluding comments

We have focused on stereotypes related to sex, race, and age. However, the ideas presented here have relevance for any stereotyped group the members of which are assumed (1) to possess characteristics antithetical to those needed to do a job well; or (2) to lack characteristics considered essential to doing a job well. In either case, the discriminatory consequences of stereotypes will be evident in personnel decision making and in self-limiting behavior. And, in either case, attending to how critical aspects of the work setting are structured can act to mitigate against discrimination.

Notes

1. Taylor, S. E., Fiske, S. T., Etcoff, N. C., & Ruderman, A. J. Categorical and contextual bases of person memory and stereotyping. *Journal of Personality and Social Psychology*, 1978, 36, 778-793.
2. McCauley, C., & Stitt, C. L. An individual and quantitative measure of stereotypes. *Journal of Personality and Social Psychology*, 1978, 36, 929-940.
3. McArthur, L. Z., & Resko, B. G. The portrayal of men and women in American television commercials. *Journal of Social Psychology*, 1975, 97(2), 209-220.
4. Katz, D. The functional approach to the study of attitudes. *Public Opinion Quarterly*, 1960, 24, 163-204.

5. Taken from Josefowitz, N. *Paths to power.* Reading, Mass.: Addison-Wesley, 1980.

6. Frieze, I. H., Parsons, J. E., Johnson, P. B., Ruble, D. N., & Zellman, G. L. *Women and sex roles: A social psychological perspective.* New York: W. W. Norton, 1978, p. 279.

7. Milton, K. *Women in policing.* Police Foundation, 1972.

8. Allport, G. W. *The nature of prejudice.* Reading, Mass.: Addison-Wesley, 1954.

9. Rosenthal, R., & Jacobson, C. *Pygmalion in the classroom: Teacher expectation and pupil's intellectual development.* New York: Holt, Rinehart & Winston, 1968.

10. Merton, R. K. The self-fulfilling prophecy. *Antioch Review,* 1948, *8,* 193-210.

11. Rubovits, P., & Maher, M. Pygmalion analyzed: Toward an explanation of the Rosenthal-Jacobson findings. *Journal of Personality and Social Psychology,* 1971, *19,* 197-203.

12. Word, C. O., Zanna, M. P., & Cooper, J. The nonverbal mediation of self-fulfilling prophecies in interracial interaction. *Journal of Experimental Social Psychology,* 1974, *10,* 109-120.

13. Rosen, B., & Jerdee, T. H. The nature of job-related age stereotypes. *Journal of Applied Psychology,* 1976, *61,* 180-183.

14. Rosenkrantz, P. S., Vogel, S. R., Bee, H., Broverman, I. K., & Broverman, D. M. Sex-role stereotypes and self-concepts in college students. *Journal of Consulting and Clinical Psychology,* 1968, *32,* 287-295; Broverman, I. K., Bogel, R. S., Broverman, D. M., Clarkson, T. E. & Rosenkrantz, R. S. Sex-role stereotypes: A current appraisal. *Journal of Social Issues,* 1972, *28,* 59-78.

15. Feldman-Summers, S., & Kiesler, S. B. Those who are number two try harder: The effect of sex on attributions of causality. *Journal of Personality and Social Psychology,* 1974, *30,* 846-855.

16. Schein, V. E. The relationship between sex-role stereotypes and requisite management characteristics. *Journal of Applied Psychology,* 1973, 57, 95-100.

17. Schein, V. E. The relationships between sex-role stereotypes and requisite management characteristics among female managers. *Journal of Applied Psychology,* 1975, *60,* 340-344.

18. Dipboye, R. L., Arvey, R. D., & Terpstra, D. E. Sex and physical attractiveness of raters and applicants as determinants of resume evaluations. *Journal of Applied Psychology,* 1977, *62,* 288-294; Dipboye, R. L., Fromkin, H. L., & Wiback, K. Relative importance of applicant sex, attractiveness, and scholastic standing in evaluation of job applicant resumes. *Journal of Applied Psychology,* 1975, *60,* 39-43; Rosen, B., & Jerdee, T. H. Effects of applicant's sex and difficulty of job on evaluations of candidates for managerial positions. *Journal of Applied Psychology,* 1974, *59,* 511-512.

19. Zickmund, W. G., Hitt, M. A., & Pickens, B. A. Influence of sex and scholastic performance on reactions to job applicant resumes. *Journal of Applied Psychology,* 1978, *63,* 252-255.

20. Rosen & Jerdee, Effects of applicant's sex and difficulty of job.

21. Terborg, J. R., & Ilgen, D. R. A theoretical approach to sex discrimination in traditionally masculine occupations. *Organizational Behavior and Human Performance,* 1975, *13,* 352-376.

22. Fidell, L. S. Empirical verification of sex discrimination in hiring practices in psychology. *American Psychologist,* 1970, *25,* 1094-1098.

23. Dipboye, et al., Sex and physical attractiveness of raters and applicants.

24. Dipboye, R. L., & Wiley, J. W. Reactions of college recruiters to interviewee sex and self-presentation style. *Journal of Vocational Behavior,* 1977, *10,* 1-12.

25. Cohen, S. L., & Bunker, K. A. Subtle effects of sex role stereotypes on recruiters' hiring decisions. *Journal of Applied Psychology,* 1975, *60,* 566-572; Cash, T. F., Gillen, B., & Burns, D. S. Sexism and "beautyism" in personnel consultant decision making. *Journal of Applied Psychology,* 1977, *62,* 301-311.

26. Rose, G. L., & Andiappan, P. Sex effects on managerial hiring decisions. *Academy of Management Journal*, 1978, *21*, 104-112.

27. Heilman, M. E., & Saruwatari, L. R. When beauty is beastly: The effects of appearance and sex on evaluations of job applicants for managerial and nonmanagerial jobs. *Organizational Behavior and Human Performance*, 1979, *23*, 360-372.

28. Goldberg, P. A. Are women prejudiced against women? *Transaction*, April 1968, pp. 28-30.

29. Pheterson, G. I., Kiesler, S. B., & Goldberg, P. A. Evaluation of the performance of women as a function of their sex, achievement, and personal history. *Journal of Personality and Social Psychology*, 1971, *19*, 114-118.

30. Deaux, K. Sex: A perspective on the attribution process. In J. Harvey, W. J. Ickes, & R. F. Kidd (Eds.), *New directions in attribution research* (Vol. 1). Hillsdale, N.J.: Lawrence Erlbaum Associates, 1976.

31. Heilman, M. E., & Guzzo, R. A. The perceived cause of work success as a mediator of sex discrimination in organizations. *Organizational Behavior and Human Performance*, 1978, *21*, 346-357.

32. Gross, E. *The sexual structure of occupations over time.* Paper presented at the meeting of the American Sociological Association, August 1967.

33. Deaux, Sex: A perspective on the attribution process.

34. Deaux, K., & Farris, E. Attributing cause for one's own performance: The effects of sex, norms, and outcome. *Journal of Research in Personality*, 1977, *11*, 59-72.

35. Deaux, Sex: A perspective on the attribution process.

36. Rosen, B., & Jerdee, T. H. The psychological basis for sex-role stereotypes: A note on Terborg and Ilgen's conclusions. *Organizational Behavior and Human Performance*, 1975, *14*, 151-153.

37. Sargent, A. G. *Beyond sex roles.* St. Paul, Minn.: West Publishing, 1977.

38. Heilman, M. E. *Information as a deterrent against sex discrimination: The effects of applicant sex and information type are preliminary employment decisions.* Manuscript submitted for editorial review.

39. Kanter, R. M. *Men and women of the corporation.* New York: Basic Books, 1977.

40. Heilman, M. E. The impact of situational factors on personnel decisions concerning women: Varying the sex composition of the applicant pool. *Organizational Behavior and Human Performance*, 1980, *26*, 386-395.

41. Heilman, M. E., & Kram, K. Self-derogating behavior in women—fixed or flexible: The effects of co-workers' sex. *Organizational Behavior and Human Performance*, 1978, *21*, 346-357.

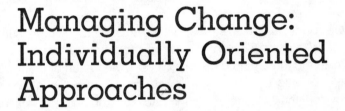

Managing Change:
Individually Oriented
Approaches

ORGANIZATIONS and their subunits are the deliberate
and accidental by-products of human endeavor. They exist to
expedite work on tasks in order that some desired goals might be
achieved. For that reason, they are expendable. When they fail to
serve their purpose, their *raison d'être*, they must be altered,
sometimes drastically. A substantial portion of the responsibility
for changing an organization is in the hands of its managers. They
are responsible for monitoring the effects that structure, technology, and human forces have on organization success, and they are
responsible for making essential changes. Very often, however,
the changes that managers propose are either never introduced or
are introduced and fail, *not* because they are unsound, but because of the human forces which are involved.

Reconsider one of the case examples offered in this book's introduction. The one labeled, *"Organization Z improves its information system."* It explained how a well-designed electronic
data-processing (EDP) system failed to achieve its full potential

because, during its installation, no effort was made to manage people's responses to the change.

In another instance, the managing director of a social services agency contacted an outside consultant because he felt "overwhelmed and was preparing to take drastic action which he might regret." He related the following story:

Nearly two years had passed since he accepted the position of managing director and simultaneously inherited a "nightmarish" management structure: 22 people reported directly to him, including the directors of 16 service agencies and 6 department heads. "My predecessor loved the arrangement," he told the consultants. "He was a wonderfully brilliant man, but an autocrat. In this way, he could keep his finger in everyone's pie." Of course, as the consultants learned too late, the "benefits" of this structure were not restricted to the managing director. With it, the 22 subordinates enjoyed direct attention and clear access to the managing director's office, giving each of them a sense of influence and control. This allowed them to avoid confronting the competition that directors felt for one another and the resentment which existed between directors and department heads.

Of course, their sense of influence and control was an illusion. In reality, the past and present occupants of the managing director's office made all the decisions. This titillated and pleased the current managing director, but it also burdened him, consuming time that he more reasonably recognized he needed for long-range planning, charting policy, and building extraorganizational linkages with public and private city, state, and national organizations.

Without recognizing this underlying drama of human forces, the consulting agency studied the management structure and filed a 30-odd page report describing a new structure with altered reporting relationships. It was an unremarkable, but very sensible idea. They suggested two new positions: An assistant managing director of service agencies, to whom all agency directors would report, and an assistant managing director of staff operations, to whom all department heads would report.

The written material was graciously accepted, the consulting agency was paid, and the suggestions were quickly buried. The managing director's ambivalence about losing control, his admiration for and competition with his predecessor, his accurate conjecture that unacceptable levels of turnover among senior personnel would result from implementing these suggestions, and his inability to imagine anyone successfully filling these intermediary positions because of subordinate antagonism and sabotage, all contributed to the proposal's demise. (As we will see later, these very same ideas, in a slightly altered form, were resurrected 18 months later through a very different process.) In this example, as in the previous one involving installation of an EDP system, an idea's technical adequacy was insufficient to promote organization change. Human forces intervened, preventing necessary alterations from occurring.

Different approaches to dealing with human forces in organization change are described in this chapter and the next. Gross distinctions almost always contain error, but they can also be extremely useful illustrations and guides. Therefore, as an aid to readers, a gross distinction between different approaches to organization change is presented in Figure 11-1. It tells us that organization efforts at managing change can be thought of as if they differed along two dimensions. One dimension is concerned with the target of the effort. Some change efforts target individual employees and try to change attitudes, values, or behavior. Others target broader issues in organization life. Taking a system's focus, they concentrate on social norms, lines of authority, and work structure. The second dimension crosscuts the first. It is concerned with the factors that regulate organization behavior. Some approaches to organization change assume that these regulators are internal to individuals and largely psychological. Values, feelings, and internalized group norms are examples. Other approaches assume that the regulators are external to individuals and are generally observable, concrete aspects of organization life. Incentive systems and formal organizational policies and procedures are examples of external regulators.

In this chapter, two individually oriented approaches are discussed. The first, T groups and related experiential approaches to training, assumes that the principal regulators of organizational behavior are internal. In contrast, the second, behavior modifica-

Figure 11-1

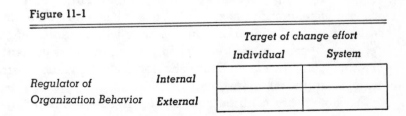

tion, assumes that these regulators are external. In the next chapter, two systems-oriented approaches are discussed. Again, one of them (called organization development) assumes internal regulation, whereas the second (called sociotechnical) assumes external regulation.

Individually oriented approaches

As assumption shared by these approaches is that, if you want to change organizations, it is essential to focus directly on individual members by attempting to change some aspect of their functioning. Individual feelings, values, attitudes, perceptions, skills, and behavior at one time or another have all been the direct target of these change efforts.[1] In general terms, the assumption has straightforward logic and a commonsense appeal. What people are doing determines how organizations are performing. Therefore, if improved organization performance is the goal, *change what people are doing.* Sometimes these efforts are roundabout and aimed at changing feelings, values, perceptions, and attitudes—the internal regulators of organization behavior. Sometimes they are more direct and aim at changing behavior by adjusting organizational rewards, an external regulator of organizational behavior.

Organizations abound with efforts that are concerned with the internal regulators. An extreme and relatively infrequent example occurs when organization members are encouraged to receive individual counseling. Much more commonplace, however, are the millions of occasions when personnel are sent to management education programs which are aimed at changing such things as how the participants communicate, make decisions, lead others, and manage intra- and interdepartmental conflict. At these programs, "staff members," "trainees," "facilitators," and "visiting experts" lecture participants on how to handle unmotivated employees, alcoholics, women, blacks, and employees approaching retirement.[2] Sometimes cases are used, and participants' diagnoses and solutions are explored and challenged. At other times, incidents are simulated, and individuals who are attending the "program" ("conference," "workshop," "seminar") play the parts of critical actors, reviewing their behavior (feelings, values, perceptions, or attitudes) afterwards.

Psychology has contributed to this approach by identifying one of the most powerful tools for creating individual change: the peer group.[3] The person most responsible for identifying this tool and developing its organizational implications was Kurt Lewin.

Lewin's consideration of peer group influence began during World War II. It was a time of food shortages and rationing, and Lewin directed an action research project aimed at influencing American housewives to use foods which were unpopular—beef heart, kidney, and sweetbreads, for example. Some of the women who participated in this project listened to a lecture which provided information about the nutritional value of these foods and how they might be prepared. That was the common procedure, and it had been used before without any substantial success. Other women in the project had a different experience, however. They participated in groups which first discussed these foods and then made a decision about using them. Subsequently, 3 percent of the women who heard the lecture reported using the unpopular foods, but 32 percent of the women in the discussion/decision groups reported doing so.[4]

These findings were confirmed in other research,[5] and through the years additional studies have demonstrated that group discussion and decision making is superior to a simple lecture or even individual tuition in changing the occurrence of such diverse events as (1) women's self-examination for breast cancer,[6] (2) the basis on which supervisors select employees,[7] and (3) the productivity levels workers set for themselves.[8] Moreover, group discussion and decision-making techniques have been shown to be effective for less noble ends, as well. They have been used as part of a program of "brainwashing" in an effort to change individuals' political and national allegiances.[9]

Why peer groups have the power to create such dramatic changes in individual behavior was captured by Lewin when he said, "As long as group standards are unchanged, the individual will resist changes more strongly the further he is expected to depart from group standards. If the group standard itself is changed, the resistance which is due to the relation between individual and group standard is eliminated."[10] Lewin's statement recognizes a psychological phenomenon which adolescents regularly display with crystal clarity. Despite pressure placed on them by parents, they are fanatic in pursuit of the latest fad. But when some subliminal cues from peers indicate that the fad is over, they drop it rapidly in order to chase after the next one with equal zeal.

Human beings cling tenaciously to the standards of groups in which they desire membership, resisting pressures to behave in ways which are contrary to those standards, until the standards themselves change. In Lewin's action-research programs, group discussion and decision making publicly altered the existing standards about food and introduced new ones which provided the basis for individual change.

In their book, *The Social Psychology of Organizations*, Daniel Katz and Robert L. Kahn, elaborate Lewin's idea by identifying several factors which underlie the benefits of group discussion and decision making:

1. Self-esteem is enhanced because people participate in creating a product which transcends their scope of concern, ability, and interest.
2. The salience of *group norms* is greater and recognition of the new social consensus is heightened.
3. Individuals crystallize their thinking and self-commitment.
4. Public commitment occurs, which enhances the likelihood of follow-through.
5. Action plans move the psychological decision into a real blueprint for behavior.[11]

Lewin pursued his interests in the power of groups to alter individual behavior after the war ended. He sought to bring this power to bear on problems of prejudice and discrimination in American society. In 1946, he and his colleagues organized a workshop for the Connecticut State Inter-Racial Commission. It was an action research project. During the day, group discussions occurred among participants aided by facilitators. In the evening, the researchers gathered in order to discuss their observations of the day's events. At one point, some participants asked for permission to observe the evening discussions. Permission was granted. They listened. Then they talked, argued, probed, and generally felt very stimulated, believing that they were learning more about *human relations* from these open-ended, self-reflective evening sessions than they were during the day.[12]

One year later, some members of the original action research team held a similar workshop in Bethel, Maine, deliberately spending more time in sessions like the evening meetings in Connecticut. This workshop heralded the birth of T groups, sensitivity training, National Training Laboratories (NTL), and the small-group movement.[13] Lewin was involved in organizing this meeting but never had an opportunity to see its fruits. He died in February 1947, eight months before his 58th birthday.

Several people have worked to advance the use of the T group[14] and its derivatives[15] as an instrument of organization change. One who moved it to new levels of public prominence through his scholarly efforts to develop clarity about the T group's role in organization change is Chris Argyris.[16]

Argyris' starting point is a common observation among organization theorists and managers: The structure of many, if not most, organizations is guided by what is variously called a bureaucratic or mechanistic model. Its component assumptions are familiar:

1. Authority and accountability are paramount in organization life. Every organization member must be accountable to his/her superior for his/her actions and for those of his/her subordinates. Every individual derives his/her authority from a superior and is responsible for obeying the directives of that superior.
2. Specialization of function is desirable and it emerges from an unambiguous division of labor which divides tasks into their smallest possible components, making jobs as simple and uninvolved as possible.
3. Task performance for separate positions is insured by a comprehensive system of rules and procedures.
4. Task performance must be impersonal, thereby eliminating disturbing individual forces.
5. Selection, promotion, and continued employment is determined by technical considerations, nothing more.

Argyris' views certainly seem to be in disagreement with Max Weber's absolute claim that a bureaucratic organization is "capable of attaining the highest degree of efficiency and is in this form the most rational known means for carrying out imperative control over human beings."[17] In fact, in a *Harvard Business Review* article, Argyris complains that experience in these organizations inculcates a set of "pyramidal" values, which can hinder attainment of organization success. These values are expressed in the following ideas: (1) "The important human relationships—the crucial ones—are those which are related to achieving the organization's objective, i.e., getting the job done. (2) Effectiveness in human relationships increases as behavior becomes more rational, logical, and clearly communicated; but effectiveness decreases as behavior becomes more emotional. (3) Human relationships are most effectively motivated by carefully defined direction, authority, and control, as well as appropriate rewards and penalties that emphasize rational behavior and achievement of the objective."[18]

These values can be important assets in organizational life, but not when they are exclusive. Then, says Argyris, they tend to have adverse consequences, causing a shift from "authentic" to "nonauthentic" behavior. Table 11-1 describes the specific behavioral changes which Argyris believes occur.

Table 11-1

Decreases	Increases
1. Giving and receiving nonevaluative, descriptive feedback about oneself and others.	1. Giving and receiving evaluative feedback about oneself and others.
2. Accepting responsibility and acknowledging ("owning") one's attitudes, feelings, and values.	2. Projecting onto others and denying one's attitudes, feelings, and values.
3. Helping others to "own" attitudes, feelings, and values.	3. Requiring others to agree with one's attitudes, feelings, and values.
4. Openness and experimentation with new attitudes, feelings, and values and permitting others to do the same.	4. Closed and nonexperimenting responses to new attitudes, feelings, and values and requiring others to behave similarly.
Authentic	*Nonauthentic*

Source: Argyris, C. *Interpersonal competence and organizational effectiveness.* Irwin-Dorsey, Homewood, IL. 1962.

From an organizational perspective, these changes reduce "interpersonal competence" and cause decreases in effective decision making, increases in organizational defensiveness, and a greater degree of "department centeredness and organizational rigidity." Overall, the result is lowered organizational effectiveness.

Argyris claims that an *additional* set of values is needed as an available alternative to the pyramidal values. He describes three specifically:

1. The important human relationships are not only those related to achieving the organization's objectives but those related to maintaining the organization's internal system and adapting to the environment, as well.

2. Human relationships increase in effectiveness as *all* the relevant behavior (rational and interpersonal) become conscious, discussable and controllable.

3. In addition to direction, controls, and rewards and penalties, human relationships are most effectively influenced through authentic relationships, internal commitment, psychological success (the experience of realistically challenging situations that tax one's capacities) and the process of confirmation (interpersonal experiences which validate one's view of the world as substantially accurate.)[19]

In order to introduce organization members to these alternative values, a process of reeducation is required. A principal instrument in that process is the T group.

T groups: What they are and how they work

It is not uncommon for a "trainer" to begin the first meeting of a T group by saying something like the following:

Hello. My name is _____. This group will meet several times over the next few days. Our purpose in meeting is to learn something about ourselves—how we affect others, how they affect us—*and* something about groups and their dynamics.

In my experience, one of the useful ways of learning about these things is for us to observe ourselves as we interact and work together. We have no agenda and I am not a leader in the traditional sense. I will not call on people or select topics for us to discuss. But I will try to use my skills to facilitate our learning about the group and each of our roles in it.

At the moment, as I observe where we are in this process, I think the problem we are facing is how to begin. . . .

Learning in a T group occurs as a consequence of doing (by participants and staff) and reflecting (by the participant, guided by the "trainer"). It is contrary to the traditional way of learning that occurs in classrooms which involves telling (by an instructor) and listening (by the student). Implicit in T group learning is the assumption that "very little can be gained if someone tells us how we are *supposed* to feel, how we are *supposed* to behave, or what we are *supposed* to do with our lives. A parallel assumption is that a great deal can be gained if we understand *what* we're feeling, if we understand the kinds of interpersonal events that trigger various kinds of feelings, if we understand how our behavior is read and understood by other people, and if we understand the wide variety of options available to us."[20]

Generally speaking, from an organizational perspective, the aim of the T group experience is to enhance a person's skills as a member of social organizations. These skills are not meant to be used to manipulate others, but rather for the work and satisfaction of self and others when functioning in groups.

After reviewing a substantial portion of the literature on T groups through the mid-1960s, John P. Campbell and Marvin D. Dunnette published an article called, "Effectiveness of T group experiences in managerial training and development."[21] In it, they identify six aims of T groups which they believe are common to most discussions of the T group method.

1. Increased self-insight or self-awareness concerning one's behavior and its meaning in a social context.
2. Increased sensitivity to the behavior of others.
3. Increased awareness and understanding of the types of processes that facilitate or inhibit group functioning and the interactions between different groups. . . .
4. Heightened diagnostic skill in social, interpersonal, and intergroup situations.
5. Increased action skill. . . . a person's ability to intervene successfully in inter- or intragroup situations so as to increase member satisfactions, effectiveness, or output.
6. Learning how to learn. . . . ability to analyze continually his own interpersonal behavior for the purpose of helping himself and others achieve more effective and satisfying interpersonal relationships.[22]

Thus, most authorities agree that T group learning aims at producing the improved interpersonal competence and resulting organizational benefit which Argyris is seeking. Edgar Schein and Warren Bennis state the matter plainly when they say, "The point is that laboratory training [A generic term which refers to combinations of T group and other experienced-based learning activities] provides the instrument whereby the normative goals and improvements set forth by organization theorists and practitioners of organizations can be achieved."[23]

But do they work? Do T group methods achieve the aims which are set for them?

Outcomes of T group experiences.   In their wonderfully thorough review of the literature, Campbell and Dunnette conclude by lamenting "the small number of studies using well-researched attitude measures and/or situational measures as criteria. If such criteria were more widely used," they say, "one might have a clearer idea of exactly what kinds of attitudes and skills are fostered by laboratory education. As it is, no conclusions can be drawn." They reinforce this unhappy finding by saying, "To sum up, the assumption that T group training has positive utility for organizations must necessarily rest on shaky ground. It has been neither confirmed nor disconfirmed."[24]

A more positive note is struck by Elliot Aronson, one of America's leading experimental social psychologists. He says, "Most of the research done on T-groups lacks the control and precision of . . . laboratory experiments. . . . It remains difficult to be certain about what causes what. At the same time, after surveying the research literature, I am compelled to draw the conclusion, albeit tentatively, that important changes do take place in T-groups, and that these changes are demonstrable beyond the individual's self-report."[25]

As support for this assertion, Aronson cites evidence from studies which were more experimentally rigorous than most. These studies demonstrated that, as compared to members of control groups who had no T group experience, people who had the experience exhibited less ethnic prejudice,[26] greater hypnotizability, (and therefore were presumably less suspicious and more trusting),[27] and an increased capacity for emphatically predicting other group members' preferences.[28]

These studies may provide impressive testimony about short-term individual change, but they say little about either long-term effects on individuals or organizational benefits that accrue as a result of T group experiences. In this regard, Argyris' findings in one study which he reported in a *Harvard Business Review* article seem typical. Argyris compared the values of 11 executives before and after their participation in a T group and other human-relations oriented, experienced-based learning activities. He reports finding a "significant shift on the part of the experimental group toward a set of values that encouraged the executives to handle feelings and emotions, deal with problems of group maintenance, and develop greater feelings of responsibility on the part of their subordinates for the effectiveness of the organization." But the effect fades out after 10 months. Argyris comments, "This was studied and data were obtained to suggest that the executives had not lost their capacity to behave in a more open and trustful manner, but they had to suppress some of this learning because the corporate president and the other divisional presidents, who were not participants in the laboratory [That is, the T group and related activities], did not understand them."[29] In another study concluded some years later, Argyris claims that the changes do not fade out altogether.[30] Rather, executives exhibit the new behaviors selectively, in settings in which they believe approval, support, and understanding is forthcoming.

It is doubtful that Argyris was surprised by this fade-out effect. It was illustrated years earlier in one of the first studies of the effects of human-relations training on supervisory behavior.[31] Immediately after the training, supervisors were showing subordinates more consideration, just as they had learned to do. Six months later, however, there was a fade out. The supervisors were behaving just as they had been before the training experience. The reason for the fade out was akin to the one which caused it to occur in Argyris' executives; these supervisors' superiors were not rewarding them for the new behaviors.

In one sense, attempts to use T groups in this fashion represent a misunderstanding of Lewin's idea. Individual change may occur during training sessions because people are involved with new group norms and standards. But when they return to their organizations, old norms and standards still prevail and, quite predictably, these forces exert irresistible pressure to return to the old ways.

Argyris recognizes this problem: Change, he says, will be neither effective nor permanent *until the total organization accepts the new values.*[32] In *The Social Psychology of Organizations,* Katz and Kahn arrive at similar conclusions. After examining T groups and other forms of training, they point out that these efforts implicitly accept a chain of "discouraging" assumptions which they describe in the following way: Some new knowledge or insight can be offered to an individual; these ideas will alter motivation and behavior; these alterations will persist when the individual return to the organization and they will be adapted to that setting; co-workers will be persuaded to accept these changes and will themselves make complementary changes. Sounding frustrated, Katz and Kahn comment that, despite the many weak links in this chain of assumptions, "we persist in attempting to change organizations by working on individuals without redefining their roles in the system, without changing the sanctions of the system, and without changing the expectations of other role incumbents in the organization about appropriate role behavior."[33]

Seeing the same issues but using different phrasing, Hornstein et al.[34] discuss four problems of individually oriented strategies of managing change which assume that the regulators of organization behavior are internal.

1. *The problem of individual versus organizational functioning.* Personal learning and growth may be a commendable and regular outcome of T group experiences, but there is no clear evidence that these kinds of changes produce organizational benefits.
2. *The transfer-of-training problem.* Experiences in T groups occur away from the organization, therefore people may *undergeneralize* the learning and not apply it in their organization, or they may *overgeneralize* it and apply it indiscriminately.
3. *The critical-mass problem.* If the primary means of changing the organization involves changing aspects of individuals, then what aspects must be changed? How many people need to be involved before organizational change occurs? Which people need to be involved?
4. *The social-influence problem.* Organizational social norms remain unchanged. Consequently, new behaviors are not supported when people return from the T group experience.

These comments by Katz and Kahn, Argyris, and Hornstein identify other organization changes which might accompany individually oriented training if it is to succeed. Changes in organization rewards and incentives, structure, (e.g., the organization of tasks, reporting relationships, and job designs for individuals and groups), and social norms must be considered as important adjuncts. The first of these (i.e., rewards and incentives) is a particular concern of another individually oriented approach, behavior modification. In contrast to the T group approach that was just considered, however, behavior modification assumes the regulators of organizational behavior are external.

The use of behavior modification in organizations

If you need to, review that part of the chapter on motivation in which reinforcement theory was discussed. This theory is the foundation of organization programs of behavior modification. The theory's central premise is appealingly simple: Behavior is controlled by its consequences. If you want a behavior to recur, then reward it. If you prefer it to be discontinued, then do not reward it. (Remember, punishing unwanted behavior by using "negative reinforcers" may have undesirable by-products and is not generally encouraged.) Praise, promotion, pay, and perks of any kind are all possible reinforcers. If a person desires some outcome and values receiving it, then it is a reward, a positive reinforcer.

Organizations that elect to manage change by introducing programs of behavior modification have a number of reinforcers at their disposal. One user of such programs at the Questor Corporation, M. W. Warren, identified five categories of reinforcers: (1) money (if it is clearly and specifically tied to performance); (2) praise and other forms of positive verbal recognition; (3) greater autonomy in organizing one's activity; (4) enhanced opportunity to see one's progress in performance, status, and value as a co-worker; and (5) power to influence others.[35] Dozens of other examples of on-the-job reinforcers are presented in a comprehensive, yet readable book on this approach titled, *Organizational Behavior Modification* by Fred Luthans and Robert Kreitner.[36] They mention "consumables" such as coffee break treats, lunches, Easter hams, Christmas turkeys, and beer parties; "manipulatables" such as desk accessories, watches, company cars, home-shop tools, and club privileges; "visual and auditory rewards" such as offices with windows, redecoration, private offices, popular speakers, and feedback about performance; "tokens" such as money, stocks, stock options, movie passes, and profit sharing. In addition to all these, which they call contrived rewards, they identify a number of natural rewards. These occur during the normal course of organization life and ordinarily will not involve additional cost. Examples include friendly greetings, informal recognition, solicitation of suggestions/advice, smiles, job rotation, extended breaks, and personal time off with pay.

Many companies have introduced programs of behavior modification, including Addressograph–Multi-graph, Allis-Chalmers, American Can, Bethlehem Steel, Chase Manhattan Bank, Ford Motor Company, IBM, Michigan Bell Telephone, Procter & Gamble, Standard Oil of Ohio, United Air Lines, Upjohn, Warner-Lambert, and Westinghouse.[37] One of the first to do so was the Emery Air Freight Company. Given a reported savings of over $2 million during a three-year period, the company's experience with this approach to managing organization change has become a classic case for managers and scholars.[38]

A former vice president at Emery, E. J. Feeny, has identified four steps which can act as a guide to management development of these efforts.[39] First, he says, it is essential to identify important indicators of performance and express them in behavioral terms. The key word here, and one which deserves to be italized, is *behavioral*. Subjective assessments of an employee's "vibes" simply will not do. Successful introduction of a behavior-modification program requires a manager to define concrete, observable behaviors that are related to job performance, and then assess current performance in terms of each of these critical behaviors. This process is called a "performance audit." Some claim that the audit motivates employees to work with the change program because it provides a clear picture of current performance. Further, it provides a point of comparison for judging future performance. Managers may be aided in completing this audit if they ask themselves four questions: (1) Can the behavior in question be reduced to *observable* behavioral events? (2) Can I *count* how often each behavioral event occurs? (3) *Exactly* what must the person do before I record a response? (4) Is this a key *performance-related* behavioral event?[40]

As a second step, Feeny suggests developing performance goals for each employee. As before, these must be expressed in specific, objectively measurable terms.[41] In practice, the method for selecting these goals varies. Managers have done it both by themselves and with employee participation. Some have used MBO as a framework, while others have been more eclectic in their effort. From the viewpoint of behavior modification, it is essential that the goals are expressed in clear, behavioral terms. From the perspective of other issues that we have examined in this book, however, it is clear that the process used to set goals is critical and will affect and be affected by human forces in a myriad of ways.

Feeny's suggestion for step three in these organization-change efforts is to provide employees with a means for tracking their own performance. This opportunity for continuous self-assessment provides feedback, an opportunity for corrective behavior when performance falls short of goals, and self-congratulation (intrinsic positive reinforcement) when it reaches them. Self-feedback of this sort is not an indispensible component of these efforts, and many practitioners use it as only one of a number of possible interventions. In effect, after identifying performance-related behaviors and assessing current success, these practitioners begin a program of rewarding desirable behaviors using one or more of the dozen of rewards at their disposal, which is step four in Feeny's plan.

For step four, Feeny suggests that, after an appropriate interval of time has passed, superiors examine the performance records of their subordinates, offering praise (or any other positive reinforcement) for successful performance, and withholding it for inadequate performance. Others have added to these four steps by reminding us that an appropriate conclusion to the program is a follow-up in which managers assess performance-related behaviors in order to see whether any improvement has occurred.

So what is new, you say. Why all the rumpus when all that is being said is reward people when they do well and withhold reward when they do not? Well, nothing is new, really. The principle is age old, even if modern behavioral science has provided some nonobvious refinement, e.g., behavior acquired under a schedule of partial reinforcement is more resistant to change than one acquired under a schedule of continuous reinforcement. What is beneficial about these programs, however, is that they encourage a systematic application of very commonplace ideas. Despite the reasonableness of these ideas and their intuitive appeal, managers often fail to employ them.[42] Indeed, there are undoubtedly times when undesirable behavior is inadvertantly reinforced. By requiring a performance audit and by clearly attaching rewards to certain behaviors, some of these problems may be avoided.

After surveying some of the companies mentioned earlier, a review of the results of their behavior modification programs was published in the Spring 1976 issue of *Organization Dynamics*.[43] It was very encouraging. Among the benefits claimed were cost efficiency, improved safety, reductions in absenteeism and lateness, gains in productivity, and increased job satisfaction. Nonetheless, introducing and maintaining these programs is not without problems.

1. Questions have been raised about the durability of reinforcers. People's view of what is reinforcing varies. Over time, the "dose" of a positive reinforcer that is required in order for it to be reinforcing may have to be increased beyond reasonable limits. Even worse, repeated exposure to some reinforcers may render them trivial and without any capacity to act as a reinforcer.

2. Not all jobs in all industries allow performance to be meaning-

fully expressed in simple, discrete behavioral terms. Such efforts may be suitable for tasks that are regular and concrete, but less so for those which require varied, fluid, creative problem solving.

3. Even when it is possible to identify critical behaviors, it may not be possible to establish the practice of providing contingent reinforcement. Company politics, union practices, and the personal skills of managers may all interfere with such an effort. Opposition to programs of organizational behavior modification may even occur because they are seen as violations of ethical and moral standards. Debates regularly rage over whether these efforts manipulate people, robbing them of freedom and dignity, as control over their behavior is placed in the hands of a small group of people.

4. Even when the behavior can be identified and the contingencies established, success may prove elusive. Organizations are complex, providing each employee with multiple, often clandestine responses to performance. Other reinforcers and pressures more powerful than the program's may operate to counteract the planned change effort. These countervailing forces frequently emanate from broader organizational sources, such as structure and social norms. These potential regulators of organizational behavior, which are largely neglected by the individually oriented approaches, are the principal concern of the two approaches to organization change that are discussed in the next chapter.

Notes

1. See Katz, D., & Kahn, R. L. *The social psychology of organizations.* New York: John Wiley & Sons, 1966; Hornstein, H. A., Benedict, B. A., Burke, W. W., Gindes, M., & Lewicki, R. J. *Social intervention.* New York: Free Press, 1971, Pt. 1.

2. Katz & Kahn, *Social psychology of organizations,* chap. 13.

3. Ibid.; Schein, E. H., & Bennis, W. G., *Personal and organizational change through group methods: The laboratory approach.* New York: John Wiley & Sons, 1965.

4. Lewin, K. Group decision and social change. In G. E. Swanson, T. M. Newcomb, & E. L. Hartley (Eds.), *Readings in social psychology* (Rev. ed.). New York: Holt, Rinehart & Winston, 1952, pp. 459–473.

5. Radke, M., & Klisurich, D. Experiments in changing good habits. *Journal of the American Dietetic Association,* 1947, *23,* 403–409.

6. Bond, B. The group-discussion-decision approach: An appraisal of its use in health education. *Dissertation Abstracts,* 1956, *16,* 903–904.

7. Levine, J., & Butler, J. Lecture vs. group decision in changing behavior. *Journal of Applied Psychology*, 1952, *36*, 29–33.

8. Lewin, K. Frontiers in group dynamics. *Human Relations*, 1947, *1*, 5–41.

9. Schein, E. H. The Chinese indoctrination program for prisoners of war. *Psychiatry*, 1956, *19*, 149–172.

10. Lewin, K. Group decision and social change. In E. R. Maccoby, T. M. Newcomb, and E. L. Hartley (Eds.), *Readings in Social Psychology*. New York: Holt, Rinehart & Winston, 1958, p. 210.

11. Katz & Kahn, *Social psychology of organizations*, p. 402.

12. Marrow, A. *The practical theorist*. New York: Basic Books, 1969.

13. Ibid.; Bradford, L., Bennis, K., & Gibb, J. (Eds.). *T-group theory and laboratory method: Innovation in re-education*. New York: John Wiley & Sons, 1964; Back, K. *Beyond words*. New York: Russell Sage Foundation, 1972.

14. Bradford, et al., *T-groups theory and laboratory method*; Schein & Bennis, *Personal and organizational change*; Rogers, C. *Carl Rogers on encounter groups*. New York: Harper & Row, 1970.

15. Blake, R. R., & Mouton, J. S. *The managerial grid*. Houston, Tex.: Gulf Publishing, 1964.

16. Argyris, C. T-groups for organizational effectiveness. *Harvard Business Review*, 1964, *42*,(2), 60–74; Argyris, C. *Interpersonal competence and organization effectiveness*. Homewood, Ill.: Richard D. Irwin, 1962.

17. Weber, M. [*The theory of social and economic organization*] (A. M. Henderson & T. Parsons, trans.). New York: Free Press, 1947, p. 337.

18. Argyris, T-groups for organizational effectiveness.

19. Ibid., p. 62.

20. Aronson, E. *The social animal*. San Francisco: W. H. Freeman, 1972, p. 240.

21. Campbell, J. P., & Dunnette, M. D. Effectiveness of T-group experiences in managerial training and development. *Psychological Bulletin*, 1961, *70*, 73–108.

22. Ibid., p. 74–75.

23. Schein & Bennis, *Personal and organizational change*, p. 204.

24. Campbell & Dunnette, Effectiveness of T-group experiences, p. 106.

25. Aronson, *Social animal*, pp. 260–261.

26. Robin, J. The reduction of prejudice through laboratory training. *Journal of Applied Behavioral Science*, 1967, *3*, 29–50.

27. Tart, C. Increases in hypnotizability resulting from a prolonged program for enhancing personal growth. *Journal of Abnormal Psychology*, 1970, *75*, 260–266.

28. Dunnette, M. People feeling: Joy, more joy and the "Slough of Despond." *Journal of Applied Behavioral Sciences*, 1969, *5*, 25–44.

29. Argyris, T-groups for organizational effectiveness, p. 73.

30. Ibid.

31. Fleishman, E. A., Harris, E. H., & Burtt, H. E. Leadership and supervision in industry. *Ohio State Business Educational Research Monograph*, 1955, No. 33.

32. Argyris, C. *Integrating the individual and the organization*, New York: John Wiley & Sons, 1964.

33. Katz & Kahn, *Social psychology of organizations*, p. 391.

34. Hornstein et al., *Social intervention*.

35. Warren, M. W. Performance management: A substitute for supervision. *Management Review*, October 1972, pp. 28–42.

36. Luthans, F., & Kreitner, R. *Organizational behavior modification*. Glenview, Ill.: Scott, Foresman, 1975.

37. Hamner, W. C., & Organ, D. W. *Organizational behavior: An applied psychological approach.* Plano, Tex.: Business Publications, 1978; At Emery Air Freight: Positive reinforcement boosts performance. *Organizational Dynanics*, Winter 1973, pp. 41-50.
38. Performance audit, feedback, and positive reinforcement. *Training and Development Journal*, November 1972, pp. 8-13.
39. Hamner & Organ, *Organizational behavior;* Where Skinner's theories work. *Business Week*, 2 December 1972, pp. 64-65; Whyte, W. F. Skinnerian theory in organizations. *Psychology Today*, April 1972, pp. 67-68.
40. Luthans & Kreitner, *Organizational behavior modification*, p. 71.
41. Sorcher, M., & Goldstein, A. P. A behavioral modeling approach in training. *Personnel Administration*, March-April 1972, 35-41.
42. Skinner, B. F. Conversation with B. F. Skinner. *Organizational Dynamics*, Winter 1973, pp. 31-40; The power of praise. *International Management*, October 1973, pp. 32-35.
43. Hamner, W. C., & Hamner, E. P. Behavior modification on the bottom line. *Organizational Dynamics*, Spring 1976, pp. 2-21.

Managing Change:
Systems-Oriented
Approaches

CHAPTER 2 of this book reported on the effect of different communication networks on individual behavior and feelings. Chapter 3 discussed some effects of a person's function and status in an organization on his/her perception of events and people. Chapters 7 and 8 considered some of the ways in which group process and structure affected individual problem-solving efforts. And Chapter 11, the last chapter, examined Kurt Lewin's observations concerning group norms and how they are capable of affecting individual reasoning, beliefs, feelings, attitudes, perceptions, and behavior. The principle that can be drawn from these discussions is straightforward. Organizations, like any social system, create a psychological environment which greatly affects individual functioning. *Conclusion:* If you want to change individual functioning in organizations, then begin by changing those parts of the organizational environment that are regulating individual functioning. This conclusion shifts the emphasis in managing change from individuals as the primary target, to systems.

Two systems-oriented strategies of managing change are considered in this chapter. Both attempt to produce changes in individual functioning, but the first, called the sociotechnical approach, attempts to do so by changing structure, an external regulator of organizational behavior, while the second, the organization-development approach, attempts it by changing social norms, an internal regulator of organization behavior.

Sociotechnical approaches to managing change

The concept of a sociotechnical system arose from the consideration that any production system requires both a technological organization—equipment and process layout—and a work organization. . . . The technological demands place limits on the type of work organization possible, but a work organization has social and psychological properties of its own that are independent of technology.[1]

Implicit in this approach to organization change is a recognition that the technology and physical environment of work sites constrain the form that a work organization may take, but they do not fully determine its shape. That idea is a critical one for managers to understand. It means that options exist. Different work organizations can be created to fit the same set of technical/environmental constraints but, according to the sociotechnical approaches, caution must be exercised in choosing among them. These alternatives possess different social psychological properties, and these properties are *not equal* in their ability to produce employee gratification or encourage productivity. Six structural characteristics have been identified as common to work organizations which produce social psychological properties that are conducive to improved performance.[2]

1. Work is organized so that it forms a psychological whole, allowing workers to experience a *sense of completion* when their work is done. The task may not be completed from an organizational perspective. More work may be required until the product is marketable. But, from an individual's perspective, some meaningful plateau in work has been reached and a psychologically completed unit exists.[3]
2. The work organization provides reasonable measures of au-

tonomy and freedom, thereby avoiding the adverse reaction which ordinarily accompanies the perception that one's activities are being excessively controlled by other people.[4]

3. Work is organized in order to create *cooperative* rather than competitive relationships among co-workers.[5]

4. Since wide differences in the skills of co-workers lessens the likelihood of cohesiveness and communication, work is organized in a manner that allows all members of the same work group to comprehend and aspire to the *narrow range of skills represented.*[6]

5. Similarly, since wide differences in prestige and status also adversely affect cohesiveness and communications as well as internal leadership, a *narrow range of prestige and status differences* is preferred.

6. Work-group boundaries are flexible, so that members of work groups who are not pleased with their group are able to freely move to another one.

In the interest of fairness, it is essential to acknowledge that many individually oriented approaches accept the importance of structural changes as an accompaniment to their efforts. Some, in fact, have even advocated structural changes which closely conform to these six characteristics. Argyris, for example, a clear enthusiast of the individually oriented approach, discusses these issues with creative consideration in his book, *Integrating the Individual and the Organization.*[7]

Argyris's organization of the future will tend to require individuals with somewhat different needs, values, or predispositions, than are customary. He identifies these as people who value psychological success, self-esteem, self-responsibility, and internal commitment. The organization of the future, he adds, will "strive to enlarge jobs." This will go beyond "doing" and "motor abilities" to include intellectual and interpersonal skills and responsibilities for "larger and larger meaningful segments of the product and its quality." The pyramidal structure will "exist side by side with several other structures," each serving predefined purposes. Similarly, leadership will also be expanded and "a set of decision rules to guide the participants in when and how to use each leadership style" will exist. Finally, controls, rewards, and penalties will be transformed from unilateral monitoring and disciplinary devices into feedback systems that aid individual learning and development.[8]

Argyris' ideas still await a test, but one of the first and most dramatic applications of the ideas underlying sociotechnical approaches to changing organizations was carried out by Eric Trist and Kenneth Bamforth nearly 40 years ago in the British coal-mining industry.[9] Just before their critical work occurred, mining coal involved extracting it from the coal face, loading and moving it, and preparing the mine shaft for additional exploration by providing roof supports and moving the conveyer forward into the mine. These operations were executed by a group that worked autonomously. Members of the group were self-selected and each one had the skills necessary for all phases of the operation. Pay was based on the group's productivity.

After the development of a new piece of technology—the face conveyer—this method of mining changed. It was replaced by a procedure called the "long-wall method." Jobs were reorganized and the autonomous work groups disbanded. In the new division of labor, each worker was limited to a single task—some cut the coal face, others loaded the coal for transport, and still others advanced the mine shaft.

Any speculation about the success of this change using the most traditional models of organizations leads to a prediction of greater efficiency. Each worker was given a single, narrowly defined task. Such a work organization facilitates training, supervision, and distribution of rewards because each person's responsibility is unvarying and comparatively simple.

Of course, the sociotechnical approach would predict a more negative outcome for the long-wall method—it violated most of the six essential characteristics of successful sociotechnical systems. The change did, in fact, fail. Miners resented the new jobs. They felt that the separate tasks were too simple and mastery of all of them could easily be attained. Therefore, differences in prestige and pay based on task specialization seemed artificial and unfair. Moreover, since pay was tied to task, not production, pay rates suddenly became a cause célebrè involving extensive negotiation and competition between groups.

Trist and Bamforth developed plans to replace the long-wall method by reorganizing the miners once again into self-selected, autonomous groups. These groups were larger than before, but in principle were structured in the same way. The plans, which were eventually adopted, also tied pay to performance.

The new system operated at 95 percent of potential, whereas the previous one was operating at only 78 percent of potential. Moreover, this increase in productivity occurred without the added cost of supervisors, an expense which was essential with the long-wall method.

Similar results were obtained by A. K. Rice in 1955, when he worked with two textile mills located in Ahmedabad, India.[10] Here, the management had introduced automatic looms but were disappointed by the absence of any improvement in productivity. The work organization that management created in an effort to keep the 224 looms in continuous operation consisted of 29 people holding 12 different specialized jobs. But the interrelationships among these workers and their responsibilities for the looms were confused. After examining the problem, Rice proposed that a small group of workers take responsibility for a single group of looms, sharing previously separate jobs and responding to an overall leader.

The plan was accepted, four groups were formed, and overall success was amazing. After two years, productivity was 95 percent of potential, as compared to only 80 percent before Rice's reorganization. Quality of production also rose, reducing the amount of damaged cloth to about half of what it had been previously. Finally, prior to the reorganization, a third work shift was regarded as impossible to initiate. After the reorganization, a third shift was introduced without difficulty.

The work of Trist and Bamforth and Rice represents a school of thought developed at the Tavistock Institute in England. It reflects a commitment to changing the design of work organization as a means of managing the human forces of organization life. In the coal mines of England and in the textile mills of Ahmedabad, India, Trist and Bamforth and Rice created autonomous work groups in which members shared a common group of skills and were paid through a scheme that stimulated cooperative ties. Tasks for these groups were organized so that they formed a psychological whole. Similar efforts have been made in Procter & Gamble, Volvo,[11] and in a pet-food plant in Topeka.[12] Through changes like these, work organizations are redesigned in accordance with the six structural characteristics that sociotechnical approaches have argued are conducive to improved performance. The success of such restructuring effort is testimony to the validity of the ideas guiding them, but it can also be misleading. Other evidence demonstrates that this form of work organization is not desirable in all circumstances and can even be dysfunctional in some.

Charles Perrow, a sociologist, has developed a simple scheme which can be used to illustrate which organizational circumstances determine when this kind of design for work is desirable and when it is not.[13] The scheme (Table 12-1) has two components. One is concerned with a task's predictability—some tasks are routine and predictable, very few exceptions occur. Consequently, operational plans are hardly ever disrupted and need revision only infrequently. Well-established assembly-line operations are an example; so are routine paper-shuffling procedures. For other tasks, however, exceptions are almost the rule. They occur all of the time, requiring frequent revisions of plans. R&D groups in most organizations, some units within hospitals and educational settings, and design groups in aerospace or any industry on the edge of knowledge breakthroughs face this situation regularly.

Table 12-1

		Exceptions	
		Few	Many
Difficulty of handling exceptions	Easy		
	Difficult		

Source: Adapted from Perrow, C. A framework for comparative analysis of organizations. *American Sociological Review*, 1967, *32*, 194-208.

The scheme's second component is concerned with the ease with which exceptions can be managed when they arise. In some operations, methods for handling the exceptions are reasonably well understood. They are simply lying on the shelf, waiting to be used. In others, exceptions to routine present more of a problem. The problems are difficult to analyze and the solutions are harder to develop.

A traditional organization of work units seems to be perfectly adequate when there are few exceptions and comparatively easy-to-solve, analyzable problems. Under these circumstances, the exceptions can be managed by preset standard operating procedures, advance planning, or referral upward in the hierarchy because the exceptions are familiar and few enough to be handled at senior levels. But, when both the number of exceptions and the difficulty of solving them increase, then a more flexible system, of the sort Trist and Bamforth and Rice created, seems advisable. Thus, the most desirable organization for work units is not fixed. It is contingent on the character of task demands confronting the group.

Others have arrived at similar conclusions. After examining the operation of a number of decision groups in manufacturing and R&D organizations, Robert B. Duncan claimed that highly structured work organizations (i.e., ones with rigid hierarchies of authority, impersonality in decision making, little participation in decision making, a dependence on static rules and procedures, and inflexible divisions of labor) predictably restrict communication and information flow. Nonetheless, this form of organization may actually be preferred when (1) an urgent need to make decisions exists, (2) decisions are routine, (3) solutions to problems are routine and clear to everyone, (4) the environment is static and uniform.[14]

From a broader perspective, interunit organization of work units (groups, departments, divisions) also illustrates the operation of the same contingency principle. An early example of this is contained in a study of the Scottish electronics industry.[15] T. Burns and G. M. Stalker illustrated how *mechanistic* organizations operate best in stable environments—i.e., those which are slow to change and are therefore highly predictable—whereas what they call *organic* organizations function best in unstable environments.

The distinctions which they draw between mechanistic and organic organizations are familiar, but worth repeating:

		Mechanistic		*Organic*
Tasks	1.	divided into very specialized units	1.	divided into larger entities which bear a clear relation to final product
	2.	rigidly defined, inflexible boundaries	2.	in flux, being redefined and readjusted as demands shift
Responsibility and authority	3.	narrowly defined, tied closely to functional roles, rules, and procedures	3.	broadly defined, loosely tied to roles, rules, and procedures
Rewards and punishment	4.	strict hierarchy of control	4.	less strict hierarchy of control—sanctions more internal and from peers
	5.	individual sense of importance and prestige derives from identification with organization	5.	individual sense of importance and prestige derives from affiliations and own skills
Leadership	6.	leader is total authority	6-7.	authority rests with knowledge, not role
	7.	power vested in role		
	8.	loyalty to leader highly valued	8.	commitment to task is highly valued
Communication	9.	vertical, from superiors to subordinates in form of decisions and commands	9.	lateral, two-way, across ranks in the form of consultation

Several years after Burns and Stalker published their findings, Paul Lawrence and Jay Lorsch arrived at conclusions which have similar implications.[16] They studied six organizations operating in a common industrial environment. Not surprisingly, they found that the structure of the sales, research, and production groups in these organizations varied. Production was the most structured, followed by sales and then research. Why should this have occurred if they were all in the same "business"? Because, in one sense, they were *not* in the same business. They faced different sets of demands, and, for that reason, success required appropriately varied responses.

One of the most comprehensive and well-conceived expositions in this tradition is by Jay Galbraith. Galbraith, formerly a professor at Wharton, presented these ideas in his book, *Organization Design*.[17] As the title implies, Galbraith's principal focus is on the design of work organizations but, unlike some sociotechnical analysts, he deemphasizes the relationship between design and social psychological properties and concentrates on the effects that design has on organizational information-processing capacities.

At the center of Galbraith's analysis of alternative organization designs is the problem of task uncertainty, which he defines as *"the difference between the amount of information required to perform the task and the amount already possessed by the organization."*[18] Task uncertainty increases as (1) goal diversity grows, (2) division of labor becomes more specialized, and (3) minimal level of performance needed for success is high.

Galbraith says, *"The greater the task uncertainty, the greater the amount of information that must be processed among decision makers during task execution in order to achieve a given level of performance. The basic effect of uncertainty is to limit the ability of the organization to preplan or make decisions about activities in advance of their execution."* On the basis of these ideas, Galbraith concludes that differences in organization design really reflect organizations' varied efforts to either "(1) increase their ability to preplan, (2) increase their flexibility to adapt to their inability to preplan, or (3) decrease the level of performance required for continued viability."[19]

Galbraith reasons that, as task uncertainty increases, the information-processing potential of the mechanistic model will inevitably be exhausted. This is guaranteed by inherent features of the mechanistic model. First, the *hierarchy* acts as a conduit, reducing the number of channels through which information flows. That benefits the organization until the flow becomes so great that people at the top are overloaded. Second, *standard operating procedures and plans* prescribe behavior in advance of events. That also provides an organization with temporary benefit by eliminating the need for information processing and decision making. This only works, however, when exceptions are few and events are routine, allowing advance prediction of their occurrence. As organizations grow in size and diversity, as specialization and interdependence of subparts increase, exceptions occur more frequently and uncertainty mounts. Information-processing needs flood the restricted, brittle structure of mechanistically designed organizations. Survival demands new ways of organizing. Five alternative designs are discussed by Galbraith.

Designs which reduce the need for information processing

Environmental management.   All organizations have transactions with their environment. For some, this means that a larger number of exceptions, and therefore uncertainty, are caused by circumstances which lie outside organizational boundaries. Fluctuations in government regulations, the activities of clients and vendors, labor and financial markets, and raw material sources may ruin forecasts and disrupt standard operating procedures, forcing decisions to be moved upward in the hierarchy. In an effort to stem the flood which may develop, organizations may attempt to influence the environment. The aim is to produce less variable, more positive responses to organization interests. Examples include attempts to eliminate competition for such things as clients, labor, and vendors; produce a favorable image through public relations; and voluntary compliance with interest-group demands as a means of avoiding their uncontrollable escalation and worse losses of autonomy. Implicit cooperation with other firms, contractual agreements to regulate behavior, and cooptation of critical individuals and groups in order to create a sympathy and stability in the environment are also examples of environmental management.

Creation of slack resources.   As organizations grow larger and more complex, uncertainties may arise because the organization lacks information which is necessary to set priorities and coordi-

nate efforts of interdependent individuals and groups. If the costs
for doing so can be tolerated, then it may be sensible to respond
by "increasing the resources available rather than utilizing existing resources more efficiently." This "creates additional resources
by reducing performance standards. These additional resources
are called slack resources. The slack process takes the form of
additional time that the customer must wait, in-process inventory,
underutilized man-hours and machine time, higher costs, etc."[20]

Creation of self-contained tasks.   An alternative response to
the uncertainty which arises because organizations grow larger
and more complex is to reduce interdependence between functional units by giving them independence and autonomy. Trist
and Bamforth did this, so did Rice. The strategy involves redesign
of tasks so that each work group (department or division) *(a)* assumes responsibility for some designated product, and *(b)* is composed so that it contains all the skills necessary to complete production. In this way, (1) "the output diversity faced by a simple
collection of resources is reduced," (2) there is a "reduction in the
division of labor and therefore fewer distinctly different resources
when work needs to be coordinated and scheduled;" and (3) "the
point of decision is moved closer to the sources of information."[21]
The most immediately obvious cost of this approach is that organizations may lose economies of scale because use of resources is
duplicated by separate units.

Designs which increase the capacity for information processing

Investment in vertical information systems.   Sometimes it is
possible to develop mechanisms which allow an organization to
increase its capacity to use information which is acquired during
task performance in order to redirect efforts. This strategy assumes that (1) someone knows which information is critical for
making decisions which will modify or completely revise a plan;
(2) information can be put into a form which makes its processing
possible; and (3) people will abide by decisions which may be
impersonally and even machine generated. In discussing this
strategy, Galbraith offers a caveat, "Providing more information
more often may simply overload the decision maker. Investment
may be required to increase the capacity of the decision maker by

employing computers, various man-machine combinations, assistants. . . . The cost of this strategy is the cost of the information-processing resources."[22]

Creation of lateral relations.   This strategy protects the upper hierarchy from overloading by moving decision making about exceptions down to local levels where the information exists. In effect, managers who must deal with the consequences of changes wrought by exceptions work together to solve the problems they produce. Decision making is decentralized by providing greater discretion at lower levels in the organization. Lateral relations take different forms including:

1. *Direct contact* between managers involved in the problem.
2. *Liaison roles* to link departments.
3. *Task forces* to solve multidepartment problems.
4. *Permanent teams* for recurring interdepartmental problems.
5. *Integrating roles* to guide difficult lateral relations.
6. *Linking managerial roles* in situations characterized by substantial differentiation.
7. *Matrix design* to place dual authority over critical organizational contact points.

Clearly, this strategy places stress on the ability of people (sometimes in great numbers) to solve problems, build teams, manage conflict, and demonstrate, with some degree of excellence, interpersonal skills which facilitate small group work. In addition, it assumes that an organization is prepared to reward these efforts and supply managers with the freedom and information they need to form creative decisions.

Conclusion

Organization design is an expedient. Its value varies depending on surrounding circumstances. Each design has costs and benefits. Each is equipped to handle some problems and not others. Designs should change as demands vary. But they don't! Burns and Stalker have commented on how organizations resist changing form even when circumstances demand it. Managers may honestly fail to see the need for change. Or they may see the need, but resist change nonetheless, because of vested interest or fear of the unknown. For these reasons, organizations stagnate, problems remain unremedied, and decay sets in.

Organization development (OD), a second systems-oriented approach to managing change in organizations, is especially concerned with resistance to change. Unlike the sociotechnical approaches, it assumes organizational behavior is internally regulated. As a consequence, OD focuses more on the *process* than on the substance of change. It is less of a commitment to a kind of solution than it is a group of approaches to identifying problems and selecting solutions. In terms of their content, OD efforts are hallmarked by variety. They employ both individually oriented and sociotechnical change technology. In fact, many OD practitioners accept the idea that both mechanistic and organic forms of organization design are useful—but *under different circumstances.* In their book, *Organization Development,* for example, French and Bell comment, "Paradoxically, however, while the thrust of an organization development effort is toward the organic mode, OD activities sometimes increase the mechanistic quality of some organization dimensions."[23] They offer an example of a work team which decides to place more reliance on a superior for coordination and control of routine tasks. "At the level of routine tasks, the team here decided to become more mechanistic." The critical issue is *how* these changes are decided upon and introduced.

Organization development approaches to managing change

The chapter titled "Managing Change: Individually Oriented Approaches" began by describing a consulting effort that failed. Its fate was sealed when the consultants neglected the maelstrom of human forces which were twisting and turning in the organization. Eighteen months after the first group of consultants left, a second group arrived. The solutions that their work eventually produced were quite similar to the first group's, but the process that they introduced to arrive at the solutions was quite different.

During their first meeting with the social service agency's managing director, the consultant group concluded that their next step would be to meet with a representative group of directors and department heads. When they met, this group listened to the managing director's view of the problem, claimed it was the first time they heard him speak of it (his perception was that it had been shared previously), and agreed to become a steering committee for working toward a solution.

Alternative approaches were discussed with the consultants and the group decided on an approach which involved interviewing the 16 directors of service agencies, the 6 department heads, and the managing director. The interview was designed by the consultants and revised by some members of the steering committee. It included questions about (1) job activities—actual and desired; (2) communication systems; (3) problem-solving and decision-making procedures, including actual and desired influence; (4) areas of cooperation and competition; (5) perceptions of leadership; and (6) views about redesigning structure.

Responses were summarized and organized into meaningful displays for feedback to the total group. This took place at the beginning of a two-day meeting and was followed by a series of large and small group meetings during which people identified problems, gathered data, and developed solutions. The solution that was eventually developed produced changes in structure, job assignment, and job definition, as well as in the rules and procedures for decision making. But, generally speaking, it was similar to the one that had been offered by the first group of consultants 18 months earlier, with one exception, on this occasion, members of the organization created it.

The process of this consultation, not the substance of its outcome, distinguishes it as an OD effort. By and large, modern OD approaches advocate that organizational units engage in a self-examination of the operating fit between external environment, task, structure, technology, and human forces.[24] Individually oriented and sociotechnical approaches are two potential forms of solution for organization problems which can be used in the context of an overall OD effort. But OD is less of a commitment to a kind of solution than it is a process of identifying problems and selecting solutions.

In the past two decades, examples of efforts like these have occurred in a number of the world's most successful organizations, including Union Carbide, Exxon, Hotel Corporation of America, NASA, Boise Cascade, Digital Equipment, Polaroid, Armour and Company, Texas Instruments, Citibank, Chase Manhattan, American Airlines, TRW Systems, General Electric, Imperial Chemical Industries, Procter & Gamble, J. Lyon and Company, and Shell Oil, as well as in a great number of smaller organizations, schools (especially medical colleges), and government agencies.

Definitions abound. Pundits and practitioners of OD have never arrived at a single definition of their approach. French and Bell claim that "Organization development is the name given to the emerging applied behavioral science discipline that seeks to improve organizations through planned, systematic, long-range efforts focused on the organization's culture and its human and social processes."[25] Then, forsaking the comparative brevity of this statement they say, "organization development is a long-range effort to improve an organization's problem-solving and renewal processes, particularly through a more effective and collaborative management of organization culture—with special emphasis on the culture of formal work teams—with the assistance of a change agent, or catalyst, and the use of the theory and technology of applied behavioral science, including action research."[26]

Other definitions of OD offered by Warner Burke and Harvey Hornstein and by Richard Beckhard echo ideas contained in French and Bell's. Burke and Hornstein, for example, define OD as "a process of planned change. It involves change of an organization's culture from one which avoids an examination of social processes . . . especially decision making, planning and communications, to one which institutionalizes and legitimates this examination."[27]

Beckhard's definition contains more operational information about implementing an OD effort than do any of the preceeding, but endorses the same concerns about the process of change. He says, "Organization development is an effort (1) *planned*, (2) *organizationwide* and, (3) *managed* from the *top*, to (4) increase *organization effectiveness* and *health* through (5) *planned interventions* in the organization's "processes," using *behavioral-science* knowledge."[28] When he expands upon the fifth component of this definition, Beckhard's commonality with French and Bell and Burke and Hornstein becomes clear:

> A strategy is developed of intervening or moving into the existing organization and helping it, in effect, 'stop the music,' examine its present ways of work, norms, and values, and look at alternative ways of working, or relating, or rewarding. . . . The interventions used draw on the knowledge and technology of the behavioral sciences about such processes as individual motivation, power, communication, perception, cultural norms, problem solving, goal setting, interpersonal relationships, intergroup relationships, and conflict management.[29]

All of these definitions are concerned with the process of change. And they all reflect the influence of Kurt Lewin's ideas about the power of groups to regulate individual member behavior: "If you want to change individual behavior you must change the group (organizational) norms which regulate the behavior." Organizations develop norms for how people are to be socialized and supervised, for conflict management, communication, problem solving, decision making, and discrimination. These norms exert an influence in every area of the *human-forces filter*. For this reason, the effective management of change in organizations requires a holistic approach in which managers are prepared to diagnose and intervene in the area of human forces as well as in the areas of task, technology, and structure.

Diagnosis and intervention.   Scrutiny of the principal explanations, expositions, and apologies of OD suggests an ideal. Like most such dreams, it is a useful target but one that is rarely, if ever, fully realized. In this case, the star that guides many OD efforts is a cyclical process which might be labeled a "holistic, action research" approach to management. As Figure 12-1 illustrates, the cycle has two phases and seven components.

Figure 12-1

| | *Diagnosis* | *Intervention* |

1. problem identification
    2. data gathering
        3. feedback of data
            4. discussion of data
                5. problem solving
                    6. action planning
                        7. implementation

              Follow-up

In never-ending iterations, the process begins with diagnosis of conditions in all organizational subsystems: (1) external environment, (2) task, (3) technology, (4) structure, and (5) human forces. Several critical components of the diagnostic process distinguish it from some more familiar forms of diagnosis (as, for example, in medicine), and, consequently, give special meaning to the character of intervention of OD work:

Relevant organization members collaborate in at least the first six steps, from problem identification through action planning.

By collecting data about human forces, the group is preparing to openly examine *how* it is functioning, its own process.

Perceptions, impressions, attitudes, and values are all essential sources of data.

Data are not used to evaluate individuals or groups, or to justify sanctions. They are used for diagnosis, problem solving, and action planning.

Mutually arrived at conclusions about the meaning of data become the basis for action. Power, tradition, and position are less potent.

Thus, in OD efforts, *collaboration* in the diagnostic and action-planning efforts becomes a basis for changing group norms, just as they did during World War II, when Kurt Lewin worked on changing the eating habits of American households.

The focus of intervention in OD work varies, but the process of intervention continues to reflect a commitment to this kind of collaboration. French and Bell identify 12 major families of OD intervention:

1. *Diagnostic:* to assess conditions within the organization.
2. *Team building:* to improve the functioning of work groups.
3. *Intergroup:* to improve the effectiveness of interunit (team, department, division) operations.
4. *Survey feedback:* a general classification of activities with use of the feedback of survey data as a basis for organizational problem solving.
5. *Education and training:* to improve the skill and knowledge of individuals, e.g., management education seminars.
6. *Technostructural:* a general classification of activities which use changes in structure or technology as a principal means of generating organization change. (Equivalent of sociotechnical in this book.)
7. *Process consultation:* a label coined by Edgar Schein to describe consultant activities aimed at helping groups to understand and change "process" events which are affecting their performance. Generally, the term is reserved for small group and one-to-one consulting activities.
8. *Grid organization development:* a six-phase approach developed by Robert R. Blake and Jane Mouton. Phase

I—starting at the top, for all organization members, special seminars which orient people to the approach and provide some feedback about leadership style; Phase II—starting at the top, team development for all groups; Phase III—intergroup meetings between units at important organizational interfaces; Phase IV—using guiding ideas developed by Blake and Mouton, the top team develops an ideal model of their organization; Phase V—temporary task forces form to implement the ideal model; Phase VI—assessment of change and follow-up.

9. *Third-party peacemaking:* to manage interpersonal conflict.
10. *Coaching and counseling:* to help individuals understand their own needs and behavior and their effects on work.
11. *Life and career planning:* to help individuals plan for the future.
12. *Planning and goal setting:* activities aimed at improving the part of the problem-solving cycle which is concerned with setting objectives.

OD's commitment to collaboration in diagnosis and intervention has prompted its adherents to contribute to the current "Quality control circle explosion." In his article of the same name in the April 1981, issue of the *Training and Development Journal*, Edwin Yager, commenting on this phenomenon, says, "No management process has so caught the fancy of so many organizations in such a short period of time as has the Quality Control (QC) Circle."[30]

QCs were introduced into Japan at the beginning of the American occupation after World War II. Their success is attested to by their numbers. In 1967, Yager tells us, some 72,000 circles were meeting in different organizations across the country. In the United States, their popularity has been equally notable. Although no numbers are available, QCs are reportedly a part of organization life at "Hughes Aircraft, 3M Co., General Motors Corp., Ford Motor Co., Westinghouse, General Electric, Bank of America, Memorex Corp., Foremost Foods, Crucible Steel, Hoover NSK, Eaton Corp., Polaroid Corp., Pentel of America, Verbatain, and perhaps a hundred other organizations."[31]

In practice, the form that these circles takes and their functioning vary. As a general rule, however, each circle is composed of employees with a common concern for some aspect of their organization's activity. This group meets periodically to identify, analyze, and solve work problems that are hindering the quality of organization performance. Placing an emphasis on data gathering and systematic problem solving, QCs try to generate solutions for management consideration. Yager comments, "The uniqueness of the Quality Circle lies in its emphasis on measurement and problem solving. Circles focus on measurement . . . how much, how often, how far, where, when, etc. They also focus on problem solving . . . why, what can be done, and similar questions. And Circles also focus on experimentation . . . what if this were skipped, ignored, done less often, done more often, etc. And they focus on evaluation. . . . What happened with each change, what was the result, what is the value."[32]

QCs are generally not intended to remove management prerogatives. Their aim is to enhance organizational problem solving by bringing together employees who have relevant information and are directly affected by the problem. This process undermines the anachronistic, organizationally dangerous illusion that "management must have all the answers." If management can provide a hospitable climate by listening to input from the circles, refraining from manipulating their functioning, accepting failures, explaining why some proposals are rejected, and supporting training of QC participants, then evidence suggests that QCs are able to produce financially valuable solutions to nagging organization problems. An additional benefit is the employee commitment that builds as a consequence of participating in these organizational problem-solving efforts.

It is evident that, in action, QCs manage human forces by embracing some important psychological principles that are also part of the practice of OD. Collaboration in diagnosis and action planning stimulates motivation and commitment. Resistance to change is lessened and cross-organizational bonds develop, providing a basis for future cooperation and conflict management. In effect, QC, as an organizational intervention, is consistent with others in the OD tool kit. Its apparent success suggests that it is a very important addition and one that can be used by individual managers and their subordinates, even when it is not employed on an organizationwide basis.

But no approach to managing organization change is without costs. OD efforts may lessen resistance to change and create in organization members a sense of ownership of solutions as well as a desire to work toward them, but they also have potential hazards. (1) Collaborative, open discussions about data and action plans inevitably produce discord. Can employees be certain that power and position will be sufficiently minimized so that individuals are not subsequently punished for their views? (2) Although OD efforts sometimes lead to a centralization of authority, there is no denying that the overall movement is toward power equalization. Before embarking on an OD approach, management must be very certain that this is a direction in which it wants to move. (3) Rising expectations about participation in decision making are a natural outgrowth of having opportunities to participate. Management must find ways to develop in employees realistic expectations about levels of participation in the future. (4) Special skills and an outsider's perspective are often needed for successful OD work. Yet this involves the risk of creating unreasonable dependency on people whose priorities may not be equivalent to management's. (5) Analysis and change of human forces is supposedly carried out in the service of work. Yet introspection of this sort if an engaging pursuit which continually involves the risk of being an end in itself, causing the maintenance of interpersonal relations to become an organization's principal goal. (6) OD efforts take time. Two questions confront management: Can we afford to take the time? Can we afford not to?

Notes

1. Rice, A. K. *Productivity and social organization: The Ahmedabad experiment.* London: Tavistock Publications, 1958, p. 4.
2. Katz, D., & Kahn, R. L. *The social psychology of organizations.* New York: John Wiley & Sons, 1966, pp. 433–435.
3. Zeigarnik, B. Das Behalten erledigter und unerledigter Handlungen, III. *Psychologische Forschung,* 1927, *9,* 1–85.
4. Brehm, J. W. *Responses to loss of freedom: A theory of psychological reactance.* Morristown, N.J.: General Learning Press, 1972.
5. Deutsch, M. *The resolution of conflict.* New Haven: Yale University Press, 1973.
6. Rice, *Productivity and social organization.*
7. Argyris, C. *Interpersonal competence and organization effectiveness.* Homewood, Ill.: Richard D. Irwin, 1962.
8. Ibid., Pt. III.
9. Trist, E. L., & Bamforth, K. W. Some social and psychological consequences of the long-wall method of coal-getting. *Human Relations,* 1957, *4,* 3–38.
10. Rice, *Productivity and social organization.*
11. Both are described by Walton, R. E. How to counter alienation in the plant. *Harvard Business Review,* 1972, *50,* 70–81.
12. Walton, R. E. Using social psychology to create a new plant culture. In M. Deutsch & H. A. Hornstein (Eds.), *Applying social psychology.* Hillsdale, N.J.: Lawrence Erlbaum Associates, 1975.
13. Perrow, C. A framework for comparative analysis of organizations. *American Sociological Review,* 1967, *32,* 194–208.
14. Duncan, R. B. Multiple decision making structures in adapting to environ-

mental uncertainty: The impact on organization effectiveness. *Human Relations*, 1973, *26*, 273-291.

15. Burns, T., & Stalker, G. M. *The impact of innovation*. London: Tavistock Publications, 1961.

16. Lawrence, P. R., & Lorsch, J. Differentiation and integration in complex organizations. *Administrative Science Quarterly*, 1967, *12*, 1-47.

17. Galbraith, J. R. *Organization design*. Reading, Mass.: Addison-Wesley, 1977.

18. Ibid., p. 36.

19. Ibid.

20. Ibid., p. 83.

21. Ibid., p. 85.

22. Ibid., p. 52.

23. French, W. L., & Bell, C. H., Jr. *Organization development*. Englewood Cliffs, N.J.: Prentice-Hall, 1973, p. 186.

24. Nadler, D. A., & Tushman, M. L. Systems, concepts and planned organization change. In N. M. Tichy (Ed.), *Organization diagnosis and improvement strategies*. La Jolla: Calif.: University Associates, 1980.

25. French & Bell, *Organization development*, p. xiv.

26. Ibid., p. 15.

27. Burke, W. W., & Hornstein, H. A. *The social technology of organization development*. Fairfax, Va.: NTL Learning Resources, 1972.

28. Beckhard, R. *Organization development: Strategies and models*. Reading, Mass.: Addison-Wesley, 1969, p. 9.

29. Ibid., p. 13.

30. Yager, E. G. The quality control explosion. *Training and Development Journal*, April 1981, p. 98.

31. Ibid., p. 99.

32. Ibid., p. 103.

Index

*This book has been set VIP, in 10 and 9 point
Memphis, leaded 3 points. Chapter numbers
are 55 point Outline and chapter titles are
24 point Memphis. The size of the type page is
26 by 47 picas.*